The Bible
Made Easy

A Book-by-Book Introduction

Timothy P. Schehr

ST. ANTHONY MESSENGER PRESS

Cincinnati, Ohio

RESCRIPT

In accord with the *Code of Canon Law,* I hereby grant my permission to publish *The Bible Made Easy,* by Timothy P. Schehr.

Most Reverend Carl K. Moeddel
Vicar General and Auxiliary Bishop
of the Archdiocese of Cincinnati
Cincinnati, Ohio
May 25, 2006

The permission to publish is a declaration that a book or pamphlet is considered to be free from doctrinal or moral error. It is not implied that those who have granted the permission to publish agree with the contents, opinions or statements expressed.

Cover design by Mike Winegardner
Cover photo: ©iStockphoto.com/Kati Neudert
Book design by Phillips Robinette, O.F.M.

LIBRARY OF CONGRESS CATALOGING-IN-PUBLICATION DATA

Schehr, Timothy.
  The Bible made easy : a book-by-book introduction / Timothy J. Schehr.
    p. cm.
  Includes bibliographical references and index.
  ISBN-13: 978-0-86716-598-2 (pbk. : alk. paper)
  ISBN-10: 0-86716-598-7 (pbk. : alk. paper) 1. Bible—Introductions. I. Title.

BS475.3.S335 2007
220.6'1—dc22

                              2006026917

ISBN 978-0-86716-598-2

Published by St. Anthony Messenger Press
28 W. Liberty St.
Cincinnati, OH 45202
www.SAMPBooks.org

Printed in the United States of America.

Printed on acid-free paper.

  08 09 10 5 4 3 2

CONTENTS

INTRODUCTION

You probably have a collection of favorite books in your library; books to get lost in; books that take you away from the stresses and strains of the day and transport you to another world. If you were asked to explain why your favorite books are so special, you would probably list things like the exciting characters, the story line or even the beauty of the words that carry the story forward.

You should know that all of this is available in the Bible. But the Bible also has something else, something that makes reading the Bible different from reading any other book. The Bible invites us into the world of faith. On every one of its pages, God speaks to us, inviting us to realize in our lives all the wonderful advantages that come with walking with God in this world.

The format of this book follows the format of the Bible. The books of the Bible will be considered in the order in which they appear in the Bible. We begin with a few preliminary chapters to give you some perspective on the Bible.

The purpose of this book is to introduce you to the amazing literature of the Bible. If you wish to learn more about the Bible, there are many good resources available. A good way to delve more deeply into a biblical book is to find a resource that appeals to you, read it and then choose something from the bibliography of that book to read. Keep following this procedure until you have satisfied your hunger for knowledge. At the end of this book, you will find some resources that will get you started on further exploration of the Bible.

PART ONE
GETTING STARTED

Getting Familiar With the Bible

You can think of the Bible as a library of many books—seventy-three altogether! In fact, the Bible was a collection of separate scrolls, or books, until the fourth century AD when it first appeared as a single book. Some of these earliest single-volume Bibles still survive. One of the most famous of them is in the Vatican library.

Like any library of books, you can pick and choose from a variety of different kinds of writing. In the Bible you can find gripping narratives about some of the great people or events from biblical times. You can also find beautiful poetry praising God or exploring the relationship between God and people.

Of course, you can read the Bible just to find out about the people, places and events described within it. Without too much effort, you can find lists of things from the Bible: famous people, famous places, guidelines for life and time lines of peak moments in salvation history.

But the most fruitful way to read the Bible is to find in each of its many pages an invitation to faith. The authors of the Bible were inspired by *the* Author of the Bible, and so they have our spiritual welfare at heart. They want to give us every advantage in our spiritual journeys.

Reading the Bible with our focus on its invitation to faith is like looking at a beautiful work of art with just the right lighting. We will be able to see and appreciate all its beauty.

Catholic readers will discover they have a larger selection of material to read in the Bible than do some other denominations. In fact, the Old Testament in a Catholic Bible contains nearly 16 percent more material. Within the historical books, this material is represented by Judith, Tobit, 1 and 2 Maccabees. Within the wisdom books, it is represented by Wisdom and Sirach. And within the prophets, it is represented by the book of Baruch. There are also additional portions for Esther and Daniel in a Catholic Bible.

In the New Testament a Catholic Bible will include the "longer ending" for Mark's Gospel (16:9–20); the account of the adulterous woman (John 7:53—8:11); and some slight additions to Matthew and Luke.

1

Catholic readers will also recognize a clear connection between the teachings of the Bible and teachings of the church. As they read the Bible, they may recognize that much of the Bible's message is familiar to them from such things as the Creed recited each Sunday, the *Catechism of the Catholic Church,* the celebration of the sacraments and the church's many devotional prayers.

The reason for this connection is that the Catholic church believes God speaks to us in the tradition from the apostles as well as from the inspired books of the Bible. Teachings not explicitly mentioned in the Bible but compatible with its message will be embraced by Catholics because they have been handed down by the tradition. This is exhibited in such teachings as the perpetual virginity of Mary, the communion of saints and the Assumption of Mary into heaven.

Great Themes of the Bible

Listed here are some of the prominent themes you will discover in the Bible. Be sure to look for them as you make your way through its pages.

God's Word Gives Life

Every word in the Bible contributes in some way to the theme of salvation. This is true of the words placed in the mouths of human characters; it is especially true of words presented in the Bible as spoken directly by God. When a biblical passage presents God as speaking, we should listen very carefully. It is like hearing the purest recording of a beautiful symphony with absolutely no static or interference of any kind. God's Word is often protective. Think, for example, of the warning God gives Adam in the Garden of Eden, protecting him from the consequences of eating the forbidden fruit. Sometimes God's Word is not easy to hear. The truth hurts. But God is always going to speak the truth.

Walking With God

While in the Garden of Eden, Adam and Eve walked with God whenever God came to visit. After the Fall, walking with God is still the ideal task of every mortal. We are told that Enoch walked with God and for doing so, he was apparently spared from death. Then we read that Noah walked with God and for doing so, he was chosen to be the father of a new generation of mortals. But what does it mean to walk with God? Just consider the story of Abraham and so many others. It means relying entirely on the Word of God. Jesus of course provides us with the most perfect example of someone who did this. If we follow him, we are definitely on the right track.

Security in God Alone

This is one of the greatest challenges for the people we read about in the Bible. People are so inclined to look for security in the things of this world. The most prominent example is the attraction Egypt has for the patriarchs. Egypt can offer them everything this world has to give: possessions, wealth, honor. But the patriarchs gradually learn to trust in God. Only then do they gain the blessings that God alone can give. The prophets challenged kings with the same lesson. But the kings did not learn so well. Jesus presents his disciples with this challenge, too. The preaching of Peter and Paul in the Acts of the Apostles demonstrates how well they learned the lesson.

Our Bond With God

The biblical word for this is *covenant*. A covenant is an agreement between two parties. In the Bible a covenant is often sealed by an elaborate ritual like the sacrifice of animals. Consider, for example, the elaborate ritual between God and Abraham in Genesis 15. The covenant theme is so prominent in the Bible it is used to distinguish between the two major sections of the Bible: The Old Testament and the New Testament. The word *testament* is based on the Latin word for covenant. The most notable covenant in the Old Testament takes place at Sinai when Israel pledges to be God's holy people. In the New Testament the bond between us and God is secured by the death and resurrection of Jesus.

Service to God

The ideal response to all that God does for us is to render humble service to God. Of course, to do this successfully we have to overcome our preference to serve ourselves. That is why the Bible is filled with narratives about people who struggled to let go of the things they would choose for themselves in order to focus on the things of God. In the book of Isaiah, the suffering servant is the ideal example of someone who did just that. And Jesus fulfilled that ideal in a way matched by no one else.

Everything Is Gift

We spend a lot of energy claiming things as our own. We think of this world as a great buffet of things to gather into our life: things, places, even people. But if we are truly honest, we will recognize that we really own nothing. Even as we cling to things, they are being claimed by the passage of time. The ideal outlook on life is expressed so memorably by Job: "Naked I came from my mother's womb, and naked shall I return there; the LORD gave, and the LORD has taken away; blessed be the name of the LORD" (Job 1:21). When you get right down to it this is the only authentically true view of our life in this world. As Jesus told the believers standing around him, "the truth will make you free" (John 8:32).

The Struggle of Faith

There is an independent streak in us. We would rather choose to go our own way than listen to God and go God's way. Just look at the obstacles so many characters in the Bible had to overcome as they learned to rely on God. A major portion of the Bible deals with this very thing: learning to rely on God. In the early days of Israel's history, Abraham and Sarah had to learn to trust in the Word of God. And in New Testament times the apostles had to learn what was involved in following the Lord Jesus Christ.

The Human Family

From the viewpoint of the Bible, we are all God's children. We can see this already in the account of Adam and Eve, which presents all of us as descendants of one loving couple. In God's call to Abraham, it is clear that all the nations of the world will eventually find blessing in that great patriarch who becomes our father in faith. This is what Paul celebrates in his Letter to the Romans. The prophet Isaiah echoes this theme with his vision of all the nations streaming to Jerusalem to worship the Lord. In the Gospels Jesus sends his disciples out to the whole world to proclaim the Good News to all the nations.

Gratitude

Think how often we find people giving thanks to God in the Bible. From Abel onward we find people in the Bible offering sacrifice or praying or singing to God. The book of Psalms is filled with songs of praise and thanksgiving to God. In Deuteronomy we find a prayer of thanks the people are supposed to render to God every year at harvest time. Some believe it even served as a kind of creed for them. It is a summary of all the wonderful things God did for Israel. All the great feasts were also times of thanksgiving to God. And for us the great prayer of thanksgiving is the Eucharist we celebrate every Sunday.

Ways to Read the Bible

People will sometimes ask how to begin reading the Bible. Here are some suggestions I have recommended over the years. Maybe one of them will work for you.

Scheduled Reading

If you are someone with a lot of discipline, you may want to set up a personal reading program. Set aside a certain time each day to read a predetermined portion of the Bible. Within a year, you will be amazed at how much of the Bible you have read through. There are Internet and print resources available to help guide you through a scheduled reading of the entire Bible.

Study Guides

Many editions of the Bible include study guides for the reader. Some of them even include elaborate programs organized according to certain themes or topics. All you need to do is set aside the time to explore all the options available in the Bible section of your local bookstore.

The Stepping-Stone Approach

Start with a part of the Bible you know already. Details about the reading will lead you to other passages. Repeating this process over and over again will connect you with much of the Bible. For example, if you begin with the miracle of the loaves in Matthew 14:13–21, the notes may connect you to Exodus 16 and 2 Kings 4:42–44. Cross-references will connect you with parallel readings in John 6, Mark 6 and Luke 9.

Exploring the Great Themes of the Bible

You may prefer to read passages connected with themes like creation, the Word of God, deliverance, covenant, judgment, wisdom, discipleship, prophecy, victory over suffering and death, and the power of the Spirit. You will probably need to use a dictionary of the Bible to point you to the parts of the Bible that exhibit these themes in a special way. There are also Bibles that identify major themes for you by assigning a certain color for each theme and using these colors as a background on the printed page.

Meeting the Great Characters of the Bible

Start reading about your own favorite characters. A quick look at a Bible dictionary will connect you with the passages where your favorite character appears. You could also let Sirach be your guide with his Praise of Israel's Great Ancestors (Sirach 44—50).

The Historical Approach

Follow the history of salvation from beginning to end by reading the historical books of the Bible in chronological order. These are the books in which you can see how salvation history unfolds. Begin with Genesis and Exodus. Then move on to Joshua, Judges, 1 and 2 Samuel and 1 and 2 Kings. Then Ezra and Nehemiah, 1 and 2 Maccabees, the Gospels (Matthew, Mark, Luke and John), and the Acts of the Apostles.

The Liturgical Approach

Let the readings for each Sunday be your guide. Some editions of the *New American Bible* include the three-year cycle of readings used at Mass. You could also buy a copy of the lectionary for Mass. There is one for Sunday readings and one for weekday readings. Many parishes have study groups that meet during the week to read together and reflect on the readings coming up on the following Sunday.

Advice From a Saint

Saint Jerome offered this Bible reading program for the granddaughter of a friend:

> Let her begin by learning the psalter, and then let her gather rules of life out of the proverbs of Solomon. From the Preacher (Ecclesiastes) let her gain the habit of despising the world and its vanities. Let her follow the example in Job of virtue and of patience. Then let her pass on to the Gospels…the Acts of the Apostles and the Epistles. As soon as she has enriched the storehouse of her mind with these treasures, let her commit to memory the prophets, the heptateuch (Genesis to Samuel), the books of Kings and of Chronicles, the rolls also of Ezra and Esther. When she has done all these she may safely read the Song of Songs.…

A Bible Calendar

One challenging aspect of reading the Bible is keeping track of the vast expanse of history between its covers. This is no easy task because the books of the Bible reach back many centuries before the time of Jesus.

That is a lot of time to keep track of as we make our way through the Bible. One way to make it easier is to concentrate on just a few special episodes in the history of salvation using them as major markers along the way. Each episode represents a time of freedom or deliverance for God's people.

The first major marker in salvation history is the deliverance from Egypt. Data within the Bible and indirect evidence from history places the Exodus about thirteen hundred years before Jesus. The exodus from Egypt is the model for deliverance.

The second major marker is the kingship of David around one thousand years before the time of Jesus. Through David's loyalty to God, the people were finally free from the tyranny of their enemies. They were able to at last enjoy the Promised Land.

Unfortunately, this era of peace did not last long. David's successors forgot about God. So they ended up oppressed again, this time during the Exile in the land of Babylon. But God led them back to the Promised Land a second time. This return from Exile took place about five hundred years before the time of Jesus.

Nearly two hundred years before the time of Jesus, there came another threat to their stay in the Promised Land. This time it came in the person of a king named Antiochus IV. He tried to erase the traditions of the Jewish people. But by God's grace, the Jewish leaders won a victory. This was the age of the Maccabees. This period is significant for the time of Jesus because the Pharisees and the Sadducees traced their origins back to the time of the Maccabees.

The big signpost for the New Testament is Easter, when Jesus won the victory over death. The church celebrates this as the New Exodus. We can readily see the connection if we think of the first Exodus as a passage from death in Egypt to new life in the Promised Land. The traditional date for this first Easter is the year AD 33. In the years that follow, the apostles proclaim the gospel and Paul sets out on his missionary journeys.

We have identified five major periods in the history of salvation. Each period is a time of freedom or deliverance for God's people. Listed in chronological order, beginning with the earliest, they are:

Deliverance from Egypt	around 1300 BC
Rise of King David	around 1000 BC
Return from Exile	around 500 BC
Victory of the Maccabees	around 200 BC
Jesus and the church	first century AD

We can fill in the gaps as we make our way through the books of the Bible. But with these five major time markers in mind, we at least have a general framework with which to work.

Our discussion of each book of the Bible will include a segment about where to place the book on the "clock"—dates when the book's events might have occurred, and other significant historical dates that help provide some context.

PART TWO

THE PENTATEUCH

The word *Pentateuch* means "the five books," specifically the five that stand at the beginning of the Bible. This part of the Old Testament introduces the exciting drama of God's relationship with people. We learn early on that people are created in the image and likeness of God. This means that men and women have a dignity that goes beyond any other created thing. And so, as we begin reading the Pentateuch, we have every reason to expect this part of the Bible to move from one happy episode to the next. Unfortunately, things go wrong right from the start.

A troubling pattern emerges early on. It can be presented this way: God blesses people; people ignore God's blessing; God seeks ways to bless people again. This sequence is repeated over and over again in the Bible. The good news in all this is that we can see how dedicated God is to staying in touch with men and women. The bad news is that people so often fail to appreciate God's love for them. But no matter how many times they fail, God picks up the pieces and starts over again. God loves us that much!

Taken in order, the first five books are Genesis, Exodus, Leviticus, Numbers and Deuteronomy. This sequence is not random; it follows a time line from creation to the arrival of God's people at the border of the Promised Land. Let's consider the books one by one just to get a feel for the drama that unfolds in them.

Genesis presents material we are most likely very familiar with already: Adam and Eve; Noah and the Flood; the city and Tower of Babel; and of course those great patriarchs of Israel—Abraham, Isaac and Jacob.

One thing that may come as a bit of surprise is that by the end of the book, in spite of all God's efforts to steer them to the Promised Land, the people of Israel end up in Egypt. And with God's people in Egypt, we know the story is definitely far from over.

Exodus records the great deliverance from Egypt and the journey to Mount Sinai where Israel enters into a solemn relationship with God. And that's only the first half! The rest of Exodus presents us with the plans and the construction of the tabernacle and the ark of the covenant. God is definitely committed to being present among the people.

Leviticus serves as a kind of guidebook for the people, providing them with instructions on how to remain in right relationship with God. Numbers starts off with a lot of promise as the people set out on the journey that will take them to the Promised Land. But somehow they end up wandering in the desert for forty years!

By the time we get to Deuteronomy, the people have still not entered the Promised Land and Moses has reached the end of his earthly life. But before he dies, Moses gives them a long lesson on the things they will need to know if they are to prosper in the land beyond the Jordan River.

Taken together these five books prepare the way for the rest of the Bible. They tell us how special we are in God's sight. They tell us God wants us to enjoy life in a world where God comes first. But we are also painfully aware that people can choose to ignore God, a choice that never leads to peace or happiness. By the end of the Pentateuch Israel has learned a lot of hard lessons. Will they remember what they learned and enjoy life in the Promised Land?

GENESIS

This book is about beginnings. As everyone knows, it tells us about the beginning of the heavens and the earth. But most importantly, Genesis is about the beginning of God's relationship with us. Key to this relationship is total reliance on God's Word. That is important because God's Word gives life. The drama builds in intensity as men and women exercise their freedom to listen to God or to others.

The material in the first eleven chapters of Genesis is sometimes identified as primeval history. This is understandable since we are reading about ancient events in these chapters. But however old the history in these chapters may be, we should not overlook the main issue in this book: God's relationship with the men and women of those times. God's entire focus is on people like Adam and Eve, Cain and Abel, Noah and his family, and the people of Babel whose plans, unfortunately, do not include God.

After the Babel account, the pace slows down as chapter after chapter follows the faith journey of just a few special men and women. We follow Abraham and Sarah as they struggle to come to complete faith in God. Their struggle derives from a desire to make things happen on their own terms rather than on God's terms. Only with time do they fully trust in God's promise that they will have a son of their own.

Isaac is very much like his father; he prefers to do things his way. But in Rebekah, Isaac has a wife who is close to God. She helps her blind husband see that Jacob should receive his blessing because Jacob is the twin who is spiritually stronger than Esau.

The remainder of the book follows Jacob's spiritual journey. Like Abraham and Isaac before him, Jacob has his own way of doing things. His favoritism toward Joseph and Benjamin—sons of his beloved Rachel—leads to jealousy within the family. The most familiar part of this story is Joseph's rise from slavery to become the second most powerful figure in Egypt. But Egypt is not Joseph's true home. In time, Jacob awakens within this favorite son a love for the Promised Land. And so, by the end of his life, Jacob has achieved success. He proves to be a worthy servant devoted to God's saving plan. As the text of the Bible puts it so memorably, Jacob "drew up his feet into the bed" (Genesis 49:33). He has reached the goal in his journey of faith.

The 50 chapters of Genesis:

Adam and Eve

As long as they listen to God, they enjoy many blessings in the Garden of Eden. We all know what happens when they listen to the serpent. But God is still with them and continues to bless them. When, for example, Eve celebrates the birth of their first child, she announces that she brought him into the world with God's help (Genesis 4:1).

Noah

Noah's ark, with its menagerie of animal life, has inspired countless artists. But the truly inspiring thing about Noah is his obedience to God's Word. He does exactly what God tells him to do. It literally saves his life. If only other characters in the Bible were like Noah.

Noah's Wife

In the account of the great flood, Noah's wife is never named. But in one of the caves of Qumran, a scroll was found that contained further details about the descendants of Adam. Specialists have entitled this scroll "Tales of the Patriarchs." This scroll includes the name of Noah's wife. It was Imzera, meaning "mother of offspring."

Joseph

Joseph has two dreams about his family showing him honor. He recalls these dreams when he becomes a great leader in Egypt. But since Joseph's dreams come from God, they probably reach beyond his success in Egypt to include his spiritual success at the end of Genesis when Joseph declares that his final resting place must be the Promised Land.

Covenant

To put Abraham's worries to rest, God includes him in a covenant ritual. The purpose of a covenant ritual was to remove any grounds for uncertainty in the relationship. God wants Abraham to have no doubts about the promises made to him. It takes Abraham some time to trust God fully. But eventually he sets aside his fears and reaches the level of unconditional faith in God.

A Ladder to Heaven

Jacob's ladder is one of the more memorable images in Genesis. It's comforting to know that the vast space between our world and heaven can be spanned—at least from God's viewpoint—by a ladder. And it is even more comforting to know there is a constant stream of heavenly emissaries going up and down the ladder to assist God in the profound and mysterious work of salvation. Jacob has God at his side to help him make the right decisions in life. In time, he will fully appreciate this and then he will be able to guide his family along the path of faith.

Why Did They Live So Long?

Many of the characters in Genesis lived very long lives. Adam, for example, lived to be 930 years old. Methuselah had the longest life—969 years! How was this possible? Some believe the biblical authors counted time differently than we do. Others point to the exaggerated life spans found in other genealogies from antiquity. Another viewpoint, and one that seems to fit well with the theme that God is life, is that even these long lives are relatively short if we recall that Adam and Eve would not have died at all if they had not eaten from the tree of knowledge. And so their long lives might be intended to remind us readers of this earlier freedom from death.

Did You Know?

The most famous representation of our creation by God is on the ceiling of the Sistine Chapel in the palace of the Vatican. God reaches out to Adam, their hands almost touching. Here's an interesting thing to think about: Did Michelangelo, the painter of that image, imagine those hands to be drawing closer or drifting farther apart?

Genesis on the Clock (BC)

Abraham   c. 1700
Joseph   c. 1500
Exodus   1290?

Does this book tell us how old the earth is? We should keep in mind that the authors of the Bible have our spiritual interests at heart and not precise calculations about the age of things, such as the earth. The Jewish calendar—working from the genealogies in the book—identifies this century as the fifty-seventh since the creation of the world. But ask a geologist and you will probably get a date reaching back millions or billions of years.

When did Abraham and Sarah live? Archeologists—those specialists who open up the earth to piece together the many layers of history—have found ancient libraries that help connect the narratives of Genesis with the ancient world. On the basis of such data, it is generally agreed the accounts about the patriarchs best fit into a time period beginning some eighteen centuries before the time of Jesus.

When was the book of Genesis written? Since no records about this are available, we have to make educated guesses based on the text of Genesis itself. Currently, specialists identify three main traditions that make up the book of Genesis. The earliest (J) is associated with the time of King David. The second (P) is dated about a hundred years later and associated with the northern kingdom of Israel (Solomon's kingdom was divided into north and south after his death). The third tradition (D) is the latest of the three; it is associated with the period of the Exile in Babylon.

As you read Genesis…

Couples often choose Genesis 1 or 2 for their wedding ceremony. What makes these passages so fitting for a wedding?

Why do you think God spends so much time speaking to Cain in Genesis 4?

How many times have you seen artistic representations of Noah and the ark? What lessons do you take away from them?

Do you think the people at Babel make the best use of language?

How is Abraham's story a lesson in finding security in God?

In chapter 13 Abraham leaves Egypt with all the things the world has to offer him. Why was this not the end of his story?

Why do you think God tells Abraham to offer up his son, Isaac?

In chapter 24, we find Abraham's servant at prayer. How well does God answer this prayer?

What are your first impressions of Rebekah? Does your impression change as you read her story?

Why is Joseph's family so filled with jealousy and hatred for him?

Do you think Joseph's family gives the best interpretation to his dreams in chapter 37?

How do you see God's hand at work in Joseph's life?

Why do you think Jacob said about Joseph, "I must go and see him before I die" (45:28)?

Joseph thought of Egypt as his new home. But at the end of his life, he requested to be buried in the Promised Land. What made Joseph change his mind?

Three Spiritual Lessons From Genesis

- We are created in God's image and so we have a special relationship with God
- We find true freedom in choosing to listen to God's protective Word
- No matter where we go, God is still with us calling us to new life

EXODUS

The title of this book means "way out," a title that could be applied to much of the Bible, which often portrays God showing people a way out of some difficulty into which they have managed to get themselves.

In the book of Exodus the way out is the one that takes Israel out of Egypt. Later, God shows them the way out of the desert. Still later, God shows them the way out of Exile. And, of course, in so many pages of the Bible, God is showing the people the way out of sin.

Egypt always seems to have had a certain appeal for God's people. Abraham goes down to Egypt when he finds Canaan too uncomfortable for him. Isaac would have gone to Egypt if God had not stopped him. And Jacob had to go to Egypt to see his son Joseph. Jacob brought his entire family with him. The original plan was that they would stay only for the duration of the famine. But years turned into decades, and decades into centuries.

What made Egypt so attractive? It had a lot to offer. In fact, Egypt possessed all the resources this world has to offer. It was a place to find security in the things of earth. But of course, Egypt could never be the home of God's people because Egypt did not recognize the God of

15

Israel. By the time the people learned this, it was far too late. They were enslaved in Pharaoh's world, which was nothing like the world God intended for them.

With God's people in Egypt, God was definitely going to do something about it. And God does some very impressive things in this book. Later generations will remember them as the great signs and wonders God worked to set the people free. Of course, the most dramatic wonder was the crossing of the sea.

But in one sense, getting out of Egypt was the easy part. After all, was there ever any real doubt that God could not lead the people beyond the reach of the king of Egypt? Pharaoh thought he could stand in God's way, but in the end, he proved to be powerless to stop God's people from marching right out of his country.

The real challenge comes after the Exodus from Egypt. Although the people had physically escaped from Egypt, it takes a long time for them to break free of Egypt's influence on them. When they grow hungry in the desert, they recall fondly the food they had in Egypt, forgetting, of course, the oppression that came with that food. But God is patient with them and offers them what they need.

At Sinai, the people take a significant step in their religious lives. They agree to enter into a special relationship with God. The covenant ceremony at Sinai marks a major turning point for them. From then on, they are God's special people. The history of this people seems to have reached a high point that we expect will be sustained for many years.

But in fact, the ideal is shattered almost immediately. On the mountain of God, things are going well. God gives Moses the Ten Commandments as well as plans for the construction of the ark of the covenant. But at the base of the mountain, things are not going well at all.

The people urge Aaron to fashion an idol for them. They want something to represent the divine presence in their midst. This of course is precisely what the tabernacle and the ark of the covenant will provide for them. But once again, the people are not patient enough to allow God to provide what they need. Once again, they pursue things their own way. We know the rest of this story. In anger, Moses shatters the stone tablets

Still, Exodus concludes on a positive note. Moses returns to the mountain of God. He prepares a new set of stone tablets containing the Ten Commandments. And Moses oversees the construction of the tabernacle and the ark of the covenant. God chooses to remain in the midst of the people in spite of their failures.

The 40 chapters of Exodus:

1 — 15	God leads Israel out of Egypt
16 — 18	The journey to Sinai
19 — 24	The covenant at Sinai
25 — 40	God's loving presence among a sinful people

A Long School Year

Israel remained at the base of Mount Sinai for nearly a year. They arrived there on the first day of the third month after leaving Egypt; they left Mount Sinai on the twentieth day of the second month of the second year after leaving Egypt. During all that time, God was instructing them on the basics of being God's people.

Mount Sinai

The precise location of this mountain where Israel encountered God is not known. The monastery of St. Catherine occupies the traditional spot. But archaeology has yet to identify the exact place.

The Burning Bush

This is an appropriate symbol of the special relationship between God and humanity. Under normal circumstances, fire would consume a bush. But God protects the bush from destruction. In a similar way, God protects the people.

The Ark of the Covenant

This was a strikingly beautiful chest about four feet by two feet square. The top of the ark was covered with a gold plate and two cherubim. God's presence was associated with the ark, which is sometimes spoken of as a divine footstool. The ark was God's gift to the people providing them with a visible sign of God's presence in their midst.

Exodus on the Clock (BC)

The Pyramids   from c. 2500
Joseph   c. 1600
Exodus   1290?

The exodus from Egypt is dated about thirteen centuries before the time of Jesus. A monument set up by one of the pharaohs

17

mentions a people called "Israel" living in what we now know as the Holy Land. The date for this monument is about the year 1220 BC. We know the people of Israel wandered in the desert for forty years. So to be in the Holy Land by 1220 BC they must have left Egypt at least by 1260 BC if not earlier.

When was the book of Exodus written? There are no records at hand to help answer this question. But the same traditions associated with the origin of Genesis are believed to have contributed to Exodus too. That dates some portions of Exodus to nearly a thousand years before the time of Jesus. Miriam's song of victory in Exodus 15 may be even older.

As you read Exodus…

The rabbis regarded the Hebrew midwives Shiphrah and Puah as spiritual heroines. What reasons would they have given to prove their point?

God appears to Moses in the image of a burning bush. What makes this image fitting for a revelation of God?

In Exodus 5, Pharaoh commands the people to gather straw each day to make bricks. Compare this with God's command—in Exodus 16—that the Israelites gather manna each day. What do you discover about God and about Pharaoh in this comparison?

What do you think is the reason for placing the month of the Passover at the head of the Israelite calendar?

The account of the crossing of the sea (Exodus 14—15) is the dominant Old Testament reading at the Easter Vigil. What makes this reading so appropriate for Easter?

In the incident of the golden calf, God announces to Moses that the Israelites will be consumed and Moses will become a great nation in their place. How does Moses respond to this? Why does he respond the way he does?

From the details in Exodus 36 and 37, make a sketch of the ark and the tabernacle of the Lord.

Three Spiritual Lessons From Exodus

- Walking with God leads to true freedom
- God's commandments are given for our benefit
- No earthly thing is an insurmountable obstacle to our relationship with God

LEVITICUS

What did you learn in school today? If this question were asked of the people of Israel encamped at the mountain of God, they might have said, "We learned about being God's holy people."

During their nearly yearlong stay at the base of Mount Sinai, the people of Israel enjoyed the great privilege of having God for a teacher. Their program of studies was entirely devoted to giving them all the information they needed to serve God faithfully.

The first item in their curriculum was a survey of all the sacrifices they were to offer to God each year. With so much time devoted to giving God praise and thanks, the people were constantly reminded of their relationship with God, the source of life. The ideal outcome of this elaborate program of sacrifice was that the people would never lose focus on God.

To aid the people in their rituals, God provided them with a family of priests. This privilege was given to Aaron and his sons. These priests had the entire tribe of Levi to assist them in their work. The name of this book derives from the name Levi.

A second item in the program of studies for Israel was purity. If they were to serve God, they would need to know what made them presentable to God and what did not. So God provided them with a detailed regimen for cleanliness. All this attention to physical purity was also a reflection of the spiritual purity that they were to exhibit in their inner lives. The people had to learn to be just as attentive to spiritual maladies as they were to physical ones.

A third item in their Sinai curriculum was holiness. Leviticus includes detailed instructions to help the people reflect the holiness of God. How would they do that? By being merciful, just and loving toward others—the very things they looked for in their relationship with God.

The final lessons of the book return to the theme of sacrifice. But this time the emphasis is on all the feasts and special seasons that made up their calendar. God did not want the people to forget that time was also one of God's special gifts to them. To show their gratitude to God for this wonderful gift of time, their calendar should be full of special intervals filled with attention to God.

With so much of their lives taken up with attention to religious things, there was ideally little chance of the people drifting away from

God who was the source of life for them. As the days for their departure for the Promised Land drew near, they had all they needed to make the journey successfully. The next book in the Torah gives the account of that journey.

The 27 chapters of Leviticus:

1 — 7	Giving thanks and praise to God
8 — 10	Serving God: Aaron and his sons
11 — 16	Being acceptable to God
17 — 22	Being holy for God
23 — 27	Setting aside time for God

Nadab and Abihu

These are definitely not household names. But the lesson we learn from them is unforgettable. These two sons of Aaron were consumed by fire as they offered sacrifice before the altar of God. We are told they offered "unholy fire" before the Lord (Leviticus 10:1). There are no details about their specific offense, but we can assume they failed to show respect for God in some way. The lesson for us is to value the gift of God's presence in our lives.

Day of Atonement (Yom Kippur)

On this day—the tenth of Tishri in the Jewish calendar, late September or early October in the Christian calendar—the high priest offered the most important sacrifice of the year. Only on this day was the priest allowed to enter the chamber where the ark of God rested. While inside this holiest of places, the priest sprinkled the blood of sacrifice on the plate of solid gold that covered the ark. This sacrifice, above all others, represented the restoration of the bond between God and people.

The Scapegoat

On Yom Kippur, after emerging from the presence of the ark of God, the high priest placed his hands on the head of a goat and confessed the sins of the people. This gesture symbolized the transfer of the sins of the people to the goat. The scapegoat was then chased off into the wilderness and away from the community now cleansed of its sins. The ceremony assured the people that as they began a new year their relationship with God was fully restored.

LEVITICUS

Jubilee Year

A year of jubilee may bring to mind a trip to Rome to visit the great basilicas and offer special prayers to God. But in the book of Leviticus, the jubilee year was a time for Israel to recall the gift of the Promised Land in a special way. In a sense, they turned the land back over to God from whom they had received it in the days of Joshua. They did not work the land that year; any portion of the land that had been sold was returned to its original owner so that the allotment in the days of Joshua was restored. There is no evidence that such a jubilee year was ever in fact observed in Israel. But if they had, we can only imagine what blessings they would have enjoyed.

Leviticus on the Clock (BC)

Exodus 1st month 1290?

Stay at Sinai/Departure from Sinai 2nd month 1291?

The people of Israel remained encamped at the base of Mount Sinai for almost one full year—from the first day of the third month after they left Egypt to the twentieth day of the second month the following year (see Exodus 19:1; Numbers 10:11). A standard date for the Exodus is the year 1290 BC. So the events in this book would fall in the year after that date. When did the book of Leviticus receive the form in which we read it today? Most specialists believe this book comes from about five hundred years before the time of Jesus and that it reflects traditions associated with the priests of Israel.

As you read Leviticus…

Leviticus 1—7 reviews the rich sacrificial practices of Israel. What rituals have a similar importance in your religious life?

What lesson is learned from the fate of Aaron's sons Nadab and Abihu? (Leviticus 10)

What makes the Day of Atonement so special in the Jewish calendar?

On the Sixth Sunday of the Year (Cycle B) the passage about leprosy (Leviticus 13:1–2, 44–46) is read as a companion text to Mark's account of the healing of a leper (Mark 1:40–45). What do you learn by comparing the two readings?

What are the great festivals of the Lord described in Leviticus 23? What great spiritual festivals do you find on your calendar?

21

Three Spiritual Lessons From Leviticus
- There is much to gain from regarding life as a valuable gift from God
- Keeping ourselves spiritually presentable is no less important than keeping ourselves physically presentable
- Maintaining a right relationship with God should stand at the top of our priority lists

NUMBERS

Don't be fooled by the title! Reading the book of Numbers is not at all like staring at a spreadsheet loaded with columns of digits and fractions. This fourth book of the Bible tells the story of Israel's journey to the Promised Land. The Hebrew name for this book means "in the wilderness," a title that reflects the physical and spiritual challenges that faced the people on this journey.

As the people set out from Mount Sinai, we expect things to go very well for them. God has been preparing them for this trip for nearly a year, organizing them into twelve divisions. They have the order and discipline of an army. This is also where the numbers come in, since God orders a census of the people before they set out.

The "army" of the Israelites is like no other. There is no mention of weapons for defense, and for a good reason! The people of Israel have God for their protection. As long as they remain in right relationship with God, they have no need to worry. Nothing can stand in their way as they proceed toward the land of their fathers.

But things go very wrong; and it happens almost immediately. The problem is that the people keep looking back to Egypt whenever they encounter any difficulty along the way. And when they reach the borders of the Promised Land, they lose heart altogether, fearing they can never claim the Promised Land as their own. At that point, they even go so far as to choose leaders to take them right back to Egypt. That's when God announces they must wander in the desert until all those without the courage to enter the Promised Land have died.

Forty years later, God directs Moses to take a second census. The results show that indeed not one of those unbelievers remains among the people. It is time to lead the rest of the people into the Promised Land. The book ends with all the people of Israel encamped on the east bank of the Jordan River right across from the city of Jericho. All they have to do now is cross that river and they are home.

The 36 chapters of Numbers:

1 — 10	Preparing for the journey
11 — 19	The weakness of the first generation
20 — 36	The strength of the other generations

Moses

This great leader of Israel dominates the pages of Numbers. But now flaws in his character begin to surface. When the people cry out for food, Moses cries out to God asking God to strike him dead because the people are too heavy for him to carry anymore. Later, Moses fails to trust God and strikes the rock twice to bring water from it. For this offense, God bans Moses from leading the people into the Promised Land.

Aaron

This brother of Moses plays a significant role in Numbers, too. He and his sons have the great privilege of caring for the ark of the covenant. But Aaron also begins to show some flaws. He is reprimanded by God for challenging Moses. Later, God directs Moses to make Eleazar high priest in place of his father. Aaron dies before the people enter the Promised Land.

Miriam

Like her brothers Moses and Aaron, Miriam also displays a darker side in this book. When she challenges the authority of Moses, God banishes her from the camp—even marking her as a leper for a time. The community awaits her return and then proceeds with its journey. But Miriam dies before they enter the Promised Land.

Korah

This prominent member of the tribe of Levi leads a rebellion against Moses. He even goes so far as to set up a rival sanctuary among the Israelites claiming that he has the authority to lead the Israelites to a land flowing with milk and honey. When he and his followers refuse to submit to Moses as God's chosen leader, they are removed in a dramatic way from the midst of the people.

NUMBERS

Caleb and Joshua

These two were among the twelve sent to scout out the Promised Land. But when the scouts return, only Caleb and Joshua firmly believe that God can lead the people safely into the Promised Land. And in fact, they are the only two out of the entire generation of adults who left Egypt and actually cross the Jordan River into the Promised Land.

Zelophehad's Daughters

You have probably never heard of them. But these five women have great faith. They trust that God will lead the people to the Promised Land. They also request an inheritance in the land since their father had no sons. Their request is so unique Moses has to take it to God. And God grants their request.

A Special Blessing

Numbers includes the famous priestly blessing we hear at the beginning of each year on the Feast of the Solemnity of Mary. It is filled with beautiful imagery expressing God's favor for the people. Clearly, the people begin their journey to the Promised Land with every spiritual advantage. We can imagine God blessing our journeys in a similar way. The full blessing reads this way:

> The LORD bless you and keep you;
> the LORD make his face to shine upon you, and be gracious to you;
> the LORD lift up his countenance upon you, and give you peace.
> (6:24–26)

Water From the Rock

If asked to identify the reason why God banned Moses from the Promised Land, most people would say that Moses struck the rock twice instead of just once. But if you read the text of Numbers 20:1–13 carefully, you will discover that Moses was told to just speak to the rock and water would flow out of it. That seems to make his offense doubly bad.

The Serpent on a Pole

This is a very familiar image from Numbers 21. By God's grace, a source of death is transformed into a sign that gives life. In his dialogue with Nicodemus Jesus compares his being lifted up on the cross to the lifting up of the serpent on the pole (John 3:14).

Numbers on the Clock (BC)

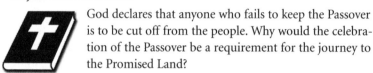

Exodus   1290?
40 Years of Wandering
Arrival at Jordan River   1250?

This book begins with Israel's departure from the base of Mount Sinai; it concludes forty years later with the people encamped on the east side of the Jordan River across from the city of Jericho. Our biblical time line would place these events to the middle of the thirteenth century before the time of Jesus. When did Numbers take the shape we have it in today?

Once again, specialists attribute this book to priestly traditions active some five hundred years before the birth of Jesus.

As you read Numbers…

God declares that anyone who fails to keep the Passover is to be cut off from the people. Why would the celebration of the Passover be a requirement for the journey to the Promised Land?

God's response to lack of faith is harsher now than it was in the days immediately after the Exodus. Why do you think this is so?

What lesson does Moses learn from the work of Eldad and Medad?

Some rabbis taught that God was not pleased with the decision to send scouts into the Promised Land. What do you think their reasons for this position would have been?

After Numbers 19, a new generation of Israelites begins to appear. What makes this new generation different from the first generation that died in the desert?

In Numbers 27, five sisters make a very special request. What does God's answer to their request reveal about the Promised Land?

Three Spiritual Lessons From Numbers

- It takes time to learn to walk with God
- Our own relationship with God has an impact on the faith of others
- God is patient with our weakness and our failures

25

DEUTERONOMY

This book comes at a dramatic moment in Israel's history. The people of Israel are right on the border of the Promised Land. All that visually separates them from the land of milk and honey is the Jordan River. But on the spiritual plane, much more formidable barriers threaten to impede their progress. Moses attempts to remove these potential spiritual hindrances by walking them through a detailed review of what it means for them to be God's people.

The Hebrew title for this book is "the words." That is a perfect title because this book is almost entirely made up of the words of Moses. Moses wants the people to understand that the land is a gift from God and will always remain so. If they ever forget that and carry on as if they no longer need God, they run the risk of losing the land and going into exile.

To make a lasting impression on the people, Moses begins with a rehearsal of all the good things God did for them up to this point in their lives. His main point is that God has always been faithful to the promises made to them. If God has been so loyal to the covenant, then they should be loyal, too.

After reviewing their history with God, Moses goes on to remind them of all the things God expects them to do. This review of the law is the reason this book has such an unwieldy name—Deuteronomy—which means "the second law."

Moses urges the people to love God with everything they have—heart, soul and strength. Any weakness in their loyalty to the terms of the covenant will weaken their relationship with God and jeopardize their stay in the Promised Land. And Moses does not leave them guessing what the rewards and punishments might be. He gives them a very detailed list of both. There is plenty of motivation to abide by the terms of the covenant.

The book concludes with a record of Moses' final moments with Israel. The great leader pronounces a blessing on the people. Then God allows him to view the Promised Land from a distance before he dies. His final resting place is unknown.

All this may leave the wary reader wondering: If someone of Moses' stature could not enter the Promised Land, how good are Israel's chances? The next book of the Bible will give us the answer.

The 34 chapters of Deuteronomy:

1 — 11   God's commitment to the people

12 — 26   Their commitment to God

27 — 30   The advantages of faith

31 — 34   Moses steps aside

Milk and Honey

Deuteronomy often describes the Promised Land as a land "flowing with milk and honey." This image uses the products of the land to represent its richness. If we were to describe the land in more conventional language, we might say it was a land of rich pastures and plentiful flowers.

Creed

Deuteronomy 26:5–10 is regarded as one of Israel's earliest creeds. It describes the patriarchs this way: "A wandering Aramean was my ancestor; he went down into Egypt and lived there as an alien, few in number, and there he became a great nation, mighty and populous" (verse 5). Lack of complete trust in God certainly did cause their ancestors to wander about and eventually end up in a place like Egypt. But God did not abandon them. By God's grace, they flourished and became "a great nation."

Shema

This word is a command meaning "hear" or "listen." It stands at the beginning of Israel's key profession of faith. The complete text is found in Deuteronomy 6:4–9. The people are to say this prayer at the beginning and end of each day. The text of the Shema is often placed in a small oblong box *(mezuzah)* near a doorway. It is also placed in small black pouches strapped to head and arm *(tefillin)*. The idea is that wherever they go the people have this prayer close by.

Deuteronomy on the Clock (BC)

Exodus 1290?

40 Years of Wandering

At Jordan River 1250?

This book is associated with the last days the life of Moses. Before the great leader dies, he addresses the people of Israel four times explaining to them how they will remain God's special people once they cross the Jordan River into the Promised Land. Moses dies shortly afterward at the age of 120. The date would be sometime near the middle of the thirteenth century BC.

When did Deuteronomy surface in the form we have it today? Most specialists attribute this book to religious leaders during the time of Israel's Exile in Babylon. Of course, these leaders drew on material reaching back years earlier in the tradition of the people. By retelling the great narrative of Israel's entry into the Promised Land, they wanted to give the people of their own time spiritual advantages as they prepared to return to the Promised Land after years of exile.

As you read Deuteronomy...

The words of Deuteronomy 6:4–5 make up the famous Jewish prayer called the Shema. By tradition, this prayer is said several times a day. What do you think makes it so meaningful?

Deuteronomy 26:5–10 is thought to have served as an ancient creed for Israel. Why does a faith community find the recitation of a creed so important?

Moses gives the people a long list of blessings in Deuteronomy 28. Which blessings are the most meaningful to you?

God does not allow Moses to enter the Promised Land because he failed to manifest God's sanctity among the Israelites. Read Numbers 20:1–13 to learn how Moses failed in this way. Do you think God was being too strict with Moses?

Three Spiritual Lessons From Deuteronomy

- We can find inspiration from key moments in our relationship with God
- To listen to the Word of God is to choose life
- God gives us every advantage to make the journey of faith a successful one

PART THREE
THE HISTORICAL BOOKS

At the end of the Pentateuch, the people of Israel are in a covenant relationship with God and ready to enter the Promised Land. The historical books pick up the story from this point and carry it all the way down to just a century or so before the birth of Jesus. This portion of the Old Testament, therefore, covers a large span of time—about twelve hundred years altogether.

We should read these books not as history for its own sake, but as history in the service of the Bible's favorite theme: the bond between God and us. We will meet many people in this extensive body of literature, so extensive in fact, that it accounts for over one-quarter of all the verses in the Bible. The people we want to pay special attention to are those men and women who look to God for their strength and security. Their lives provide us with models to follow as we make our own faith journeys.

The book of Joshua picks up where Deuteronomy left off. As successor to Moses, Joshua leads Israel into Canaan. God's promise to the patriarchs is now fulfilled. God is certainly loyal to the people. But by the end of his book, Joshua is worried about the people's loyalty to God.

Joshua's fears are confirmed in Judges where we see big cracks beginning to show up in the perfect picture of God and Israel together in the Promised Land. But God does not give up. God gives them leaders—the judges—to steer them in the right direction. Yet even with all this help from God, the tribes, by the end of the book, are in disarray and even fighting against each other.

A welcome break from all this distress comes with the beautiful story of Ruth. Her strong faith leads to benefits for herself and for the people of Israel. This woman of faith is the great-grandmother of David.

There is promise of restoration as we read about the great spiritual leader Samuel. He serves God faithfully throughout his life. Samuel's spiritual success is the subject of much of the first book that bears his name. Samuel's legacy continues through the able leadership of David whom he anoints as king of Israel. The story of David's kingship and his relationship with God is the main theme of 2 Samuel. David's career soars until he neglects God. By the end of his long reign, conditions have worsened.

David was the ancestor of a long line of kings. But unfortunately, his successors could not match his candor with God. The slow decline of the kingdom is recorded in 1 and 2 Kings. By the end of 2 Kings, the kingdom has collapsed and the people are in exile.

A more idealistic view of all that we have read thus far is offered in 1 and 2 Chronicles. These two books concentrate on David's spiritual gifts; how David prepared the way for the restoration of the people after their exile. Ezra and Nehemiah carry this hopeful theme forward with the account of events that followed Israel's return from Babylon to the Promised Land.

At this point in the Bible, we come across three smaller books—Tobit, Judith and Esther—providing us with close-ups on certain spiritual giants associated with this history. Each of these was protected by God against a powerful earthly kingdom.

The book of Tobit reaches back to the years after the fall of the northern kingdom when the empire of Assyria dominated the scene. Tobit's life demonstrates what good can come about when people turn to God in times of difficulty.

Next, we meet Judith. This woman of faith saves her people from the earthly power of the army of Babylon. The story of Esther takes place in the time of the Persian Empire. Like Judith, Esther saves her people through her reliance on God.

The time up to the final centuries before the time of Jesus is covered in 1 and 2 Maccabees. In these books, we see how determined the people are to secure their faith and their traditions against assault by an enemy determined to overpower them.

Put on your spiritual walking shoes and begin this journey through time: the history of God's people. We will meet a host of fascinating characters along the way. We will also learn a host of lessons about how to make such a journey successfully.

JOSHUA

Could anyone really take Moses' place? This question may be on our minds as we begin reading this book. It was certainly a question on Joshua's mind. Little wonder God tells the new leader three times to be "strong and courageous." As things turned out, Joshua proved to be quite the leader for the people of Israel. Of course, it was all due to the fact that God was truly with him.

After forty years of wandering about in the desert, the people of Israel finally cross into the Promised Land. But their spiritual journey is far from over after they make that crossing! There are plenty of obstacles to overcome before they can settle down in the land of milk and honey.

The real obstacles are not the obvious ones. The walls of Jericho tumble down. Surprise attacks against Joshua's people fail. Even several kings uniting their armies as one cannot defeat the Israelites. God is definitely on Israel's side. And as long as God is on their side, nothing on the outside can interfere with their claims to the land.

The real obstacles come from deep within the hearts of the Israelites. Just as a lack of faith in God slowed down their progress toward the Promised Land, so does a lack of faith threaten their claim to the land once they are within its borders.

Joshua proves to be such a loyal servant of God that he is able to strengthen the hearts of the people. The central chapters of the book record the allotment of the land to the tribes of Israel just as God had promised.

But by the conclusion of the book, Joshua is not so sure that after he is gone the people will remain loyal to God. Already they seem to be losing focus on God—the very thing Moses had warned about before they crossed the Jordan—and are beginning to serve earthly interests. Joshua tries his best to motivate the people. He professes his own loyalty to the God of Israel and challenges them to do the same. They speak the right words, but Joshua seems less than confident in their resolve. When the book finishes, we wonder what lies in store for the people.

The 24 chapters of Joshua:

31

A Strong Ally

When Joshua saw the commander of the Lord's army, he asked whose side he was on. The answer Joshua got was "neither" (5:14). The significance of this response seems to be that God does not observe national boundaries but is rather on the side of faith and justice.

The Longest Day

The sun and the moon remained stationary in the sky on the day Israel fought against the Amorites (Joshua 10:12–14). God granted Joshua and the people the time they needed to win the victory. The lesson in this passage is that all the resources of heaven are available to those who seek to remove obstacles to their journey of faith.

A Woman of Faith

Rahab was a Canaanite and a citizen of Jericho, but she was also a woman of great faith. She understood even more than the two Israelite spies who stayed at her home that nothing could stand in the way of God's plan for a faithful people. No wonder her name appears in the family tree of Jesus in the first chapter of Matthew's Gospel.

Final Resting Place

The bones of Joseph are finally laid to rest at Shechem in a plot of ground purchased by his father Jacob many years earlier (Joshua 24:32). This fulfilled the oath Joseph made his brothers take before his death (Genesis 50:24–26). Joseph's burial in the Promised Land at last brings to a close the account of the Exodus from Egypt.

Joshua on the Clock (BC)

Exodus 1290?

Crossing the Jordan and Settlement in Canaan c. 1250

The victories described in Joshua reach back some twelve centuries before the time of Jesus. Archeological evidence suggests that there were considerable social changes going on in Canaan at that time. In the form we have it now, Joshua is most likely the work of writers associated with the royal court in Jerusalem in David's time and later. After the Exile, editors reworked the book to accent lessons learned during those years outside the Promised Land.

As you read Joshua…

God encourages Joshua repeatedly in the first chapter. What do you think is the reason for this?

Read over Rahab's declaration to the spies in Joshua 2:8–13. What do her words reveal about her deepest convictions?

What lesson can be drawn from the collapse of the walls of Jericho?

Joshua warns the people of the dire consequences of rebuilding the city of Jericho. In fact, Jericho was rebuilt (see 1 Kings 16:34). What reasoning would lead people to restore that city?

Considering the things Achan took from Jericho, what do you think his intentions were?

Why are the Gibeonites successful in their bid for survival?

How does God show favor to the people of Israel in chapter 10?

Note Joshua's treatment of royalty in 10:22–27. Why do you think he does this?

What progression do you observe in the opposition to Israel from chapters 6 to 11 of Joshua?

What is your estimation of Caleb after reading chapter 14?

What do you think of the tribe of Joseph after reading chapters 16 and 17?

How do you think the tribes from Gilead feel when they have to leave the Lord's land where the rest of the tribes are settled (Joshua 22)?

Do you think Joshua is justified in his fears that the people may not be able to serve the Lord (Joshua 24)?

Three Spiritual Lessons From Joshua

- The Promised Land is a gift from God
- People who trust in God enjoy advantages in life
- Illusions of self-sufficiency weaken our relationship with God

JOSHUA

JUDGES

This book introduces you to some of the most colorful characters in the Bible. You meet a decisive woman who leads her people to victory, an unassuming young boy who becomes a mighty warrior, and a strong man who can destroy a temple with his bare hands.

These are just a few of the judges of Israel. The three referred to above are Deborah, Gideon and Samson. Each of them was gifted by God to lead the people to victory against their enemies. And lead they did!

But in almost every account of a judge in Israel there is something a little out-of-balance, something that makes the character, no matter how brave, a little less than a complete model of faith.

Of course, there are exceptions. Deborah is definitely one of them. She speaks for God. Her associate Barak, the chosen leader of Israel, knows that he needs Deborah at his side to win the battle. When they have won the victory with God's help, they sing a song together to celebrate all that God did for them. You will find the text of their song in Judges 5.

But other judges are not so clearly models of faith. Gideon, for example, does indeed become a great leader as we noted above. But he also seems to allow his successes to go to his head. When Gideon dies, the country suffers because he gave more attention to himself than to God, even though he owed all his success to God.

Probably everyone is familiar with Samson's story, at least the part about him and his beloved—and dangerous—Delilah. For all his strength, Samson cannot resist beautiful distractions in his life—like Delilah. By the time he gets refocused on God, he has the strength for one last mighty deed, but he gets himself killed in the process.

After Samson's time things really begin to go downhill for Israel. Instead of uniting in a common effort against their enemies, the tribes of Israel end up fighting each other.

It is clear by the end of the book that unless the people learn to focus on God first they will be caught up in an endless cycle of death and destruction. And their claim to the Promised Land will grow progressively weaker.

The 21 chapters of Judges:

1 — 16   Israel struggles to survive under a series of leaders including:

Othniel and Ehud	3
Deborah and Barak	4 — 5
Gideon	6 — 8
Abimalech, Tola, Jair	9 — 10
Jephthah	11 — 12
Samson	13 — 16

17 — 21   Israel is still in need of a real leader

Judges

The heroes and heroines in this book are not judges in the ordinary sense. They do not wear black robes and sit at a bench in a court of law. The term "judge" in this book refers to a temporary ruler over Israel chosen by God to defend the people from their enemies.

A Fable

You will find one of the few fables of the Bible in Judges 9:7–15. It clearly presents the dangers of giving someone royal power. The trees go in search of a king to rule over them. All the good candidates are satisfied with what they do already. In desperation, the trees must turn to a bramble, which has nothing to offer them but everything to gain. The fable is a clear warning about the dangers of royal power.

Women of Substance

Several women prove to be true leaders in this book. We already know about Deborah. There are others. A woman named Jael has the strength to strike down the enemy (Judges 4:17–22). The daughter of Jephthah bravely accepts the sacrifice of dying for her people.

A Refrain

A refrain we hear over and over again in the final chapters of Judges is this: "In those days there was no king in Israel; all the people did what was right in their own eyes." The people actually do have a king—the Lord God of Israel! But they choose to ignore God and instead go their own way.

JUDGES

Judges on the Clock (BC)

Settlement in Canaan   c. 1250

Judges defend Israel   c. 1250 – 1050

The Song of Deborah in Judges 5 is regarded by many as one of the most ancient portions of the Bible, perhaps reaching back twelve hundred years before the birth of Jesus. The archeological evidence we mentioned in the previous chapter indicates a good amount of social change during that period. This seems to fit the picture we get from the book of Judges, with all the struggles going on between the Israelites and others in Canaan. As with Joshua, in its current form, the book of Judges is most likely the work of writers associated with the royal court in Jerusalem during and after David's time. After the Exile, editors reworked the book to accent lessons learned during those years outside the Promised Land.

As you read Judges…

Why do you suppose the people of Israel choose to serve other divinities instead of the God of Israel?

What kind of person do you think Deborah was? Which actress would you choose to play the role of Deborah in a stage production of her story?

What changes take place in Gideon as his story unfolds?

What kind of person do you imagine Jephthah's daughter was?

In your estimation, how successful is Samson as a judge?

What thoughts fill your mind as you read about tribal relationships in the final chapters of this book?

Several times the author of Judges tells us there was as yet no king is Israel. What do you think the author meant by this?

Three Spiritual Lessons From Judges

- Anyone can be a hero or a heroine for God
- True courage is measured by loyalty to the values of heaven
- Personal ambition can interfere with service to God

RUTH

Ruth was the great-grandmother of King David. This alone would be reason enough to merit her story a place in the Bible. But her loyalty to the God of Israel provides an even stronger reason for including her story among so many other books devoted to leading people closer to God.

Her story begins with so much sorrow it seems to weigh us down with grief. The widow Naomi loses her two sons. With her world seemingly deprived of all hope for happiness, Naomi encourages her two daughters by marriage—Orpah and Ruth—to leave her and pursue their own dreams.

Orpah leaves; Ruth stays. She expresses her devotion to her husband's family in one of the most memorable lines of the Bible: "Where you go, I will go; / where you lodge, I will lodge; / your people shall be my people, / and your God my God" (Ruth 1:16).

From that point forward Ruth's story—and Naomi's, too—takes a positive turn. On the surface, this might appear to be the result of good fortune. But on a deeper level, we can almost feel the hand of God directing things to Ruth's advantage because of her great faith.

Ruth ends up working in the field of a man named Boaz, who proves to be the perfect match for her. They marry and God blesses them with a son. And so a story that began with such sorrow ends with great joy. All this because Ruth was loyal to her family and loyal to God.

The 4 chapters of Ruth:

1	Trust in God
2 — 3	Blessings
4	New life

Mara

This name means "bitter." It is the name Naomi assigned to herself after all her losses. But of course, all that changes because of Ruth's faith and love. By the end of the story, Naomi is holding a grandson.

Obed

This is the name the people give to Ruth's son. This child helped Naomi forget about all the bitterness that once filled her life. Obed became the father of Jesse. And Jesse, of course, became the father of David.

Boaz

Boaz is a person of fine character in this story. He is kind and generous. He is the perfect match for Ruth. He loves Ruth dearly but marries her only when all the legal requirements of the day have been fulfilled.

Pentecost Connection

By tradition, this book is one of five read at important festivals in the Jewish calendar. Ruth is read at the Feast of Weeks. Because this feast is celebrated fifty days after Passover, it is also known as Pentecost (a Greek word meaning fifty). Crops were harvested at that time and of course harvesting plays an important part in Ruth's story.

Ruth on the Clock (BC)

The days of the Judges   c. 1250 – 1050

The rise of King David   c. 1000

Since Ruth was the great-grandmother of David, her story could conceivably come from the dawn of kingship in Israel, about one thousand years before the time of Jesus. Some believe her story was preserved because it contributed favorably to David's kingship. That would seem to argue for a very early date for this book. On the other hand, some believe the language of the book brings it closer five hundred years or so in time.

As you read Ruth...

How many signs of emptiness can you identify in the first chapter of Ruth?

How many signs of plenty can you find in the final chapter of the Ruth?

What is your first impression of Ruth? Do you have the same impression of her at the end of the book?

How is God involved in this book?

Can you see parallels between Ruth's story and life today?

Three Spiritual Lessons From Ruth

- God's love knows no boundaries
- Loyalty to God leads to unforeseen blessings
- No hardship should lead us away from God

1 AND 2 SAMUEL

The two books of Samuel offer us some of the most captivating narratives in the Bible. The scenes are breathtaking, the characters are utterly realistic and the plot is absolutely gripping because it is about the interaction between God and people.

As you might guess from the title of the book, the principal character is Samuel. He is so big a personality that one title alone cannot capture all that he is. Samuel is first of all a priest in the service of God's sanctuary. Samuel is also a judge like all those judges who went before him, but of course he is a far better judge than most of them had ever been. Samuel is also a prophet who confronts his people with the truth of God's Word.

A second character playing a major role in Samuel's life is Saul. At God's command, Samuel anointed Saul as the first true king of the Israelites. Samuel gave King Saul every advantage in learning to appreciate what kingship in Israel was really all about. But Saul never learned to appreciate the spiritual values so crucial to being a success as king over God's people. Saul's world was the physical and the tangible. If Saul could not see something or get his hands on it, it had little value for him. Saul regarded kingship in Israel like kingship in any other country. But that could never be the ideal in Israel.

So God sent Samuel to anoint a replacement for Saul. This is where David enters the picture. David has all the potential to be a great king in Israel. He is devoted to the Lord God. Everyone is familiar with his victory over the giant Philistine Goliath. And David—so different from Saul—gave God all the glory for that victory.

David enjoyed great popularity among the people of Israel and that led to trouble. Saul, unwilling to step aside for David, sought every means to kill him. Eventually it all came down to a great battle and Saul died.

The second book of Samuel covers the kingship of David. But the theme of this second work, like all books of the Bible, remains the relationship between God and people. As we follow David's career, we discover valuable lessons in the journey of faith.

As long as David remained loyal to God, he grew stronger and stronger. Soon into this second book, David is declared king over all the tribes of Israel. With the help of God, David also brings security to the land. The people no longer have to live in fear. Soon David is even making plans to build a temple to the God of Israel. But God counters with an alternative plan. God will build a dynasty for David. The line of David will lead to the birth of the Messiah.

But then David's story takes a sad turn. Confident in his successes, David begins to forget that God was the source of his blessings. From that point on, David, so masterful in his reign over the outside world, fails to master the world within himself. He becomes a slave to his desires. His adultery with Bathsheba and the murder of Uriah, her husband and his own faithful servant, lead to a host of troubles in the kingdom.

David's sons prove to be just as unruly as he is. One of them—David's beloved Absalom—even leads a rebellion against his father. By the end of the book, David's relationship with God is weaker and his kingdom suffers.

The 31 chapters of 1 Samuel:

1 — 7	Samuel restores Israel's strength
8 — 15	The failures of Saul
16 — 31	The successes of David

The 24 chapters of 2 Samuel:

1 — 9	God's gifts to David
10 — 12	David's ingratitude to God
13 — 24	The decline of David's family

Hannah

Hannah had no children. But when she asked God to give her a child, God listened to her prayer. She became the mother of Samuel. She spent the rest of her life in total gratitude to God. And God blessed her with even more children.

Shiloh

The ark of the covenant was kept at this place in the days of Samuel. Samuel apprenticed there under the direction of Eli, the priest of Shiloh. But when Samuel was an adult, the Philistines captured both Shiloh and the ark. This was a lesson for Israel. If they truly wanted to be secure, they had to live holy lives and not merely rely on holy places.

A Loyal Servant

Joab was David's most trusted commander. Joab did all he could to secure the kingdom by force of arms. He even struck down the king's son Absalom because he posed a threat to the state. David never forgave him for this and directed his son Solomon to exact vengeance on Joab.

Endor

At this place, Saul consulted with a woman who claimed to communicate with the dead (1 Samuel 28). Unfortunately, Saul valued the words of Samuel only after the great prophet was dead. Had he listened to Samuel during the prophet's lifetime, Saul's kingdom would have remained secure.

Rabbah

This was the site of a great victory for David. David knew how to win a war on the battlefield. Unfortunately, he was not as successful at winning spiritual battles. It was while his army was winning the war with Rabbah that David lost his battle with pride. He took the beautiful Bathsheba for himself and arranged to have her husband killed.

Samuel on the Clock (BC)

Samuel   c.1070

King Saul   c. 1040

King David   c. 1000

The two books of Samuel cover the lives of three major figures in the decades before the first millennium BC: Samuel, Saul and David. The account may come from a skilled writer in the royal court of David. Some call his work "The Succession Narrative" since it dramatizes the question, "Who will succeed David as king?" The books of Samuel probably received their present form in the years following the Exile in Babylon.

As you read the books of Samuel...

How would you describe the character of Hannah, mother of Samuel?

How did the people of Israel lose the ark? And why could the Philistines not keep it?

What sets Samuel apart from his contemporaries, especially the priestly family of Eli?

What is your first impression of Saul as a suitable candidate for kingship over Israel?

How does 1 Samuel 15 alter your opinion of Saul?

What lesson does Samuel learn from God in 1 Samuel 16?

What are your first impressions of David as a suitable successor to Saul?

How does David defeat the great Philistine champion in 1 Samuel 17?

How loyal a friend to David is Saul's son Jonathan?

What are your impressions of Abigail in 1 Samuel 25?

How does David display his loyalty to Saul's family in the opening chapters of 2 Samuel?

How does the prophet Nathan win so candid a response from David in 2 Samuel 12?

What does 2 Samuel 13—20 reveal about David's family?

How does David display his devotion to God in the final chapters of 2 Samuel?

Three Spiritual Lessons From 1 and 2 Samuel

- God is always ready to forgive our offenses
- Gratitude to God is a sound basis for security
- The highest dignity comes from serving God

1 AND 2 KINGS

Royalty has a certain star quality. We get a double dose of it in these books because there are two kingdoms: Israel and Judah. But we should remember there is really just one star, one king for the people—the Lord God. Ideally, the rulers over the people were supposed to serve God's interests. For that reason an ideal title for these two books—at least from the biblical viewpoint—might be something like 1 and 2 Servants.

But in fact, few kings truly did serve God. Most of the time they pursued their own interests; they pretty much ignored God's interests altogether. So in fact, the standard title for these books is adequate after all because it accurately expresses the prideful ways of these mortal monarchs.

Surprisingly, this material begins on a hopeful note. The wise Solomon succeeds David to the throne of Israel. This son of David and Bathsheba displayed a great deal of promise. At the beginning of his reign, he had a dream in which he asked God to give him "an understanding heart." God was so pleased with Solomon's request that God gave him much more than just that. And a definite high point during Solomon's reign was the construction of the Jerusalem temple.

But Solomon forgot that a right relationship with God was the true source of all his successes. The once-wise king even resorted to building shrines to other gods right there within the Promised Land.

By the time Solomon died, the kingdom was in disarray. In fact, Solomon's kingdom split apart so that from this point on in Kings we have to bear in mind that there are now two kingdoms. The northern kingdom retained the name Israel; its capital was Samaria. The southern kingdom was called Judah after its principal tribe; the capital of Judah was Jerusalem.

The northern kings were especially neglectful of God. Each king was worse than the one who preceded him. And the worst of all was Ahab. Just listen to the way the Bible introduces his reign:

> Ahab son of Omri did evil in the sight of the LORD more than all who were before him.
>
> And as if it had been a light thing for him to walk in the sins of Jeroboam son of Nebat, he took as his wife Jezebel daughter of King Ethbaal of the Sidonians, and went and served Baal, and worshiped him. (1 Kings 16:30–31)

It's fairly clear from this preface to Ahab's story that this king was far from being the kind of ruler who would lead the people closer to God. Jeroboam, the first northern king, set the standard for faithlessness in the kingdom. But clearly, Ahab surpassed that king's record. And Ahab capped it all off by choosing the wicked Jezebel to be his wife. Little wonder the northern kingdom, weakened by decades of idolatry, collapsed. The people were exiled and the land resettled by foreigners.

The kings in the southern kingdom of Judah seem better by comparison. But in time they, too, drift farther and farther away from God and seek security in earthly resources. By the end of the second book, the Kingdom of Judah had also collapsed and many of its people, including a member of David's royal house, are exiled to Babylon.

Two definite bright spots in this gloomy record of royalty are the prophets Elijah and Elisha. Their careers span the material from 1 Kings

1 AND 2 KINGS

17 to 2 Kings 13. Both men did all they could to steer king and people closer to God. They had better success with individuals in the kingdom whose positive response serves as a model of faith for readers of every generation. Among these spiritual giants are the widow of Zarepath (1 Kings 17); the woman of Shunem (2 Kings 4); and Naaman the general (2 Kings 5).

The 22 chapters of 1 Kings:

I — 11	The rise and fall of Solomon
12 — 16	The kings ignore God's prophets
17 — 22	Ahab ignores the prophet Elijah

The 25 chapters of 2 Kings:

I — 13	Kings ignore the prophet Elisha
14 — 17	The northern kingdom collapses
18 — 25	The southern kingdom collapses

Elijah

He came suddenly like a whirlwind. He was sent by God to warn King Ahab of his evil ways. By his word, the rain stopped; by his word, the rains came back. Elijah seemed to prefer calling down fire from heaven to ignite an altar of sacrifice or to consume a company of disbelievers. But he could also offer life and plenty to those who would turn to God. In the end, he went up in a whirlwind back to heaven, but not before he anointed his successor.

Elisha

Elisha asked for and received a double portion of the spirit of God that was upon his teacher Elijah. When he turned in anger to hurl a curse at a jeering band of youngsters, not one but two bears came charging out of the forest. Elisha never again so misused the word of God. He fed the hungry, healed the sick and even raised the dead back to life. Such life-giving power emanated from this agent of God that mere contact with his bones was enough to bring the dead back to life!

Deliverance

Some of the kings of Israel took no lesson from the history of their people. They oppressed others as Egypt once oppressed Israel. Over 150 years ago, archeologists discovered a large stone of black basalt commemorating Moab's rebellion against an overbearing Israel. The Bible's record of this oppression is in 2 Kings 3:4–27.

Survival

The tunnel of Hezekiah was an engineering marvel. Excavators began at opposite ends, one team at a spring, the other in the city. Together they cut a shaft over sixteen hundred feet long. The year was about 700 BC. If only Hezekiah had been as equally enterprising when it came to putting faith in God.

Josiah

The reign of this king, in the final decades of the seventh century BC, was one of the bright spots in Israel's history. When a copy of God's law—perhaps a portion of Deuteronomy—was discovered in the temple, Josiah initiated a series of reforms in the kingdom. He died at Megiddo defending his country against Egypt.

A Great Woman

The Bible gives this title to an unnamed woman from Shunem. In a world so obsessed with things, this woman looked for something more. She welcomed the Word of God into her home. Her trust in God opened the way to new life. You can read her fascinating story in 2 Kings 4:8–37.

Bethel

King Jeroboam (pronounce it Je-ro-BO-am) built a shrine in this city to keep his subjects in the north from going down to the true temple in Jerusalem. A prophet warned him against doing such a thing. According to 1 Kings 13 even the road to Bethel was to be avoided. Jeroboam set the standard for faithlessness by which all his successors were measured.

I AND 2 KINGS

Kings on the Clock (BC)

David   c. 1000

Fall of Samaria   721

Fall of Jerusalem   587

There are actual royal archives surviving from biblical times. Unfortunately, they do not come from Israel but from her neighbors. Assyrian and Babylonian texts are especially interesting. Some of them mention biblical kings by name—a fact very satisfying to the historian in us. The books 1 and 2 Kings record events over the four-hundred-year span of time from David to the collapse of the kingdom in 587 BC. The reign of the King Josiah (640–609 BC) is a likely time for the production of Kings. This original work was later revised to reflect lessons learned during the Exile in Babylon.

As you read 1 and 2 Kings…

Solomon's reign as king begins with such promise. Why is the kingdom in such disarray when he dies?

What is the theme of Solomon's prayer at the dedication of the temple in 1 Kings 8?

Describe Solomon through the eyes of the Queen of Sheba (1 Kings 9).

What does 1 Kings 13—15 reveal about the power of God's Word?

Elijah has such life-giving powers as God's prophet. What do you think keeps King Ahab from relying on Elijah and other prophets?

Elisha requested a double portion of the spirit of Elijah. Do you think he actually became twice the prophet Elijah was? What details from his life support your position?

Elisha directed Naaman the leper to wash seven times in the Jordan River (1 Kings 5). The number draws attention to his dramatic healing. Find other instances of the number seven in the Bible. What do they dramatize?

The narrator of Kings tells us that King Hezekiah displayed a great deal of promise at the beginning of his reign (2 Kings 18:3–9). Could this be said of him at the end of his life?

Why did the kingdom collapse in spite of all the reforms introduced by good King Josiah?

Three Spiritual Lessons From 1 and 2 Kings

- The true character of leadership is measured in terms of service to God
- The only limitations on what God can do for us are the ones we present to God
- God's Word always steers us toward life

1 AND 2 CHRONICLES

The history of God's people as recorded in Samuel and Kings could benefit from a makeover. The two books of Chronicles provide one, giving us a second look at the relationship between God and the Israelites. For the most part, they retell the story, this time concentrating on the ideals. In this second telling, the people are much more successful at living up to the standards of the covenant.

The first nine chapters fast-forward from Adam to the time of David. At that point, the narrative pace slows down considerably as the material recasts David as the ideal king and spiritual leader. All the darker episodes in David's career—his personal sins and the failures in his family—are removed. In their place, Chronicles adds material about David's keen interest in the Jerusalem temple and his advice to Solomon about how to build the temple (1 Chronicles 22—29).

The effect of this rewriting is to cast David as the one who did the most to make God the focus of the kingdom. This of course had always been the ideal, but in Chronicles, it is finally realized.

The second book illustrates how David's religious program was carried forward by his successors. Good King Jehoshaphat rises as the model monarch in this book (2 Chronicles 19—20). The positive tone of this material is achieved by omitting the sad decline of the northern kingdom that received so much attention in 1 and 2 Kings.

Chronicles shows us an Israel working hard to keep its focus on God. Kings like David and his successors rise as the spiritual leaders they were always supposed to be. Of course, the kingdom still struggles with sin. Even Chronicles cannot erase the fact that the kingdom finally did collapse. But Chronicles ends on the positive note of a royal edict from Persia announcing plans to rebuild the house of the Lord. And so David's fine example continues to inspire.

The 29 chapters of I Chronicles:

I — 9	Human history leads to Jerusalem
I0 — I6	David and the ark
I7 — 29	David's plans for the temple

The 36 chapters of 2 Chronicles:

1 — 9	Solomon fulfills David's plans
10 — 20	Kings in David's likeness
21 — 36	Human failure, divine grace

Asa

This king showed signs of being a worthy descendant of David. When this king began his reign, the Chronicler could say of him that he did "what was good and right in the sight of the LORD his God" (2 Chronicles 14:2). Asa removed idols from the kingdom; he heeded the words of a prophet. But Asa's faith weakened in later years. He looked for security in other nations instead of God.

Jehoshaphat

Like his father Asa, Jehoshaphat began his reign with a great deal of promise. He was just thirty-five years old when he took the throne and he reigned for a quarter of a century. In a scene reminiscent of Solomon's great prayer at the dedication of the temple, Jehoshaphat stands in the house of God and asks God to protect the kingdom (2 Chronicles 20). The king's prayer was granted. But in later years, Jehoshaphat's faith began to weaken just as his father's did.

A Change of Heart

In the book of Kings, Manasseh's reign is singled out as the one especially responsible for the collapse of the kingdom. However, 2 Chronicles 33:12–13 records a change of heart in this king. While in exile, he turned to God in prayer. The text of his prayer was preserved in some copies of the Bible. It was placed after 2 Chronicles and bore the title "The Prayer of Manasseh." Because this prayer was not present in all manuscripts of the Vulgate, the fathers at the Council of Trent did not include it in their list of canonical books.

Early and Often

According to 2 Chronicles 36:15, God "persistently" tried to reach the people through the words of the prophets. God kept the conversation going even when it seemed no one was willing to listen. But even Chronicles with all its positive emphasis could not alter the fact that the kingdom did fall because the people refused to listen to God.

Paralipomenon

Paralipomenon is a Greek term meaning "omitted." It is the title for 1 and 2 Chronicles in the Greek Bible. The title reflects the fact that these books add further details to the material we find in other historical books of the Bible. They add this material with a definite purpose: to highlight the potential for good in that history.

Chronicles on the Clock (BC)

Adam and Eve to the Fall of Jerusalem   587

Kingdom of Persia   c. 650

In biblical time these books span the ages from Adam and Eve all the way down to the beginning of the Persian Empire. But when were 1 and 2 Chronicles actually written? The genealogy traces the line of David some ten generations beyond the last king of Judah (1 Chronicles 3:17–24). This suggests 1 and 2 Chronicles may have been written around the middle of the fourth century before the birth of Jesus.

As you read 1 and 2 Chronicles…

David directed his musician Asaph to sing a hymn of thanksgiving when the ark was transferred to Jerusalem. This hymn must have been very popular because it appears again in the Psalter. Find out where by checking the cross-references in a Bible.

What is your impression of David as he is portrayed in 1 Chronicles 19—20? How does the material in 1 Samuel 10—12 alter this impression?

How does 1 Chronicles 22—28 portray David as devoted to the Lord?

How does 2 Kings 21:1–18 portray King Manasseh? How does 2 Chronicles 33:1–20 portray him?

What themes in 2 Chronicles 36:14–23 make it a good companion text for the Lord's dialogue with Nicodemus in John 3:14–21 (Fourth Sunday of Lent, cycle B)?

What differences do you see between the final verses of 2 Kings and the final verses of 2 Chronicles?

I AND 2 CHRONICLES

Three Spiritual Lessons From 1 and 2 Chronicles

- The most meaningful life is one lived for God
- We have the potential to do great things for God
- Prayer can change us for the better

EZRA AND NEHEMIAH

How does one rebuild a nation? Ezra and Nehemiah have the answer. We can consider these two leaders together because in fact their story—contained on one scroll—is counted as one book in the Hebrew Bible. The same is true for other books of the Bible: 1 and 2 Samuel; 1 and 2 Kings; 1 and 2 Chronicles; and the twelve Minor Prophets.

We must admit right from the start that Ezra and Nehemiah are not household names. But it should come as no surprise that the message of these books fits right in with the message of the rest of the Bible, providing one more piece to the intricate puzzle that makes up the Word of God.

Back to the question about how to rebuild a kingdom—Ezra and Nehemiah give this answer: with the help of God! Let's explore this answer by giving a quick overview of the book.

These two books are busy with rebuilding. First comes the rebuilding of the altar and temple in Jerusalem. Then there is the reestablishment of religious traditions, all overseen by Ezra the scribe. Then comes the rebuilding of the walls of the city, overseen by Nehemiah the governor.

But all this rebuilding is not enough. These projects, impressive as they are, relate to externals only. They do not touch the soul. For the people to truly be restored there must be an internal rebuilding. That is why a prominent scene in this material is the public proclamation of the law by Ezra (Nehemiah 8). It is so important that Nehemiah is present for it, too. In fact, this is the only time these two figures appear together in the book.

It should come as no surprise that there are also two elaborate prayers in this material. The first is Ezra's appeal asking God to preserve the remnant of the people as they try to remain loyal to their covenant (Ezra 9:6–15). The second is Ezra's appeal asking God to forgive the people and allow them to enjoy a plentiful harvest (Nehemiah 9:6–37).

The 10 chapters of Ezra:

I — 6   Rebuilding the temple

7 — 10   Rebuilding the tradition

The 13 chapters of Nehemiah:

I — 6   Rebuilding the walls

8 — 13   Rebuilding the community

Ezra

Ezra carries the title "the Scribe." He is not merely well versed in matters of the Law of Moses. He is also deeply committed to the spiritual welfare of his people. In rabbinic tradition, he is regarded as the founder of Judaism.

Nehemiah

Nehemiah is the governor who oversees the reconstruction of the walls around the city of Jerusalem. He had formerly served as butler to the kings of Persia. But when his distress over the conditions in Jerusalem became known to the Persian court, he was entrusted with the task of governing Judah.

Kings of Persia

Three kings are mentioned in this material: Cyrus, Darius and Artaxerxes. Through their various decrees, they aided in the restoration of Jerusalem and Judah. From the point of view of the author of Ezra-Nehemiah, these mighty kings were merely in the service of the God of Israel.

Zerubbabel

This fascinating name belongs to the governor of restored Judah. He was the one overseeing the reconstruction of the temple. But he is more memorable as a descendant of King David. That is the reason why he is included in the genealogy of Jesus (Matthew 1:12–13; Luke 3:27).

Ezra-Nehemiah on the Clock (BC)

Return from Exile   537

Ezra   after 458?

Nehemiah   after 445?

These books record events from the return of the exiles from Babylon down to the middle of the fifth century. Some of the material—the decrees from the Persian court, for example—may go back to those times. Ezra 7:7 tells us the famous scribe arrived in the seventh year of King Artaxerxes. If this king is Artaxerxes I, then the year 458 BC seems likely. Nehemiah arrived in Jerusalem in the twentieth year of Artaxerxes I, which is 445 BC on our calendar. In its present form the book of Ezra-Nehemiah seems to come from a later period, perhaps just three centuries before the time of Jesus.

As you read Ezra and Nehemiah...

 Ezra begins with a royal proclamation to rebuild the temple at Jerusalem. What do you think this meant to King Cyrus of Persia? What did it mean to the people of Israel?

When the foundation of the temple is constructed, the elders who had seen the first temple began weeping (Ezra 3:10–13). Why do you think they were so moved?

What argument do opponents raise to stop the building program in Ezra 4?

On what grounds is this opposition reversed by Darius I in Ezra 6?

What does Ezra request of God in his prayer in Ezra 9:5–15?

Nehemiah 1—7 recounts the building of the walls of Jerusalem. How much stronger are these walls than the walls that protected Jerusalem in the time of David?

What themes in Nehemiah 8:2–10 make it a good companion text for the Lord's visit to Nazareth in Luke 4:14–21?

What does Ezra request of God in his prayer in Nehemiah 9:6–37?

When you finish reading the final chapter of Nehemiah, do you have the feeling there is still more to be done?

Three Spiritual Lessons From Ezra and Nehemiah

- The surest foundation for a nation is service to God
- Recognizing our need for God is the first step toward restoration
- Prayer is never out of place

TOBIT

Tobit is the story of a good man who gets even better. His book can easily be read in one sitting. And it teaches us some wonderful lessons about our relationship with God.

The story takes place in Nineveh, the same city to which Jonah preached. Tobit is one of the people taken into captivity after the Assyrians conquered the northern kingdom of Israel. Tobit was successful in his new surrounding but he always remains a faithful Israelite. He spends a lot of time doing good deeds. He even leaves the dinner table to bury the body of a fellow Israelite. Later that same night he is blinded by bird droppings. That is just one of the unforgettable scenes in this book!

Tobit seems too good to be true. And before long, we wonder what motivates him to do the good things he does. It turns out that, like the famously patient Job, Tobit will benefit from being less anxious about things and trusting more in the mysterious ways of God.

When Tobit believes he can endure his life no longer—he is blind and feels reproached by his wife—he pleads with God to take his life. He even prepares to die by sending his son Tobias to a friend in Media to collect some money. But God sets in motion a plan to extend Tobit's life and bless his family in ways Tobit could never imagine. In the end, Tobit discovers that God's plan for him was far superior to his own plans.

One special way God blesses Tobit is by sending an angel to guide Tobit's son on his journey to Media. The angel Raphael helps Tobias find Sarah and even arranges for their wedding. The angel also prepares a healing remedy for Tobit's blindness.

A special feature in the book of Tobit is its use of overlapping scenes. Here are some examples: Tobit prays for death at the same time Sarah does. While Sarah and Tobias are praising God for the gift of each other on their marriage night, Sarah's father is secretly digging a grave beside the house in the night. While Tobias and Sarah enjoy a wedding celebration, Anna and Tobit worry if Tobias will ever return.

Out of stories so preoccupied with fear and death, God weaves a beautiful story of life. In the end, Tobit discovers that the most meaningful years of his life came after the year he prayed for death.

The 14 chapters of Tobit:

1 — 3   Tobit prays for death
4 — 14   God responds with life

Anna

Anna is Tobit's loving and resourceful wife. After her husband is struck with blindness, Anna helps support the family by weaving cloth. One day a family presents her with a goat as a sign of their gratitude. When Tobit insists that she return the gift, Anna's response suggests he still has a lot to learn about righteousness. The rest of the story proves her right.

Raphael

This is the name of the heavenly agent whom God places in Tobit's life. But Raphael introduces himself as Azariah and does not reveal his true name until the end of the story. Raphael's God-given task is to heal Tobit not just from his physical blindness but, more importantly, from his spiritual blindness. Through the agency of Raphael, Tobit learns to let go of his own plans and trust instead in God' plan for his life.

Faithful Companion

Among the many memorable details of this biblical story is Tobias's dog. Only in this book of the Bible does a dog appear as a pet. This dog is Tobias's loyal companion throughout his journey to the land of Media to retrieve a sum of money entrusted to a friend by Tobias's father. Saint Jerome seems to have been especially intrigued with this dog. In his Latin translation of Tobit, he adds a verse about the dog wagging its tail.

Sarah

Sarah's story parallels Tobit's in many ways. Like Tobit, Sarah thinks there is no reason for her to continue living in this world. But God has plenty of things in store for her. By the end of the book, she is married to Tobias. They have a number of children. Tobias and Sarah have a long and happy life together.

Ahikar

His name means "my brother is honorable." The name is a good fit for this character, a nephew of Tobit. Ahikar has good connections with the royal house and helps his uncle get back into favor with the king. It seems a person named Ahikar actually did serve in the court of the Assyrian kings. His biography was famous in Assyrian literature long before the book of Tobit was written.

Sennacherib

This throne-name means "Sin (an Assyrian deity) strengthens my brothers." King Sennacherib ruled over Assyria for more than twenty years. His palace was in the city of Nineveh. A surviving imperial chronicle records the assassination that ended his career. According to 2 Kings 19:37, the deed was done by his own sons. The history of Sennacherib's family stands in stark contrast to the close relationship between Tobit and his son Tobias.

Tobit on the Clock (BC)

Fall of Samaria   721

Reign of Esarhaddon   681–668

Fall of Nineveh   612

From world history class we may recall names like Shalmeneser, Sennacherib or even Esarhaddon. They were rulers of the Assyrian Empire during its zenith more than seven hundred years before the time of Jesus. Tobit's story takes place in their world. The book begins with Assyria's conquest of Tobit's homeland. But at the end of the book, Assyria's power is doomed with the fall of the great city of Nineveh. The book of Tobit as it has come down to us was probably composed some four hundred years after the events it records.

As you read Tobit…

Imagine what it would be like to live away from home as Tobit does.

What kind of person was Tobit's wife, Anna?

Have you ever felt like Tobit as he prays to be set free from his troubles?

Does God's response to Tobit's prayer give you insights about how God works in your life?

The fish in chapter 6 plays a role in Tobias's faith journey. Can you think of similar "fish stories" in the Bible?

Some translations add the text of Raguel's blessing at 7:13. What blessing would you have for Tobias and Sarah?

Some couples choose the prayer of Tobias and Sarah (Tobit 8) as one of the readings at their wedding ceremony. What do you think makes this prayer so appealing to them?

Can you think of people in your own life who have played a role similar to the role of Azariah and Raphael in the book of Tobit?

Near the end of the book, Raphael reveals that he was right beside Tobit when he was doing his good works (12:13). Have you ever felt that heaven was watching over you as you went about your daily tasks?

In his prayer of rejoicing, Tobit gives this advice, "So now see what he (God) has done for you…" (13:6). How has Tobit changed from the beginning of his story?

We often find the characters in this book offering a prayer to God. Is this true for your life too?

One special feature of this book is the description of two separate scenes in the same time frame. What examples of this technique can you find in Tobit?

Three Spiritual Lessons From Tobit

- It is good to understand our real motives for doing good
- Suffering does not mean God has abandoned us
- We should always be open to God's plans

JUDITH

You have probably seen a picture of Judith. Artists down through the ages have given this great beauty many faces. Michelangelo included Judith in his series of great moments from the Bible on the ceiling the Sistine Chapel. What was Judith's great moment? It came when she struck off the head of her enemy! This is not a book for the faint of heart. But we are getting ahead of the story.

As the book begins, Nebuchadnezzar, king over the ancient empire of Assyria and planning war against a rival, commands all the surrounding kingdoms to make an alliance with him; they refuse. In retaliation, Nebuchadnezzar determines to punish all the kingdoms that dared offend his pride. He places his army under the command of his able general Holofernes and gives them orders to destroy the offending nations. Nebuchadnezzar is not satisfied to rule over the world; he wants the world to worship him alone. Any reader of the Bible knows this is not going to sit well with the people of Israel.

Holofernes arrives at last at the homeland of the Israelites. Learning that the Israelites have prepared to put up a fight, the great general is curious to know what kind of people they are. A man named Achior warns Holofernes not to engage the Israelites in battle. He explains that God protects the Israelites and no mortal army could ever defeat them unless they were unfaithful to God.

Holofernes refuses to believe Achior and tells him confidently "...you shall not see my face again from this day until I take revenge on this race that came out of Egypt" (6:5). Achior is handed over to the Israelites in the city of Bethulia, a city Holofernes plans to destroy with Achior in it.

The people of Bethulia are at first confident that God will protect them. But as the siege continues, their faith begins to weaken and they consider surrendering to the Assyrian army. That is when Judith steps forward. She asks for their prayers but refuses to reveal the details of her plan to save them until she has finished what she intends to do.

God has given Judith great beauty. She uses this gift to save her people. Holofernes is so vain he believes Judith has found him irresistible. After a night of feasting and drinking in celebration of his good fortune Holofernes collapses onto his bed dead drunk. Judith quickly dispatches him and carries his head in a sack back to Bethulia.

With their leader dead, the Assyrians are easily vanquished. Achior, by the way, does see Holofernes's face again, just as the boastful general said he would, but, of course, the circumstances are quite different.

Judith's story is one more illustration of the prevailing biblical theme that true security is found in a right relationship with God. Consider the way the book begins and the way it ends. The opening lines of Judith describe in some detail how the king of the Medes built a massive wall around his city to protect himself from an attack by the king of Assyria. The book ends with Judith singing a hymn of praise to God. Which source of security proved stronger? The wall? Or trust in God? Of course trusting in God is the only answer.

All the way through this book, there is contrast between earthly resources and heavenly resources. Assyria trusts in its military might; Judith trusts in God. Defenders find safety in walls; believers find safety in God. Some speak with arrogance; others pray humbly to God.

JUDITH

This match between two very different viewpoints generates some humor in the book too. In her dialogue with the Assyrian general, Judith speaks about her profound trust in God, but Holofernes is so self-absorbed he believes she is speaking about him.

At one point, for example, Judith confesses to the general's servant, "Who am I to refuse my lord? Whatever pleases him I will do at once, and it will be a joy to me until the day of my death" (12:14). Judith of course is speaking about defending her people with the help of her divine Lord. But Holofernes interprets her words to mean she finds him irresistible.

The 16 chapters of Judith:

1 — 7   Assyria's impudence and pride

8 — 16   Judith's humble service to God

A Day's Work

In his preface to the book of Judith, Saint Jerome announces that he translated the book from Aramaic into Latin in just one night. No copy of Judith in Aramaic has survived. But we do have Judith's story in Greek and, of course, in Jerome's one-day Latin translation.

Empty Boast

General Holofernes asks in 6:2, "What god is there except Nebuchadnezzar?" The rest of the book will give a very definite response to that question.

A Generous Woman

Before she died at the age of 105, Judith set her loyal servant free and gave away all her earthly belongings (Judith 16:23–24). But her story really celebrates her spiritual generosity. She shared her spiritual wealth with her people and freed them from fear and from their enemies.

Lost City

Judith's hometown of Bethulia is described as occupying high ground overlooking the valley of Esdraelon (Judith 4:6–7). This valley runs east and west in the Holy Land some forty miles or so below Galilee. The actual site of Bethulia has yet to be discovered.

Persuasive

Judith is famous for her great beauty. But the account of her in this book also celebrates her skill as a persuasive speaker. When her fellow citizens are prepared to surrender and worship the gods of Assyria, Judith argues that it is time for them to display the same kind of trust that Abraham, Isaac and Jacob did (8:26).

Judith on the Clock (BC)

Nebuchadnezzar's campaign in Judea   588–587

Return from Exile   537

Judith wins her victory during the reign of the great Nebuchadnezzar, who ruled over Babylon from 605 to 562 BC. A more specific date comes with the detail that the Babylonian army entered her homeland in the eighteenth year of the king. This would place Judith's victory around the year 588 BC on our calendars. But such historical precision does not seem to be important for the author since verses in the book (4:3; 5:19) clearly place the action after the return from Exile in 537 BC. Regarding the date for the actual composition of Judith, vocabulary and geographical details in the book place Judith about a century before the time of Christ.

As you read Judith…

Nebuchadnezzar's name can be translated "May the god Nabu (a god of wisdom) protect my kingdom." What does this contribute to your reading of the book?

What is your first impression of Achior when you meet him in chapter 5? Does it change as you learn more about him? Have you ever met anyone like Achior?

How do you picture Judith in your mind? What kind of person could portray her in a play or a movie?

What is your assessment of Judith's address to the rulers of her people in Judith 8:11–27?

Irony is present when one meaning is intended but another meaning can be taken. How many examples of irony can you find in the dialogue between Judith and Holofernes in Judith 11 and 12?

Judith's hymn is one of the canticles sung by the church in the Liturgy of the Hours. What makes this hymn so appropriate as a prayer?

Three Spiritual Lessons From Judith
- We can accomplish great things when we rely on God
- Earthly obstacles are no match for the will of God
- True strength is found in a right relationship with God

ESTHER

Every one of us has the potential to do wonderful things. Queen Esther's story is proof of that! She rises from obscurity to become a favorite in the royal household of Persia. That alone would make this quite a success story. But for Esther it is only the beginning because, like any biblical account, the real message is not about what people gain for themselves but about how they serve God in this world. But let's not get too far ahead in the book.

On the surface, the story is fairly straightforward. A young Jewish girl becomes the favorite wife of the king of Persia. A member of the royal court, Haman by name, plots to have all the Jews in the kingdom killed on a certain day. His motive is jealousy over the promotion of a certain Mordecai, also a Jew and the uncle of Queen Esther. Mordecai convinces Esther that she must use her influence with the king to put a stop to Haman's evil scheme.

After some hesitation, due to the fact that she has not been in the king's company for some time and approaching him uninvited could lead to a sentence of death, Esther finally agrees to seek a royal audience no matter what the consequences for herself.

As it turns out, the king welcomes her visit. She invites the king and Haman to a series of feasts. When the moment is right, she reveals Haman's sinister plot to have her people annihilated. In a rage, the king orders Haman to be hanged on the very gallows he had prepared for Mordecai.

That is the story as it appears on the surface. Of course, since this is a book of the Bible, there is a deeper story. All of this takes place by God's design. One indication of God's involvement in the account is Mordecai's dream that God will see to it that the humble will prevail against the proud. Another indication can be found in Mordecai's words to Esther that her royal status is no accident. As he says to her, "Who knows? Perhaps you have come to royal dignity for just such a time as this" (Esther 4:14).

The protective hand of God can likewise be seen in the circumstances that lead to Mordecai's recognition by the king just when Haman was prepared to ask the king for a death sentence against him (6:1–11). And most significantly of all, Mordecai and Esther explicitly turn to God to help them. Mordecai prays for the protection of his people in 13:1–7; Esther prays for success when she makes her appeal to the king in 14:1–19.

Mordecai and Esther live in a world seemingly controlled by people with great power and ambition. The king of Persia hosts a banquet that lasts for seven days. He dismisses his queen when she refuses to be an ornament at his feast. Haman decides to destroy all the Jews because one of them refused to show him the honor he expected from the subjects of the empire. Haman even prepares a gallows seventy-five feet high to seek his revenge on Mordecai (5:14).

In this world of extremes, Mordecai and Esther enjoy the protection of God. Mordecai escapes the trap prepared for him by the most powerful figure in the kingdom. Esther succeeds with her appeal to a king so unpredictable in his response to things. Of course, all of this is due to the protective hand of God.

The 10 chapters of Esther:

1 — 5   Threats from mortals
6 — 10   Protection from God

A Problem Book

According to tradition, the rabbis debated about whether or not Esther should be included in the Bible. One reason was that in the Hebrew version of the story the name of God never appears in the book. Another reason was the absence of any reference to the land of Israel.

The Greek Esther

The version of Esther in the Catholic Bible comes from the Greek version of Esther. It includes over one hundred verses beyond the Hebrew version. These verses include prayers of Esther and Mordecai. The Greek version thus adds religious features lacking in the Hebrew version.

A Feast

Esther is read on the feast of Purim celebrated in early spring. The name comes from the lots (*purim* in Hebrew) cast by Haman to determine the best day for him to carry out his plan to exterminate the people of Israel (Esther 3:1–11). Purim celebrates the day God set in motion events to save the people.

Susa

The royal city of Susa is the setting for Esther's story. It is one of oldest cities in the world. It was the favorite residence of the Persian king Darius the Great who rebuilt the city during his long reign (522–486 BC). Apparently, Susa was also the favorite of his son Xerxes, called by his Persian name Ahasuerus in the book of Esther.

Esther on the Clock (BC)

Xerxes I   485–465

Maccabean Revolt   167–164

Ptolemy XII   80–51

The Persian backdrop for Esther's story takes it back to the fifth century before the time of Jesus. Esther's King Ahasuerus, known to history as Xerxes I, ruled from 485 to 465 BC. The final verses of the book refer to the fourth year of Ptolemy and Cleopatra. If this couple is Ptolemy XII and Cleopatra V, then a date around 77 BC seems likely. This suggests a date for Esther not long before New Testament times. Incidentally, Ptolemy XII was the father of Cleopatra VII, so familiar to students of Roman history.

As you read Esther…

How do you interpret Mordecai's dream in the opening chapter? Check your answer against the interpretation in the final chapter.

What are your first impressions of Mordecai and of Haman?

Was Queen Vashti right to refuse to obey the king's command?

What motivates Haman to issue a decree against the Jews?

What do the prayers of Mordecai and Esther reveal about their relationship with God?

What points of comparison and contrast can you see between the beginning and the end of the book of Esther?

God is so hidden in this book that some rabbis wondered if it should be included in the Bible. Would you agree with them?

This book is very popular with children on the feast of Purim. What features in it do you think make it so attractive to them?

Three Spiritual Lessons From Esther

- Prayer can be the first step toward great achievements
- Mortal schemes are no match for the plan of God
- God can do great things with those the world would overlook

1 AND 2 MACCABEES

Some say the title *Maccabeus* means "chosen by God," others say it means "hammer." Either meaning suits the character of Judas, son of Mattathias. This Judas was the most prominent leader in the Jewish struggle against oppression known as the Maccabean Revolt.

It all began when a king named Antiochus IV wanted to unite his sprawling empire by encouraging his subjects to accept the Greek culture. The Jewish people resisted this policy and the trouble began. Antiochus IV eventually sent armies into Palestine to force the issue.

Violence against faithful Jews escalated. Then Mattathias and his seven sons broke out in open rebellion against the empire. Judas became the military leader. After a series of victories against increasingly powerful forces, Judas was able to reclaim the temple and restore worship to the God of Israel. It was spring, just 163 years before the birth of Jesus.

Jonathan succeeded his brother as leader of the people. Like Judas, Jonathan proved a capable leader. But the narrative of his work reads more like the military exploits of any nation. Jonathan makes alliances with one nation and then another. Ultimately, he dies at the hands of a supposed ally.

This same pattern is repeated with Simon, brother of Jonathan. The book concludes with Simon's son John narrowly escaping death. The final verses encourage us to pick up the rest of the story in the chronicles of John's high priesthood.

This first book of Maccabees concentrates mainly on the human initiative in that struggle, especially the bravery of Judas and the lesser achievements of his brothers Jonathan and Simon. The second book of Maccabees concentrates on the spiritual aspects of the struggle and

brings God into the picture in nearly every paragraph, accenting especially the devotion of the Jewish people to their faith and their tradition.

The second book of Maccabees begins with a pair of letters. The Jews
in Jerusalem invite their fellow Jews in Egypt to join them in celebrating
the dedication of the Jerusalem temple. We know this as the feast of
Hanukkah, a Hebrew term meaning "dedication." The joy of these two
letters sets the tone for the book.

This book highlights the spiritual successes enjoyed by Israel during
the difficult years of their struggle for renewed freedom. Even as we read,
for example, about theft, intrigue and murder by those who held the
office of high priest, we also read about a wonderful miracle of God to
keep the temple treasury out of the hands of the wicked.

The second book of Maccabees cannot ignore the cruelty of
Antiochus IV, king of Syria, as he tries to impose the Greek ways on the
Jews. But in this book, the king's power to harm is overshadowed by the
great faith of ordinary folks: an old man who dies a noble death for God;
a mother and her seven sons martyred for their convictions. The rest of
the book details the story of the victories won by Judas Maccabeus
against Antiochus IV and his generals, especially one named Nicanor.

All this makes 2 Maccabees a more spiritually satisfying read than 1
Maccabees. This second book looks for all the spiritual gemstones in the
seemingly bleak story of the Israelites' struggle for independence. We get
the definite feeling that God's people will prevail over all the greed and
wickedness in the world.

When 1 and 2 Maccabees are viewed together—like overlaying one
image on another—a profound spiritual lesson can be recognized. The
swords of warriors can win only a limited kingdom; trust in God can
lead to everlasting life in the kingdom of heaven. Viewed in this way,
1 and 2 Maccabees make yet another contribution to the prevailing
biblical message of seeking security in God alone.

The 16 chapters of 1 Maccabees:

1 — 9	Judas leads the struggle for religious freedom
10 — 16	The qualified successes of Jonathan and Simon

The 15 chapters of 2 Maccabees:

1 — 2	Celebrating the purification of the temple
3 — 10	How God protected the temple
11 — 15	How God protected the people

A Digest

The second book of Maccabees is a digest of a five-volume work on the Maccabean Revolt by a certain Jason of Cyrene. The author of 2 Maccabees accents God's role in human history. He wants his readers to enjoy his work. He announces in the final verse, "…the style of the story delights the ears of those who read the work. And here will be the end."

Hanukkah

The Hebrew word *Hanukkah* means "dedication." It refers to the eight-day celebration that took place after the faithful Jews freed the Jerusalem temple from the control of the enemy and restored the worship of God in the temple. The feast included the lighting of lamps in the temple. Jewish families celebrate this feast in December of each year.

Praying for the Dead

In 2 Maccabees 12:42–45 Judas Maccabeus takes up a collection to provide for a sin offering in the temple on behalf of those who gave their lives in battle. The text explains that he did this out of the conviction that they would rise again from the dead. This passage contributes to the church's teaching on purgatory.

Intercession of the Saints

As the devout high priest Onias was praying for his people, the prophet Jeremiah appeared alongside of him doing the same thing (2 Maccabees 15:14). This is a passage clearly exhibiting the conviction that the saints intercede for us.

Nicanor Day

This day in the month of Adar (our February) celebrated the victory against one of the more notorious enemies of the Jews. Nicanor was a high-ranking officer especially ruthless in his anti-Jewish policies. Nicanor Day was observed until the fall of Jerusalem in AD 70.

Hasideans

The Hasideans are "the faithful ones." This title refers to Jews noted for their loyalty to the Law of Moses. They are mentioned for the first time in 1 Maccabees 2:42–48. Their spiritual descendants were the Pharisees of the time of Jesus.

1 AND 2 MACCABEES

1 and 2 Maccabees on the Clock (BC)

Victory of Seleucus   312

Judas Maccabeus   167—160

Roman Palestine   after 63

The first book of Maccabees probably comes from the beginning of the first century. It certainly comes from a time after the Maccabean Revolt of 167–164, which it records. The favorable attitude toward the Roman Empire in 1 Maccabees—unlikely after the Roman occupation of Palestine—argues for a date before AD 63 when that occupation began.

The second book of Maccabees may be older than 1 Maccabees. It begins with a letter dated "in the one hundred eighty-eighth year" (2 Maccabees 1:9). This calculation begins with the year that Seleucus, a general of Alexander the Great, established a kingdom eventually controlling most of the lands of the Bible. On our calendar, the founding year of that kingdom is 312 BC, thus dating the letter to 124. This date is generally accepted as being close to the time the author completed a one-volume digest of Jason's five volumes on the Maccabean Revolt. This digest is what we now call 2 Maccabees.

As you read the books of Maccabees...

What circumstances led to the rebellion of Mattathias and his sons?

What lesson does Judas give his followers in 1 Maccabees 3?

The restoration of the temple is recorded in 1 Maccabees 4:36–59. Why do you think Judas and his brothers decided to celebrate this event every year?

What lesson does King Antiochus IV learn at his death in 1 Maccabees 6:5–13?

What new threat surfaces in 1 Maccabees 7 and how is it removed?

Where do the brothers of Judas look for security in the final chapters of 1 Maccabees?

How do the writers of the letter in 2 Maccabees 1:10—2:18 feel about the new feast of purification (Hanukkah)?

In what way does the author compare his task to the task of a painter in 2 Maccabees 2:29?

How does heaven protect the temple in 2 Maccabees 3?

What events lead up to the desecration of the temple (2 Maccabees 5)?

The account about Eleazar (2 Maccabees 6) is thought to be the earliest example of a martyr story. What lesson does the author draw from it?

The author of 2 Maccabees urges his readers to understand that the hardships recorded in his book were designed to discipline the people (2 Maccabees 6:12–17). As you read the succeeding chapters, do you find yourself in agreement?

What themes in 2 Maccabees 7:1–14 make it a good companion reading for the Lord's confrontation with the Sadducees in Luke 20:27–38?

What details in 2 Maccabees 8 reveal the spiritual convictions of Judas Maccabeus?

What lesson can be found in the elaborate account of the death of Antiochus in 2 Maccabees 9?

The final chapters of 2 Maccabees chronicle a number of battles between Judas Maccabeus and the enemies of the Jews. How does the author give a spiritual tone to this material?

Read the concluding verses of 2 Maccabees. Do you think the author accomplished what he set out to do?

Three Spiritual Lessons From 1 and 2 Maccabees

- The best defense can be found in doing things God's way
- Our bond with God is not broken by death
- A great miracle can take place wherever we are open to God's plan

PART FOUR

THE WISDOM BOOKS

The wisdom books apply the lessons of the Bible to our daily lives. The basic message here is that a life lived in service to God is a life worth living.

We begin with Job who rises above the most unimaginable tragedies to proclaim his faith, startling testimony to the truth that no experience in life should lead us away from God.

The Psalms exhibit the full range of emotions we feel as we make the journey of faith. These beautiful hymns to God are probably the part of the wisdom books most familiar to us.

Proverbs offers countless practical insights into everyday living, advocating a life close to God as the ideal.

In the book of Ecclesiastes (another title is "Qoheleth"), King Solomon tells us of his pursuit of happiness in this world. At the end of it all, he discovers that the most meaningful thing in life is to enjoy all the gifts God presents to us with each passing day.

At first reading, the Song of Songs sounds like nothing more than love poetry between a man and a woman. But because it is included in the Bible, it also serves the noble cause of expressing the love between God and people.

Solomon addresses us again in the book of Wisdom. This time he urges us to join him in the pursuit of wisdom. He illustrates the many advantages a servant of God enjoys in life. He draws much of his inspiration from the Exodus out of Egypt.

Finally, Sirach (another title is "Ecclesiasticus") offers us an insightful review of the history of God's people concentrating on famous figures from the past who distinguished themselves as models of faith.

Saint Jerome believed the books of wisdom were the perfect place to start reading the Bible. He valued the practical guidelines for life included in these books. He believed the wisdom books offered readers a good foundation for the rest of the Bible, especially the Gospels. After reading this material, you can decide whether you agree with Saint Jerome.

JOB

Every one of us at some point in our lives feels like Job. Like Job we wonder, "Why did God let this happen to me?" If we have not asked that question yet, we probably will. And when that time comes, Job's story will be of help. It will give us the strength to face our own stories.

Job is a very religious man, blessed with all the best the world has to offer. Then tragedy strikes. At first he is strong enough to accept it. But in time he convinces himself that God is playing a cruel game with his life. At that point, Job sets out on a long journey that leads him far away from God and then back again.

But let's go back to the beginning. God is so convinced of Job's unfailing devotion that God accepts a challenge to put it to the test. In spite of devastating losses, Job's devotion remains unshaken and he even blesses God who gives and takes away. But a further test reveals a change in Job. He still speaks of devotion to God but he does not give a blessing. We wonder what might be going on deep inside of him.

At this point in the account, three devoted friends turn up to comfort Job. Shocked by the change in Job when he curses the day he was born, the three friends urge him to repent. They are convinced his great suffering is a sign of some moral failure on his part. Job, of course, cannot accept their advice because he knows he has done nothing to deserve such suffering.

As the dialogue between Job and his friends continues, their efforts to force him to admit some degree of guilt serve only to strengthen his resolve to prove his innocence before God. Eventually the dialogue breaks down as Job becomes more and more convinced that God is treating him unjustly.

Then another figure speaks up. His name is Elihu, a young man who remained silent all this time out of respect for the friends who are older than he is. Elihu says he has been listening very carefully to what Job says. He heard Job defend his innocence before God. But Elihu believes Job is pressing against the boundaries of propriety when he points to his innocence to make God look like the guilty party.

At the end of his remarks, Elihu directs Job's attention up to the heavens. He seems to succeed in preparing Job to listen to God. And God does at last speak to Job pointing out to him all the wonders of creation and the weakness of demanding strict justice in the world.

In the end, Job returns to the position he held at the very beginning of the book. He no longer holds up his innocence as proof against God. Instead, Job accepts the truth that everything is a gift from God and should be received as a gift. As the book concludes, we see Job enjoying the gifts he has from God, especially the birth of three beautiful daughters.

The 42 chapters of Job:

1 — 2	The Lord gives and takes away
3 — 14	Job's dialogue with the three friends begins
15 — 21	The dialogue becomes more intense
22 — 28	The dialogue breaks down
29 — 31	Job's final challenge to God
32 — 37	Elihu disposes Job to listen to God
38 — 41	God enlightens Job
42	Job enjoys God's gifts to him

The Adversary

The Hebrew expression *ha-satan* means "the accuser." In Job, this figure is a loyal member of the court of heaven. Like all God's servants, the accuser is dedicated to promoting true worship of God. He seeks to probe Job's innermost being in order to disclose the deepest motivations for his piety.

Leviathan

Leviathan represents all that is out of control. In the poetry of the ancient world, Leviathan is pictured as a monster with seven heads. At the beginning of his argument, Job wants Leviathan's help in blotting out the day he was born (Job 3:8). At the end of the book, Job admits that Leviathan is better left in God's control.

An Old Story

The ancient world knew of a work called the Legend of King Keret. His story is preserved on three clay tablets dating back some fourteen centuries before the birth of Jesus. Like Job, Keret endured terrible losses during his lifetime. But eventually the gods took pity on him and restored everything.

Priceless

Chapter 28 of Job describes the priceless character of wisdom. All the treasures of the earth, even the purest gold, cannot compare with the

JOB

gleaming brilliance of wisdom. Where can such a treasure be found? It is a gift from God.

Job on the Clock (BC)

Ezekiel   c. 593–573

Aramaic copy of Job   c. first century AD

Job's experiences were already legendary in the lifetime of the prophet Ezekiel who preached nearly six hundred years before the time of Jesus. But it is difficult to determine just when the book of Job was written since the book contains no references to known historical events. An Aramaic translation of Job dating from the first century AD was discovered in one of the caves at Qumran.

As you read the book of Job…

In the first two chapters the scenes shift back and forth between heaven and earth. What do we gain by watching Job from the vantage point of heaven?

Job's response to his tragedy is "the Lord gives and the Lord takes away. Blessed be the name of the Lord." What do his words reveal about his outlook on life? Do you share Job's outlook?

We hear from Job's wife only at verse 2:9, but she stays with him through it all. What kind of person do you think she was?

Three friends spend time with Job. What friends would you choose to share your pain? What would you want them to say?

Read over Job 7. This passage is sometimes read at funerals. What comfort would mourners find in it?

Job describes how God made him in 10:8–12. What images would you use to describe how God made you?

What do you think of Job's litany of things God does in 12:17–25?

Note how abandoned Job feels in chapter 19. When you feel abandoned or alone, what images do you use to describe your feelings?

In 27:1–6, Job is so confident of his innocence that he swears to it by God. But what do you think of the way he speaks of God in this oath?

Where do you look for wisdom? Find an answer in Job 28.

In chapter 29 Job describes his former life. What kind of person was he?

Job gives concrete examples of his moral character in chapter 31. What do you find most noble about his character?

God appears to Job after Elihu speaks. Has Elihu said anything to prepare Job for God's arrival?

Do you see any difference in Job's outlook on life at the end of his story?

How would this book help you face your suffering and losses?

Three Spiritual Lessons From Job

- Suffering can lead to a deeper relationship with God

- God never abandons us

- The most perfect response in life is to bless the name of God

PSALMS

A gymnasium for the soul—that is how Saint Ambrose described the book of Psalms, also called the Psalter. We moderns would probably use the term fitness center. But this saint's point is that in the psalms people will find a wealth of inspiration to make their faith lives stronger.

For example, there are psalms offering spiritual guidance, psalms to help people express how they feel about their relationship with God, even psalms to help people work through anger or frustration, and of course psalms to help people celebrate all the good things God does for them.

If we are looking for insight on walking the journey of faith, there are psalms known as instruction, or "torah" psalms. Examples are psalms 1, 19 and 119. They teach us that the Word of God is a dependable guide for life. If we follow its guidelines, we will find ourselves on the path that leads to life. If we ignore the Word of God, we run the risk of walking along a path that may prove hurtful for us.

There are psalms to help us work through times of doubt. Especially helpful here are psalms 37 and 73. They begin with the psalmist wondering if there really is any advantage to living life in faithful relationship with God. People who ignore God altogether still seem to be living meaningful and prosperous lives. Yet there is greater promise in walking with God. The sands of time can shift without warning. But a life lived for God will find the strength to endure any hardship.

There are psalms to help us celebrate times when we are full of confidence. A series of psalms known as the Psalms of Ascent seem suited for times like these. Some believe psalms 120 to 134 were originally associated with mounting the steps leading to the Jerusalem temple. Whatever their origin, they do seem to carry us upward with their words and images of celebration and faith. And if we are feeling especially joyful, there are the Alleluia Psalms that serve as a grand finale to the Psalter.

At the other end of the emotional scale are the penitential psalms. Traditionally there are seven of them—6, 32, 38, 51, 102, 130 and 143. The most well known of these is Psalm 51, associated with David's repentance over his sin with Bathsheba. David's powerful images of cleansing and purification will resonate with anyone seeking spiritual freedom. And in return for his restoration with God, David promises to inspire others by telling them of the all the advantages he now sees in a right relationship with God.

If we are in a reflective mood, there are psalms that look back on all the good things God has done for us. Psalm 78 reviews the highs and lows of Israel's relationship with God, a pattern we may recognize in our own life with God. Psalm 104 finds inspiration in the countless gifts we take for granted each day in creation.

If asked to identify our favorite psalms, we could probably name a few without hesitation. "The LORD is my shepherd" (Psalm 23) would be on the top of the list for most of us. But, however familiar we may be with individual psalms, there is also an advantage in gaining an overview of the entire book as the following paragraphs seek to do.

The tone for the book is established by the very first psalm. It introduces us to two ways in life. One leads to life; the other to trouble and sadness. Naturally, the one whose way is illuminated by the Law of Moses will find happiness. And those who scoff at God will discover a less satisfactory way in life.

The five books of the Law of Moses is probably the basis for the division of the psalter into five books. Bibles clearly mark the five with headings.

Themes of struggle and hardship seem to prevail in the first three sections of the book of Psalms. Think of the penitential psalms (6, 32, 38 and 51) or the number of psalms associated with some hardship in the life of David.

In the fourth section, things get a little brighter with all the psalms celebrating the power of God to save. Of course the final section is dominated by psalms of ascent leading us up to God—psalms 120 to 134—and psalms of alleluia like psalms 146 to 150.

So when we read the psalms it is as if we are making a gradual progression from struggle to freedom. So the book seems to celebrate the very theme exhibited in the first psalm: a life focused on God will lead to joy. And, of course, if you are reading the psalms you are focused on God.

The 150 chapters of the book of Psalms:

1 — 41	Book One—the challenge of walking with God
42 — 72	Book Two—struggles along the way
73 — 89	Book Three—pleas for help
90 — 106	Book Four—God's power to save
107 — 150	Book Five—songs of praise

A Suggestion

You may find it helpful to concentrate on the images used by the psalmists. Consider for example the very first psalm. It uses the image of a tree to represent someone who is close to God. What is it about a tree that makes it a fitting image for a person? You could probably identify a few rather quickly. They might include things like having roots, growing up toward heaven, supplying fruit for the hungry or shade for the weary. After a little while, you may discover an entirely new way to pray the psalms simply by reflecting in this way on the many images in the Psalter.

Longest Psalm

With 176 verses, Psalm 119 is by far the longest psalm in the book. Its length derives from the fact that it devotes eight lines to each of the twenty-two letters of the Hebrew alphabet. As we read this psalm, we follow the psalmist's journey of faith. It begins with a prayer asking for God's help in facing the everyday challenges to faith; it concludes with the psalmist confident that God has heard the prayer.

Shortest Psalm

With just two verses, Psalm 117 is the shortest of the psalms. But it has a far-reaching message. It invites all the nations of the world to praise God because God's faithfulness lasts forever.

PSALMS

Cursing Psalms

It may come as a shock that there are psalms asking God to bring harm to others. Psalms 58, 83, 109 and 137 include very strong language directed against perceived enemies. In real life, people do struggle with such feelings. But letting those feelings out and turning them over to God is an important step in the healing process.

Laughter

In psalms 2:4 and 37:13, we find God laughing. What does God find humorous in these psalms? The answer: the pretensions of people who ignore heaven or think they can really interfere with God's plan to bring salvation to the world.

Royal Psalms

Some psalms seem to have connections with the lives of the kings. Psalm 20 was perhaps a royal prayer before battle. And Psalm 45 may have been for a royal wedding. Psalms like 72 and 110 seem to look forward to a future king who will fulfill the divine promise to David that his line would go on and on.

Psalms on the Clock (BC)

David   c. 1000
Return from Exile   c. 500

More than seventy psalms are said to have David as their composer. That would make some of them nearly three thousand years old. Many psalms—the royal psalms especially—may be associated with the weddings, coronations and battles of David's successors. Other psalms, like Psalm 137, echo the sad days of the Exile in Babylon. Although precise dates are difficult to come by, some of the psalms do seem to be among the oldest compositions in the Bible.

As you read the book of Psalms…

What do you think makes Psalm 1 a suitable introduction to the book of Psalms?

In his Pentecost sermon (Acts 2), Saint Peter turned to Psalm 16 for proof from Scripture that Jesus would rise from the dead. What verse from Psalm 16 do you think he found especially relevant to his message?

Note the powerful images in Psalm 29. What do you think inspired the composer of this psalm?

Each line of Psalm 34 begins with a letter of the Hebrew alphabet. Could you compose a hymn of praise to God using the English alphabet?

Psalm 44 celebrates what the people have learned from their ancestors about God. What could you add to this lesson from your own family history?

Psalm 51 is one of the most celebrated psalms of repentance. Read it over and discover its beauty for yourself.

Psalm 69:9 is quoted when Jesus cleanses the temple (John 2:17). Read the entire psalm to discover the object of the Lord's zeal.

Every day the Liturgy of the Hours may begin with Psalm 95. What makes this psalm a fitting start to each day?

Psalms 113 to 118 were sung at Passover. What makes them appropriate for that feast?

Psalms 120 to 134 are thought to have accompanied a procession to the temple. What makes them appropriate for such a procession?

Psalm 136 is a litany of the good things God did for Israel. What would you include in a litany based on your experience of God?

Psalms uses many vivid images for God. Which images do you find most meaningful?

Would you agree with Saint Ambrose's teaching that the psalms are a gymnasium for the soul?

Three Spiritual Lessons From Psalms

- Praying the Psalms gives us strength for the spiritual journey
- Any human emotion can be the starting point for reaching out to God
- The whole range of life is an occasion to offer praise to God

PSALMS

PROVERBS

Here is your practical guide for everyday living. Proverbs is not the sort of book a person sits down with and reads straight through from beginning to end. It is rather something like a coffee table book, the sort of book you browse through looking for items that catch the eye.

And there is plenty to catch the eye in Proverbs. The range of subject matter is quite impressive. The book's scope includes the sort of material we might expect to find in the self-help section of the local bookstore. Just consider the following items taken from the verses of Proverbs:

The character of a true friend:
Some friends play at friendship
    but a true friend sticks closer than one's nearest kin. (18:24)

The value of self-control:
Like a city breached, without walls,
    is one who lacks self-control. (25:28)

The danger of substance abuse:
Who has woe? Who has sorrow?
    Who has strife? Who has complaining?
Who has wounds without cause?
    Who has redness of eyes?
Those who linger late over wine,
    those who keep trying mixed wines. (23:29–30)

The danger of being too nosy:
Like somebody who takes a passing dog by the ears
    is one who meddles in the quarrel of another. (26:17)

The unpredictability of life:
Three things are too wonderful for me;
    four I do not understand:
    the way of an eagle in the sky,
    the way of a snake on a rock,
the way of a ship on the high seas,
    and the way of a man with a girl. (30:18–19)

And here is a clever piece on the greatness to be found in small creatures:
Four things on earth are small,
    yet they are exceedingly wise:

the ants are a people without strength,
    yet they provide their food in the summer;
the badgers are a people without power,
    yet they make their homes in the rocks;
the locusts have no king,
    yet all of them march in rank;
the lizard can be grasped in the hand,
    yet it is found in kings' palaces. (30:24–28)

No doubt, similar proverbs could be found in the wisdom literature of many cultures. But what makes this book distinctive is its spiritual character. The wisdom of the sages of Israel reaches beyond the boundaries of human interaction to include a right relationship with God. Even advice about as worldly a thing as money will, in this book, bring the standard of heaven into the picture:

One who augments wealth by exorbitant interest
    gathers it for another who is kind to the poor. (28:8)

Proverbs has a very interesting framework that gives its contents a special focus. The book begins and ends with poetry about women who bring countless blessings to people.

In the opening chapters of Proverbs, Lady Wisdom invites us to the sumptuous banquet that only a right relationship with God can provide for us. Our wise hostess explains that she is superior to everything else in creation because she was created first of all. Wisdom witnessed all that God created to make the world fit for humanity. But Wisdom's true joy is found in us because she wants to lead us back to God.

The final chapter of the book sings the praises of the ideal wife. Her wisdom and creativity bring countless blessings to her family. As we read about all the blessings she brings others, we realize she is the perfect representation of all that was said of wisdom in the chapters of this book.

The 31 chapters of Proverbs:

1 — 9	The value of wisdom
10 — 30	A treasury of proverbs
31	Wisdom, the perfect partner

In a Nutshell

If you are looking for one proverb that sums up all the rest, you cannot find a better example than this: "The fear of the LORD is the beginning of wisdom, / and the knowledge of the Holy One is insight" (9:10).

Life

Some proverbs seem to reach beyond the limitations of this world. Consider this example: "The fear of the LORD is a fountain of life, / so that one may avoid the snares of death" (14:27).

A Riddle

Can you solve this riddle found in Proverbs 30:4?

> Who has ascended to heaven and come down?
>> Who has gathered the wind in the hollow of the hand?
> Who has wrapped up the waters in a garment?
>> Who has established all the ends of the earth?
> What is the person's name?
>> And what is the name of the person's child?
>> Surely you know!

An Egyptian Connection?

Some of the sayings in Proverbs are close to sayings in ancient Egyptian wisdom collections. This is true of Proverbs 22:17—24:22, which resembles in some respects a work by an Egyptian sage named Amenemope. But whatever earthly influences might be represented in them, the proverbs of Israel are unique in that they promote the higher purpose of drawing people closer to God.

Proverbs on the Clock (BC)

Solomon   c. 960–922

Hezekiah   715–687

Tradition associates many proverbs with the court of Solomon, the legendary wise king of Israel. That would mean some proverbs may go back a thousand years before the time of Jesus. Other proverbs are connected with King Hezekiah, who ruled about two hundred years later. It is difficult to come up with precise dates for this material, but Proverbs does seem to reach back into the glory days of the kingdom.

As you read Proverbs…

Proverbs teaches that "fear of the LORD" is the beginning of wisdom. What does this mean to you? Would you substitute anything else as the starting point for wisdom?

What do you think of the description of wisdom in 3:13–18? Would you want to add anything to this description?

Of the seven things God hates (6:16–19), discord in the family tops the list. What would you put at the top of the list?

Proverbs 8 gives a celebrated portrait of wisdom. What do you think of it?

Proverbs 9 gives a portrait of two very different people. Which one appeals to you?

Find three proverbs that are especially meaningful to you. Talk about them with a friend.

The final verses of Proverbs describe the perfect partner. Why do you think the book concludes this way?

Three Spiritual Lessons From Proverbs

- Respect for God is the beginning of wisdom
- We are the apple of God's eye
- The world is filled with stepping-stones to God

ECCLESIASTES

If you are looking for an honest opinion about life in this world, you will find it in this book. The first line of the book identifies the author as "the son of David, king in Jerusalem." This, of course, is King Solomon, famous for his wisdom. But Solomon carries a new title in this book; he is now called "the Teacher." This is fitting since the book reads as a lesson about what really matters in life.

The teacher tells us of a search for true happiness in this world. In this pursuit, he flooded his senses with satisfaction, lost himself in building projects, and amassed a great fortune. But when all this was finally accomplished, the teacher still had a queasy feeling deep down inside.

The teacher admits that he knew no more happiness in the end than he had known from the start. All this obsession with the things of this world left him still feeling empty.

So what is the teacher's advice to us: Life is something to be enjoyed not controlled. In the end, we simply must admit that there are limitations to everything we do.

The teacher encourages the young to enjoy life to the fullest. But he does not condone a life spent in self-indulgence and self-seeking. He tempers his words with this advice: Remember your Creator. His point is that we must remember that we are creatures in a great big world. No matter what degree of independence we might want to claim for ourselves, we must finally come to the realization that our freedom is only relative. In the end, we must yield everything to the one who created us.

There is something refreshing about this book. Solomon the teacher wants to save us from obsessions. Solomon sets out to experiment with all the things of this world. He discovers that the best thing in life is to enjoy life as it comes.

The 12 chapters of Ecclesiastes:

1 — 8	The experiments
9 — 12	The discovery

An Alias

This book also goes by another name. In the Hebrew Bible it carries the title Qoheleth. No matter which name we use, the meaning is the same: the assembly figure. In some traditions, this figure is given a more precise role in the assembly as "the preacher."

A Festive Book

By tradition, this book is one of five books read at important festivals in the Jewish calendar. Ecclesiastes is read at the joyful Feast of Tabernacles because the book urges its readers to enjoy life.

Under the Sun

This is a favorite phrase for the author of this book. It seems to go along with the author's viewpoint which accents how restricted our efforts are in this world. All our grand achievements are marked by the sun's progress from east to west. It helps readers keep a proper perspective on things.

Time

Everyone is familiar with the beautiful reflection on time in chapter 3. The theme of this poem on time is not fatalism as if we have no control over what we do. Instead, the words call us to realism. All that happens is measured by time. Keeping this in mind preserves us from obsession with the things of earth.

Vanity

We use the word *vanity* today to express an exorbitant preoccupation with self. But this book uses the word to express the transitory nature of things in this world. Obsession with this world makes little sense; it is far better to just take the world as it comes and enjoy its beauty.

Ecclesiastes on the Clock (BC)

Solomon   c. 960–922

Egypt controls Judea   c. 300–200

The opening line of this book tells us it was the work of the son of David. Tradition therefore associates Qoheleth with King Solomon, making this a very old book indeed—a thousand years before the time of Jesus! But many specialists, considering the late Hebrew character of its language, place the book in the third century before Jesus. Some find Egyptian influence in the book, which also makes the third century a good choice, since Judea was a province of Egypt throughout that century. Fragments of this book were found in one of the caves at Qumran; they are dated between 175 and 150 BC.

As you read Ecclesiastes...

What do you think of the author's observations about life in this world in 1:12—2:26? Is there anything you would add to them?

Some mourners find comfort in the passage about time in Ecclesiastes 3:1–9. Read it over to see what they might find comforting in that passage.

Verses 5:9—6:9 occupy the very center of the book. What is the theme of this central passage?

The author of this book records all the efforts taken to find satisfaction in this world. What efforts have you taken to find satisfaction in this world? How successful has your experiment been?

Choose several Bibles and compare the way they translate Ecclesiastes 12:1–8. Which translation do you prefer and for what reasons?

Some regard the author of this book as pessimistic about life on this earth. Do you share this opinion?

The rabbis taught that at the end of life God will require each of us to explain why we failed to enjoy all the good things we saw in life. What would your response be?

Three Spiritual Lessons From Ecclesiastes

- Life is a gift from God to enjoy
- There is wisdom in accepting our limitations
- Obsessions hinder us from enjoying life to the fullest

THE SONG OF SOLOMON

Saint Jerome thought this should be the very last book of the Bible on a young student's reading list. He feared that inexperienced readers would fail to appreciate the spiritual message of this book because of its vivid imagery about marriage.

Whatever we may think of Saint Jerome's advice, he certainly was right about the powerful language of this book of the Bible. These love songs freely celebrate the intense feelings that love arouses between a man and a woman.

As the verses of this book dart back and forth from the feelings of the woman to the feelings of the man, we may see no explicit connection between their love and the love between God and people. But the inclusion of this book within the Bible certainly justifies making that connection. Prophets like Hosea and Isaiah also compared God's love for Israel to the love between a man and a woman.

Much of the energy in the book comes from anticipation. The woman yearns to be with the one she loves. In the very first line of the book, she wishes she could feel his kisses on her lips. Unable to sleep because of her longing, she rises in the middle of the night in search of him. She pleads with her friends to help her in the search, providing them with a description of the man for whom they are looking.

The man in turn yearns to be with her. He runs to her home and steals glances at her from a distance. His love for her is so strong that he fears getting lost in it. He asks her not to look at him too intensely for fear he would be consumed by his love for her.

When they describe each other, they draw their inspiration from the beauty of creation. He is a like a tall cedar tree; she is like a palm tree. His eyes are soft like those of a dove; her eyes are deep like pools of water.

They see in each other a royal dignity. She regards him as King Solomon surrounded by riches and devoted followers ready to die for their king. He believes she is so beautiful she would stand out in a room filled with women dressed in regal clothing.

All the yearning these two have for each other seems to be rewarded in the closing chapter where we see them walking together one leaning upon the other. Then suddenly the two are apart again anticipating the moment they will be together once more.

The 8 chapters of the Song of Solomon:

1 — 6   Love's search

7 — 8   Love's power

The Author
According to 1 Kings 4:32, King Solomon composed over one thousand songs. Tradition regards this one as his greatest song or, in the idiom of the Hebrew language, "the song of songs."

Written in Gold
One of the verses in this book is so popular that it is commonly engraved on wedding bands. It reads: "I am my beloved's and my beloved is mine" (Song of Solomon 6:3).

A Popular Book
Rabbi Akiba, a first-century Jewish teacher, had this to say about the Song of Solomon: "The whole world is not worth the day on which the Song of Solomon was given to Israel." Origen, an early church Bible scholar, so admired this book he wrote a ten-volume commentary on it. He found its lyrics to be a beautiful expression of the bond between Jesus and the church.

THE SONG OF SOLOMON

Passover Connection

By tradition, this book is one of five books read at important festivals in the Jewish calendar. The Song of Solomon is read at Passover because its lyrics remind people of spring, the time of year when Passover is celebrated.

The Song of Solomon on the Clock (BC)

Solomon   c. 960–922

Persian Period   c. 550–330

Solomon composed over a thousand songs, according to 1 Kings 4:32. If the Song of Solomon is one of them, then it is very old indeed. But the late Hebrew style and the Persian vocabulary in this song suggest it was composed about five hundred years before the time of Christ.

As you read the Song of Solomon...

An early Christian commentary by Origen (c. 184–254 AD) said the kisses in 1:1 were given by Christ when he came to save us. Can you identify other passages in the Song of Solomon that could represent the love between Jesus and the church?

How do you picture the house described in verse 1:17? Is it in keeping with other images in this book?

In verse 5:7 the city guards mistreat the woman as she searches for her love. Can you think of passages in the Bible where people searching for God are mistreated?

Compare the woman's description of the man at 5:10–16 with his description of her at 7:1–5. In what ways are they similar? In what ways are they different?

In verse 8:6 the poet says that love is "as strong as death." What does this mean to you?

Do you agree with Saint Jerome that the Song of Solomon belongs only at the end of a reading list of books from the Bible?

The poetry of this book includes a lot of references to fruit and spices. What does such language suggest to you?

How many different colors can you identify in this book? What does each one suggest to you?

Three Spiritual Lessons From the Song of Solomon
- The search for God takes a lifetime
- God's love for us is definitely stronger than death
- Our lives should be a beautiful song to God

WISDOM

The title says it all. This is our manual for learning how to become wise. There is no need for us to send away for any extra materials. It's all here. And we are just three steps from finding wisdom:

- Believe that you are special to God.
- Pray for the gift of wisdom.
- Keep in mind that the benefits go beyond this world.

This is probably the youngest book in the Old Testament. The book of Wisdom may have been composed just fifty years before the birth of Jesus. That makes it very close to New Testament times. On one ancient list of books, in fact, Wisdom is even listed right along with the books of the New Testament!

The author of this book is wise King Solomon himself. Well, maybe he was not the actual author, but whoever wrote it certainly speaks with the kind of wisdom for which Solomon was famous. Solomon wants us to succeed in life. Of course, his definition of success may be a lot different from our own.

For Solomon, true wisdom comes with a close relationship with God. To acquire this sort of wisdom, people must recognize that they are totally dependent on God. Any pretending that we can make it on our own simply will not do. Solomon has plenty of examples of people who rely only on the limited resources of this world. They will always end up disappointed because this world is framed by time. It is much wiser to trust in God, and then we gain benefits that never end.

The book begins by comparing the lives of the just with the lives of the wicked. Of course, someone who values a right relationship with God will live a far superior life to someone obsessed with the things of this world. The central portion of Wisdom (chapters 6—9) encourages the reader to seek wisdom. This is where "Solomon" describes his own

WISDOM

search, finally coming to the realization that wisdom is something one has to seek from God. The final chapters return to the business of comparing the lives of the just with the lives of the wicked. This time the lessons are taken from the book of Exodus. Although never identified by name, it is clear the just ones are the Israelites and the wicked ones are the Egyptians.

The 19 chapters of Wisdom:

1 — 5	Wisdom leads to immortality
6 — 9	Wisdom is a gift
10 — 19	Wisdom saves

A Popular Book

If this book sounds somewhat familiar, there is a good reason for it. Eight readings during the church's three-year Sunday cycle are taken from the book of Wisdom.

Alexandria

Some believe the book of Wisdom comes from Alexandria, an Egyptian port city on the Mediterranean Sea, its lighthouse is one of the seven wonders of the world. One of its five sprawling districts was home to many Jews, refugees from the Holy Land. Little wonder that it was at Alexandria that the Bible was translated from Hebrew into Greek.

A New Title

In verse 11:26 the author of Wisdom creates a new title for God: Lover of Souls. It belongs to a passage explaining how patiently God works with us to steer us toward the good. This part of Wisdom is the companion text for the story of Zacchaeus in Luke 19:1–10.

Idols

In verse 15:7–8 the author of Wisdom describes the production of clay artifacts in a potter's workshop. He finds it amusing that the potter uses the same clay to make a vessel for household use and the figurine of a god or goddess.

Your Name Here

In chapters 11 to 19 the author of Wisdom draws spiritual lessons from the Exodus from Egypt. But as you read through these chapters not once will you find the title Israelite or Egyptian. This makes it easier for readers to apply the lessons to themselves.

The Greek Bible

Just over two hundred years before the birth of Jesus, Jewish scholars began translating the Hebrew Bible into Greek. This was necessary because large Jewish communities, especially those in North Africa, spoke Greek. This Greek version of the Old Testament was the one taken up by the early church.

Wisdom on the Clock (BC)

Exodus   c. 1290

Solomon   c. 960–922

Hellenistic Period   c. 330 – 50

The central chapters of Wisdom have been attributed to Solomon, and its final chapters look back to the days of the Exodus. But Wisdom actually comes from a much later period. It was written in Greek by an unknown author very familiar with the Greek culture that dominated the Mediterranean world after the conquests of Alexander the Great who died in 323 BC. We call the centuries after his death the Hellenistic Age. The author was also familiar with the Greek Bible, begun c. 250 BC, but does not seem to have been familiar with Greek authors writing in New Testament times. For these reasons, a date in the early to middle first century BC seems most likely for the book of Wisdom.

As you read Wisdom…

What connections can you see between 2:12–20 and the account of the Lord's passion and death in the Gospels?

Chapter 3 is often read at funerals. What would families find so comforting in its message?

Think about the images for this passing world in 5:9–15. Which one do you find most powerful?

Wisdom 7:21–22 is famous for its string of adjectives describing wisdom. Which way of describing wisdom most appeals to you?

Wisdom 7:29–30 says that Wisdom outshines the sun. What does this mean to you?

What can you learn from Solomon's prayer in chapter 9?

Read chapter 10 without looking at the footnotes and see if you can identify all the people who were saved by wisdom.

WISDOM

What does Wisdom 11:23—12:2 reveal about God?

How effectively does the author lampoon idolatry in 13:11–19?

In chapters 16—19 the author uses the Exodus story to illustrate the advantages and disadvantages of faith. Can you identify the Exodus passages referred to by the author? (The footnotes will give you plenty of clues.)

Three Spiritual Lessons From Wisdom

- God created us to enjoy eternal life in the kingdom of heaven
- Wisdom is something we find in prayer to God
- The most meaningful life is a life lived for God

SIRACH

One of the biggest attractions at a family reunion is viewing photographs of ancestors. The older the picture, the better. Familiar names, the heroes and heroines of so many stories handed down from one generation to the next, suddenly have a face. They stand or sit in their frames looking confidently out at us. We admire their courage. We wonder what kind of people their parents and grandparents were. We listen to tales about them, eager to snatch up even the slightest hint of nobility or even royal blood in the family.

Jesus ben Sira ("Sirach") has a family album to show us too. In the chapters of his book are portraits of our spiritual ancestors. We can definitely be proud of them because their number includes patriarchs, kings, prophets, even composers! But whatever else these ancestors accomplished, Sirach is proud of them because they had wisdom; they were wise in matters of faith.

Sirach does not open the portrait album right away. He first wants us to appreciate what it takes to be included in his portrait gallery. And so he patiently explains to us what really counts for wisdom in his eyes. And for Sirach true wisdom is putting God first. Such wisdom includes devotion to God, devotion to parents, charity, justice, detachment from the things of this world, and loyalty to the covenant and the Law of Moses.

The 52 chapters of Sirach:

I — 43   The search for wisdom

44 — 52   A list of those who found it

The Grandson

Sirach's grandson took on the difficult task of translating his grand-father's works from Hebrew into Greek. He pleads with his readers to be patient: "You are invited therefore to read it with goodwill, and to be indulgent in cases where, despite our diligent labor in translating, we may seem to have rendered some phrases imperfectly" (Sirach, Prologue).

Jesus ben Sira

Sirach was a teacher. Some think he may have even been the head master of an academy in Jerusalem. His students may have been the children of leading citizens in that holy city. The main concern of his curriculum was to instill in his students a genuine appreciation for their Jewish her-itage. This was important in an age—the early part of the second cen-tury before Jesus—when the Greek way of doing things was all the rage.

The True Friend

Sirach includes some sound advice about friendship. It is best to simply let him speak for himself on this subject. "Faithful friends are beyond price; / no amount can balance their worth. Faithful friends are life-saving medicine…" (Sirach 6:15–16).

Another Name

The traditional name for this book was Ecclesiasticus meaning "of the church," *ecclesia* being the Greek word for "church." This title is a tribute to the book's popularity in the life of the church. After the book of Psalms, Sirach is the wisdom book most frequently read in the church's liturgy.

Praise of Creation

Be sure to read Sirach's beautiful reflection on creation in 42:15—43:33. He marvels at the way the majesty of God is exhibited in the harmony of it: "All things come in pairs, one opposite the other…." Sirach is think-ing of pairs like the sun and the moon, or the warm weather and the cold weather.

SIRACH

Sirach on the Clock (BC)

Death of Simeon   c. 196

Translation of Sirach into Greek   c. 124

This book comes late on our Old Testament clock. In his list of spiritual notables, Sirach includes Simeon II, a high priest in Jerusalem. On the one hand, Since Simeon died about 196 BC, Sirach must have written his book after that date. On the other hand, Sirach's book was already well known by 124 BC when his grandson translated it into Greek. So a date sometime around 180 BC seems most likely for this book of the Bible.

As you read Sirach…

Verses 3:2–14 are the first reading for the feast of the Holy Family. What makes it appropriate for that feast?

Sirach has some memorable things to say about friends in 6:5–13 and 19:13–19. What valuable lessons do you find in these passages?

There are some wonderful images in chapters 14 and 15 as Sirach reflects on the advantages of wisdom.

What do you think of Sirach's reflections on the dignity of humanity in 17:1–14?

Chapter 20 includes some striking contrasts between the wise person and the fool.

Sirach identifies ten roads to happiness in 25:7–11. Is there anything to add to his list?

What do you think of Sirach's advice on testing the character of the people you meet (27:4–7)?

What connections do you see between the teaching of Jesus on true sacrifice and Sirach's reflection on it in chapter 35?

In 38:24–34 Sirach honors people who provide the basic needs in life. Would you want to add anyone to his list?

Choose two figures from Sirach's list of notables in chapters 44 to 50. Then read their stories in the Bible.

Three Spiritual Lessons From Sirach

- True fame is found in living for God
- Our faith tradition is a priceless resource
- Respect for God leads to real wisdom

SIRACH

PART FIVE

THE PROPHETS

The prophets were God's special representatives among the people. Their purpose was to speak the Word of God. Think of them as agents of heaven trying to turn the attention of their people to God, the source of life.

You may recognize many of the people appearing in this portion of the Bible. The reason for this is that you have met some of them before as you read the historical books of the Bible. The books of the prophets often connect with the history of the people. This connection reveals how much God loved the people. God was constantly speaking to them through these special representatives, urging the people to choose life.

The books of the prophets clearly look back over the long story of God's relationship with Israel. But these books also look forward. With their many prophecies about the days to come, they prepare the way for the New Testament.

The Major Prophets

Each of the major prophets—Isaiah, Jeremiah, Ezekiel and Daniel—has his own scroll. That is, these books of the Bible have traditionally been treated as complete works in themselves. By contrast, the minor prophets are so called for the simple reason that traditionally all twelve share a single scroll.

We begin with the words of Isaiah, who preached some eight centuries before the time of Jesus. Isaiah tried to steer kings and people toward God. They resisted his message and weakened the nation. In the end, the kingdom collapsed. But God remained loyal to the covenant. And so the oracles in the second half of Isaiah are filled with promise as God invites the people to return to the Promised Land.

The books of Jeremiah and Ezekiel take us back to the years just before and after the collapse of the kingdom. Jeremiah preached in Jerusalem; Ezekiel preached in Babylon. While others looked to superpowers like Egypt to save them, these two prophets challenged them to look to God for security.

Two smaller books follow the book of Jeremiah. The first is Lamentations. As the title suggests, this book takes a mournful look at all that was lost when Jerusalem was destroyed because of the nation's refusal to rely on God. The other small book is Baruch. Baruch was secretary to the prophet Jeremiah and so his book follows the oracles of that great prophet. Baruch urges a shattered people to find hope in a return to faith.

The fourth major prophet is Daniel. His book puts earthly kingdoms—so troublesome for his predecessors—in proper perspective. Throughout his life, Daniel served in the courts of mortal kings. But his success was due to his loyalty to God. He overcomes every obstacle presented him, proving that God protects those who rely on heaven.

ISAIAH

Children have a special place in this book. We are all familiar with Isaiah's famous prophecy about Immanuel, a child whose very name declares, "God is with us." A moment's reflection may bring to mind other references to children in Isaiah. For example, there is the passage immortalized in Handel's *Messiah* as "For unto us a child is born" (9:6). And there is the beautiful image of God's love in 66:13: "As a mother comforts her child, / so I will comfort you...."

In the very first words spoken by God in this book, God laments over the children of Israel who have abandoned their heavenly Father who raised them and cared for them. But the book concludes on a happy note with the children of Israel addressing God as Father and begging to be forgiven for their past offenses.

We could read Isaiah as an elaborate presentation of the Lord's parable of the Prodigal Son. At first, the people insist on going their own way. But then after years of hardship they finally come to their senses and return to the Father who welcomes them with open arms.

The oracles in this book span a long stretch of time. At the beginning of the book, we read about the efforts of Isaiah to steer the kings of his day back to the Lord. In spite of all the promises he held out to them if they would only respond with faith, the kings chose to pursue their own interests. And so by the time we reach the midpoint of the book we understand that the kingdom will collapse.

The oracles in the second half of the book urge the people to leave behind their place of exile and turn to the Promised Land. These oracles present the people with a new ideal figure. The prideful kings are gone. In their place stands the humble servant of the Lord. This servant is so dedicated to doing God's will he is even ready to suffer death for the sake of his people.

And so as it now reads, the book of Isaiah uses a wide chunk of history to teach the important spiritual lesson that our most noble purpose in life is to serve the Lord because we are the Lord's children.

The 66 chapters of Isaiah:

| 1 — 39 | God's children turn away |
| 40 — 66 | God's children return |

The Vineyard

One of the most memorable passages in Isaiah is the famous song about the vineyard in chapter 5. God plants the best grapes, but the crop fails. It represents the people of Israel. God wanted them to be the best, but they failed because of their sinful pride.

Seraphim

In the great vision of chapter 6, Isaiah sees the throne of God surrounded by the seraphim. This is the only time in the Bible these special servants of God appear. Their name suggests some connection with fire. No wonder one of them purifies the lips of the prophet by touching them with a fiery coal from the altar of God.

Prophet and Son

In chapter 7 Isaiah is sent by God to King Ahaz to announce the prophecy of Immanuel. The prophet brings with him his son. Together the two of them—father and son—represent the ideal: people of Israel walking with God their Father.

Prophetess

The wife of Isaiah is unknown to us by name. But she is one of the few women in the Bible to hold the title "prophetess." Others who share this distinction are Miriam (Exodus 15:20); Huldah (2 Kings 22:14); and Deborah (Judges 4:4).

Gifts

The seven gifts of the Holy Spirit are listed in Isaiah 11:2–3. They are wisdom and understanding, counsel and fortitude, knowledge, piety and the fear of the Lord. The prophet tells us these fine spiritual qualities will belong to the ideal king on the throne of David.

Suffering Servant

In Isaiah 52:13—53:12 we find the most famous portrait of the suffering servant of God. Despised and rejected by the world, he surrenders his life for the salvation of many. Christians see this oracle fulfilled in the passion, death and resurrection of Jesus.

Security

The tunnel of Hezekiah, completed about 700 BC, was quite an engineering achievement for its time. Visitors today still marvel at it. Hezekiah had it constructed to secure the water supply against a siege by the army of Assyria. He had his excavators begin at opposite ends, one team at a spring, the other in the city. Together they cut a shaft over sixteen hundred feet long.

Isaiah on the Clock (BC)

Uzziah   784–742

Fall of Jerusalem   587

Return from Exile   537

The eighth century before the time of Jesus was a very busy time for prophets. Isaiah was one of four preaching at that time; the others were Hosea, Amos and Micah. Isaiah's long years of service to the Lord spanned the reigns of several kings, beginning with Uzziah (783–742) and including the notable reigns of Ahaz (735–715) and Hezekiah (715–687). During much of Isaiah's lifetime, the kingdom was threatened by Assyria's seemingly insatiable appetite for wealth and power. But Isaiah always advised reliance on God for security. After Isaiah's death, his message was expanded by others so that the present book of Isaiah extends into the years after the Exile in Babylon.

As you read Isaiah…

How would you describe the relationship between God and people after reading the first chapter of this book?

The people of Israel are often represented by a vineyard in the poetry of the Bible. What is the lesson from the Song of the Vineyard in Isaiah chapter 5?

The rabbis held Isaiah in high esteem as a prophet because of his response to God in the vision of Isaiah 6. What do you think they found so impressive about his response?

Isaiah 11:2–3 describes the character of the ideal successor to the throne of David. What distinguishes him from so many other kings in Israel?

How different are Shebna and Eliakim as described in Isaiah chapter 22?

After he recovered from a life-threatening illness, King Hezekiah addressed a prayer of gratitude to God (Isaiah 38). What do you think of his prayer? Have you ever prayed as he did?

What is comforting about the prophet's message in chapter 40?

Isaiah 44:9–17 contains a famous satire on the worship of false gods. What point is Isaiah trying to make with this passage?

Read the biography of the Suffering Servant in Isaiah 53. How does Jesus fulfill the role of this special servant of God?

Jesus read Isaiah 61:1–2 in the synagogue of his hometown of Nazareth. Then he announced this passage was fulfilled that day. What did he mean?

What do the people ask of God in chapter 64? And how does God respond in the next chapter?

Three Spiritual Lessons From Isaiah

- Our purpose in life is to learn to become servants of God
- The world can hinder us from seeing the riches of heaven
- Trusting in God can transform the world into a beautiful place

JEREMIAH

We are clay in the hands of God. Jeremiah tried so desperately to teach this truth. In an unforgettable scene from this book (Jeremiah 18), God sends Jeremiah to a studio to observe how a potter works. He sees the potter trying to fashion a lump of clay on the wheel. When the clay does not cooperate, the potter breaks it down and starts all over again.

This example of the potter and the clay represents what God is doing with the people. Through the words of Jeremiah, God is trying to build them into something beautiful. But if they resist Jeremiah's words, God will break them down and start all over again.

Unfortunately, Jeremiah did not meet with much success in his efforts to transform the people with the Word of God. They constantly resisted his message, choosing to listen to the lies and fabrications of others instead of the truth of God.

The latter half of the book tells the story of Jeremiah's efforts to convince the kings in Jerusalem that their only hope of survival was to listen to the Word of God. Their constant refusals led the kingdom down the path of destruction. The last king even went so far as to seek security in an alliance with Egypt. This of course was precisely the wrong thing for a people God had once delivered from Egypt. Knowing the inevitable outcome of this policy Jeremiah announced that Jerusalem would fall.

The 52 chapters of Jeremiah:

| 1 — 24 | God seeks to shape the kingdom with the truth |
| 25 — 52 | The kingdom resists and shatters |

Broken Cisterns

Jeremiah warned the people that the earthly resources they turned to for security would eventually fail them. He said it was like relying on broken cisterns for water. Just when needed most, they would be found empty. But God—to borrow a line from Jeremiah—was like an unfailing spring of fresh water.

The Temple

Jeremiah also said that for all its beauty the temple in Jerusalem all by itself was not enough to secure a relationship with God. If the people really wanted to be secure, they had to put their religion into practice. You will find his great temple sermon in chapter 7.

Personal Best

Of all the prophets in the Bible, we probably know Jeremiah best. This is so because Jeremiah's book includes very personal reflections in which he complains to God about the burden of serving as a prophet. You can find these so-called "confessions" at 11:18—12:6; 15:10–21; 17:14–18; 18:18–23; and 20:7–18.

Book Burning

In an effort to reach the king, Jeremiah dictated his oracles to his secretary, Baruch, and had them delivered to the royal palace. But as each three or four columns of text were read, the king cut them from the scroll and tossed them into a fire (Jeremiah 36).

New Covenant

Only at Jeremiah 31:31–34 does the expression "new covenant" appear in the Old Testament. This expression became very important for the way Christians look at the Bible. Jesus is the one who fulfilled this oracle of Jeremiah and so the books that proclaim the message of Jesus are rightly referred to as the New Covenant or, in more familiar terms, the New Testament.

JEREMIAH

Jeremiah on the Clock (BC)

Thirteenth Year of Josiah   627

First Siege   597

Fall of Jerusalem   587

Jeremiah began preaching in the thirteenth year of King Josiah, just thirty years before the first attack on Jerusalem. Babylonian records tell us the first siege of Jerusalem began around January of 597 and ended three months later in March. Ten years later Jerusalem was attacked a second time. This time the city was taken, but Jeremiah remained in the city. The last time we "see" Jeremiah was around two years later when fugitives force him to go along with them to Egypt.

As you read Jeremiah…

How does God overcome Jeremiah's reluctance to serve as a prophet?

Jeremiah describes false gods as "broken cisterns." What makes this image so effective?

Jeremiah has his own version of the creation account in verses 4:23–26 of his book. What do you think of it?

In Jeremiah 7:1–15 you will find the prophet's famous temple sermon. What is his message?

In Jeremiah 13, how does the prophet use a simple piece of clothing to teach a profound message?

Why does God, in chapter 16, tell Jeremiah not to marry?

What lesson does the prophet learn from the potter in Jeremiah 18?

Have you ever felt as Jeremiah does in 20:7–18? Were you able to express your feelings to God as he did?

Jeremiah 28 presents a contest between a true prophet and a false one. What do you think makes Jeremiah so sure the words of Hananiah are untrue?

Read Jeremiah's description of the ideal covenant in Jeremiah 31:31–34. How was this passage fulfilled in Jesus?

What do you think of the man named Ebed-melech (Jeremiah 38:7–13)?

What do you think of King Zedekiah in light of his discussion with Jeremiah in 38:14–28?

Three Spiritual Lessons From Jeremiah
- If we allow it, God's hands can shape us into something beautiful
- Listening to God's Word leads to life
- We can share our deepest feelings with God

LAMENTATIONS

This is a book for the homesick. It contains the lyrics of sad songs lamenting the fall of Jerusalem. Perhaps they were some of the songs mentioned in Psalm 137 and sung by the people as they sat along the canals of ancient Babylon pining for happier times in the Promised Land.

The songs reveal how much the people learned from their mistakes. The hardships of the Exile made them wiser. Now they recognize the profound truth that the only lasting source of security is a right relationship with God.

In Jewish tradition, these songs were always sung on a special day set aside to mourn the destruction of the temple in Jerusalem. Such ruin happened the first time some six hundred years before the time of Jesus. The enemy then was the empire of Babylon. In the year 70 AD, it happened again. This second time the enemy was the empire of Rome.

In Christian tradition, these songs were sung as the church recalled the passion and death of the Lord Jesus. The ritual was called Tenebrae (darkness). As the ritual progressed, candles were snuffed out one at a time eventually leaving the assembly in complete darkness. The symbolism captures the feeling you get as you read the lyrics of these laments, still powerful in their imagery some twenty-five centuries after their composition.

The vivid images in this poetry lead many to believe these songs must have been composed shortly after the sad event of the destruction of Jerusalem and the beautiful temple constructed by Solomon that stood for more than four hundred years.

In their Hebrew original, these songs are alphabetic in order. Each line begins with a successive letter of the Hebrew alphabet. Chapter 3 has the most elaborate construction of all with three lines assigned to each of the twenty-two letters of the Hebrew alphabet. But this design, perhaps a way to bring order out of chaos, breaks down in the final chapter. Uncontrollable grief seems to have won out in the end.

The 5 chapters of Lamentations:

I   Jerusalem weeps

2   A day of wrath

3   A word of hope

4   Images of death

5   A plea for restoration

The Alphabet

All but the final lament have an alphabetic structure; each verse begins with a successive letter of the Hebrew alphabet. This is difficult to capture in translation. One English translation of Lamentations that *is* alphabetic is the one by Monsignor Ronald Knox. If you can find a copy of his Bible, read his rendering of Lamentations and see what you think.

Jeremiah's Laments?

The Greek translation of this book names Jeremiah as the author. This may be due to the fact that 2 Chronicles 35:25 mentions that Jeremiah composed a lament for a dead king of Judah. Although there is no evidence to really connect Jeremiah with the lamentations in this book, they certainly do echo his oracles about the impending destruction of the city. Jeremiah 41:5 records the arrival of mourners in Jerusalem. Did they come to lament the city's capture by the Babylonians?

Here is a selection of the striking images in this poetry. They are as stark as those black-and-white photos of civil war battlefields so familiar to us from our history books.

Mother Jerusalem

She sits in the dust, clothed in the filthy shreds of her once beautiful garments. She grieves over her loss, filled with painful memories of happier times (1:9).

The Dead

Her citizens lie dead in the streets of the city, even the precious children mother Jerusalem once bounced on her lap (2:22).

Fragments

The noble people of the city, once gleaming like gold, now lie in the streets broken like pieces of discarded pottery (4:1–2).

Crushed Grapes

This is how the poetry describes the young people of the city struck down by the swords of Babylon's soldiers (1:15).

Lamentations on the Clock (BC)

The Fall of Jerusalem   587

The Return from Exile   537

As anyone knows, grief really has no calendar. No matter how many years have passed we can mourn for someone just as strongly as we did the day we lost him or her. The strong feelings for Jerusalem in Lamentations could have been written soon after the city was taken or long after. Many specialists believe the Late Hebrew idioms and the connections with the second half of Isaiah make likely a date before the return from the Exile around 537 BC.

As you read Lamentations…

Note the powerful images in the opening lines of chapter 1. What emotions do they evoke in you?

As you continue reading chapter 1, you suddenly find yourself being addressed by Jerusalem herself. How does this affect you?

In the second lament, how does the author show that Jerusalem's tragedy touches the lives of all her citizens?

Notice the downward thrust in chapter 2 with its references to "the ground" and to "pouring out."

What images for suffering do you find especially moving in the third lament?

Note that as you read 3:4–9 you can almost feel what is being described.

What is your reaction to the strong images for God in 3:10–13?

How effectively does the fourth lament use contrast to portray Jerusalem's tragic state?

Note the many references to color in chapter 4. What impression does each color make on you?

What images of suffering in chapter 5 do you find especially moving?

What does this final lament reveal about the people's relationship with God?

Apart from the final lament, all the verses in this book are arranged according to the Hebrew alphabet. Compose your own prayer arranged according to the alphabet.

Three Spiritual Lessons From Lamentations

- Pain and suffering do not separate us from God
- Past failures can draw us closer to God
- Faith is a sure foundation for the future

BARUCH

We all appreciate second chances, opportunities to go back in time and redo the things we did. This was true for the people of Israel too. Lost in exile, they yearned for the chance to return to their homeland, determined not to make the mistakes they made in the past. This book speaks for them. It is filled with the sort of insights we might expect a people to have learned when all mortal schemes have failed: the need for prayer; the foolishness of relying on our own resources; the wisdom of relying on God.

Who was Baruch? He was a scribe to the great prophet Jeremiah. You can find him in Jeremiah 36 taking down one of Jeremiah's oracles and then reading it before the royal court. During that great prophet's lifetime, Baruch was in the background. But in this book, Baruch has a chance to record his own words.

Baruch speaks for a people chastened by the collapse of their world. Far away from their homeland, they now look back on it with longing. They are at last ready to seek security in God alone. He begins his book with a beautiful prayer admitting the faults of the past and asking God to recognize the hardships of the people in exile. This prayer is followed by a moving poem on true wisdom and all the benefits that flow from it. Then Baruch explains to the people that God has not abandoned them but is already preparing for them a brighter future. The final chapter exposes the foolishness of idolatry and the wisdom of seeking the one true God.

The 6 chapters of Baruch:

1:1 — 3:8	Prayerful appeal
3:9 — 4:4	Wisdom's value
4:5 — 5:9	Take courage! God loves you
6:1 — 6:72	Find security in God

A Model Prayer

Baruch places in the hands of his people the text of a beautiful prayer to God. It begins with a candid admission of sin, especially pride. Then the prayer moves along to a sincere appeal asking God not to overlook their change of heart and to bring them home again (1:15—3:8).

Avoiding Illusions

Chapter 6 of Baruch appeared in older Bibles as a separate book called "The Letter of Jeremiah." It was supposedly a copy of a letter the prophet sent to the exiles in Babylon explaining idolatry as the fundamental cause for their hardship.

Baruch on the Clock (BC)

Fall of Jerusalem   587

Maccabean Revolt   167–164

According to its first chapter, Baruch read this book to the exiles in Babylon. That would date it some six hundred years before Christ. But experts today believe this book was actually composed much later than Baruch's lifetime, perhaps around the time of the Maccabean Wars since it echoes parts of Daniel in tone.

As you read Baruch…

Baruch tells us the exiles sent contributions for sacrifices. What was their purpose in doing so?

How does Baruch make an argument for searching for wisdom in 3:9—4:4?

How does Baruch encourage a broken people in 4:21—5:9?

How effective for you is Jeremiah's satire on idols in Baruch 6?

Three Spiritual Lessons From Baruch
- True repentance leads to a stronger bond with God
- The Word of God leads to life
- Faith is a better foundation for life than earthly ambitions

EZEKIEL

Imagine Solomon's temple abandoned by God! We may find this unbelievable, accustomed as we are to associating the temple with God. But the prophet Ezekiel did not have to imagine it; he saw it! It was revealed in a dramatic vision that came to him a few years before the collapse of the kingdom.

God, of course, did not want to abandon the people, but their rebellion—and God calls them rebels!—against God was so complete there was little reason for God to remain in their midst. Of course, God had plans to return to the people. But that would happen only after a time of purification.

This powerful drama of judgment and restoration is the theme of the book of Ezekiel. We can follow its progress by concentrating on the vision of God's glory that comes to Ezekiel three times in the course of this book.

As the book begins, the vision comes to Ezekiel while he lives among the exiles along the waterways of Babylon. It is an overpowering vision filled with fearsome creatures, lightning and burning coals. The throne of God sits above this fiery display as if intentionally removed from the earth. The overall impression of the vision is that God has come in judgment. This impression is confirmed when God announces to Ezekiel that the people are rebels because they refuse to hear the life-giving Word of God.

Ezekiel sees the vision of divine glory again after being transported by the power of God from Babylon to Jerusalem to witness God's departure from the temple (Ezekiel 8—11). The idolatry of the people has gone so far they have in effect driven God away. With God removed from their midst, it is only a matter of time before the people suffer defeat at the hands of their enemies. This in fact happens when Jerusalem is captured by the army of Babylon a few years later.

When Ezekiel sees the vision of divine glory the third time, God is returning to the holy city (Ezekiel 43). God has restored the city as only God could. Its dimensions and its beauty surpass anything mere mortals could accomplish. When God enters the new temple, it is clear that God intends to stay. In the very last line of the book, we learn that the name of the city is "the LORD is there." And so a book that began with God distant from the people ends with God very close to them.

Ezekiel's role in all of this is to warn the people of the inevitable collapse of the kingdom if they continue to ignore God. By God's design, Ezekiel is appointed to serve as a watchman for the people. It is his task to preach the Word of God. It is up to the people to choose whether they will listen to the Word of God or not.

The oracles of this prophet are remarkable for their sharpness and color. His most recognizable oracle describes the valley of the dry bones that come back to life through the power of the life-giving Word of God (Ezekiel 37). Another notable oracle is Ezekiel's retelling of Israel's history as the story of an ungrateful child whom God raises from poverty only to have her abandon God to live a life of depravity (Ezekiel 16).

The 48 chapters of Ezekiel:

1 — 7	The vision of judgment
8 — 32	The vision and the old temple
33 — 48	The vision and the new temple

Lioness
Ezekiel portrays the decline of Israel as the sad story of a pride of lions, once free and powerful, now caged for the amusement of the king of Babylon.

False Prophets
Ezekiel has a perfect description for false prophets. He calls them people who daub a weak wall with whitewash to make it look impressive when in fact it is in danger of collapse. They do the same thing on a spiritual level with their false words of hope.

A Doomed City
The spiritual condition of Jerusalem was so bad in Ezekiel's view that if the three most righteous people imaginable—Job, Noah and Daniel—lived in it, their righteousness would still save only themselves (Ezekiel 14).

Grace

Ezekiel 18 is well known for its emphasis on the mercy of God. God regards the worthiness of each person. The door is always open for repentance. No one is trapped by a sinful past. Nor can sinners presume forgiveness on the basis of good deeds done long ago.

Water of Life

In Ezekiel 47 the prophet sees waters of life flowing from the temple in Jerusalem. At first, it is just a small stream, but it becomes a wide river so deep the prophet cannot cross it. Where this river flows, it transforms the earth into a beautiful garden of life.

Shepherd

In chapter 34 Ezekiel describes God as the good shepherd. Mortal kings shepherded the people badly because of their self-indulgent policies; God shepherds them well because God is dedicated to the welfare of the flock.

Watchman

God appointed Ezekiel to be a watchman for the people. From his vantage point as an agent of God, it was Ezekiel's task to warn the people of any approaching danger. Ezekiel took this assignment very seriously. His book even includes a very detailed chronology of his visions and pronouncements. We may think of it as a watchman's log recording the faithful performance of his duties.

Ezekiel on the Clock (BC)

First Deportation to Babylon   598

Fall of Jerusalem   587

End of Exile   537

Ezekiel's book is filled with precise dating from 598 down to 571 BC. God entrusted Ezekiel with the task of watchman over the people. His book has the character of a logbook recorded by a watchman carefully keeping track of events. Babylon kept notes too. Archaeology has unearthed texts from the reign of Nebuchadnezzar that contain details about a king of Judah (Jehoiakin) held prisoner in Babylon along with members of his family and court.

As you read Ezekiel…

The rabbis restricted the public reading of the first chapter of Ezekiel. What reasons do you think they had for this position?

God appoints Ezekiel to be a watchman for Israel (Ezekiel 3:16–21). Identify as many reasons as you can why watchman is a good title for a prophet.

In Ezekiel 10, the prophet sees the glory of God abandon the temple in Jerusalem. What do you think this meant for Jerusalem's future?

How does Ezekiel describe false prophets in chapter 13?

How does Ezekiel develop the image of the vine in chapter 15? What does this mean for the people?

The parable of the ungrateful child in Ezra 16 is well known. What lessons do you find in it?

Tyre was a renowned port on the Mediterranean Sea in ancient times. What do you think of Ezekiel's lament over Tyre in chapter 27 of his book?

What are the characteristics of a good shepherd according to chapter 34?

The vision of the valley of bones in Ezekiel 37:1–14 is probably the best-known passage in the book. What makes this vision so powerful?

In Ezekiel 47, the prophet's heavenly guide shows him a stream of water flowing from the temple. What becomes of this stream and what does it mean for the people?

Three Spiritual Lessons From Ezekiel

- God is always seeking ways to be close to us
- No one is trapped by past mistakes; the door is always open for repentance
- Strive to become a person who brings comfort to others

DANIEL

When we hear the name Daniel, we think right away of his famous escape from the den of lions (Daniel 6). How did he do it? Daniel would be the first to tell us "God did it!" Daniel understood perfectly that God is the judge of all. In fact, Daniel's name means, "God is my judge." And Daniel certainly lives up to his name.

Daniel spent much of his life in the service of kings. But for Daniel there was just one king: the Lord God of Israel. Daniel knew that earthly kingdoms, so limited by time, eventually fade away; Daniel served a kingdom that endures forever.

Right from the start, we see that Daniel finds life in God and not in the favor of earthly kings. He and his friends announce they do not need to eat the rich foods prepared in the royal kitchens of the King of Babylon. They prefer nourishment provided by God's creation, simple foods like vegetables. To the surprise of all in the royal house, Daniel and his friends "appeared better and fatter than all the young men who had been eating the royal rations" (1:15).

Daniel and his three companions Hananiah, Mishael and Azariah—better known by their Babylonian names Shadrach, Meshach and Abednego—are special to God. Daniel not only interprets dreams but even reveals the details of a dream without any clues from the dreamer. Daniel alone can read and interpret the writing on the wall during the famous feast of King Belshazzar. Daniel's three friends do not even smell of smoke when they emerge from the fiery furnace!

But the most important news in this book is that this pattern of divine protection extends beyond Daniel and his three friends; it applies also to all who believe in God. What we see as true for Daniel is also true for God's faithful people. This news comes in four visions Daniel sees during his lifetime. Each one shows him how the great kingdoms of the earth will fade away and God's kingdom will prevail.

But Daniel cannot interpret these visions himself. He has to rely on a messenger from heaven to do that. And if dreams as interpreted by Daniel come true, certainly the visions interpreted by Gabriel will come true.

When we last see Daniel, we find him as the champion of truth. He saves the virtuous Susanna from the schemes of two wicked elders. He exposes the foolishness of believing in earthly idols instead of the living God. The author of Daniel wants us to understand that Daniel's world is the real world. God's enemies may seem to enjoy success for a while, but in the long run, their kingdoms will fall. The future belongs to God and God's faithful people.

The 14 chapters of Daniel:

1 — 6	Daniel and his friends enjoy God's protection
7 — 12	Daniel sees how God protects the people
13 — 14	Daniel protects others with God's truth

Gabriel

This is the name of the heavenly messenger who interprets the visions for Daniel. The name means "God is strong." In the third vision Gabriel tells Daniel about an "anointed one" who will come after a long time of waiting (Daniel 9:25). No wonder Gabriel is the one who appears to Mary to announce the birth of Jesus (Luke 1:26).

Hananiah, Mishael and Azariah

If you do not recognize them, it is because you are probably more familiar with their other names: Shadrach, Meshach and Abednego. These are Daniel's three friends. God takes care of them just as God takes care of Daniel. In Daniel 3, you will find the famous song they sing while inside the fiery furnace. It begins "Blessed are you, O Lord, God of our ancestors, / and to be praised and highly exalted forever..." (Daniel 3:52–90).

Susanna

This woman of virtue would rather die than sin before God. She is the victim of a cruel plot by two wicked elders who wanted to ravish her because she was so beautiful. Daniel, as God's agent of life, defends her and sentences the two elders to death connecting their fate with words they had used in their false testimony.

A New Style

In Daniel 7—12, we encounter a special kind of writing called apocalyptic. The word *apocalypse* in its literal sense means "uncovered." In the book of Daniel, this kind of writing appears in chapters 7 to 12 which "uncover" things that will happen later in time. One common feature of apocalyptic literature is contrast, especially between good and bad, light and darkness, heaven and earth. Another common element in this kind of literature is the presence of heavenly messengers serving as interpreters of visions.

Daniel on the Clock (BC)

Nebuchadnezzar of Babylon   605–562

Maccabean Revolt   167–164

In real time, Daniel comes from the difficult years of the Jewish Revolt begun by the Maccabees. The major conflict was from 167 to 164 BC, but the struggle continued for many years afterward. Daniel's fourth vision, for example, includes details that match the reign of King Antiochus IV (175–164 BC) against whom the Jews fought for independence.

In narrative time, Daniel's successes occur in the glory days of the Babylonian Empire. Placing Daniel's witness to God that far back in time may have been a way to disguise the book's real purpose which was to encourage the Jewish people to hold on to their faith in spite of the efforts of Antiochus IV to intimidate them.

As you read Daniel...

What do we learn of Daniel from the very first chapter?

What is the king's dream in Daniel 2 and what is Daniel's interpretation of it?

Read the prayer of Azariah in Daniel 3:26–45. What does he request of God?

Daniel's three companions sing their famous hymn of praise (Daniel 3:52–90) while they are surrounded by flames. What does the hymn reveal about their faith?

The church sings this hymn of the three young men all through the first week of Easter. What makes this hymn appropriate for the season of Easter?

The expression "handwriting on the wall" comes from the account about Belshazzar's feast in Daniel 5. What is the significance of the phrase in this original setting?

Daniel was protected in the den of lions (Daniel 6). What other examples of divine protection do you know of in the Bible?

Daniel 7:13–14 is read on the feast of Christ the King. What does this passage reveal about kingship?

The archangel Michael makes his biblical debut in Daniel 10 and 12. What is his role in these chapters?

In some Bibles the account about Susanna in Daniel 13 was placed at the beginning of the book of Daniel. What do you think was the reason for this?

As you read about the different rulers in this book, do you see any evolution in their attitude toward the God of Daniel?

Three Spiritual Lessons From Daniel

- Mortal schemes are no match for God's plan of salvation
- God wants to protect us from harm
- Loyalty to God is a firm foundation for life

DANIEL

THE MINOR PROPHETS

This group of twelve may not be quite as familiar to us as the twelve tribes of Israel or the twelve apostles, but the minor prophets certainly make a major contribution to God's message.

Why are they known as the "minor" prophets? It is not because their message is less weighty or because they are lesser known to history. As we learned in our introduction to the major prophets, the minor prophets are so called only because traditionally all twelve of them shared one scroll.

If we step back and look at the scroll of the minor prophets, we find similarities with the scrolls of the major prophets. There is a similarity in content. All the prophetic scrolls include oracles of salvation, oracles of judgment and oracles against the nations. There is also a similarity in structure. Like the scrolls of Isaiah and Ezekiel, the oracles against the nations in the minor prophets are gathered near the middle of the scroll where you find Obadiah, Jonah, Nahum and Habakkuk. Also like Isaiah and Ezekiel, the scroll of the "twelve" begins with a heavy concentration of oracles of judgment (especially Amos and Joel) and ends with a heavy dose of oracles of salvation (notably Haggai and Zechariah).

All of this suggests that there is something to be gained by reading the twelve minor prophets as a unit. It will echo the same sort of message gained from reading one of the other prophet scrolls: a gradual movement from challenge to promise.

The minor prophets bring the Old Testament to a close. Their oracles cover a large span of time from the ninth century down to the fifth century before the time of Jesus. Like the major prophets, they affirm God's commitment to the welfare of the people in spite of the fact that the people refuse to listen to God and choose to go their own way. By this time in our reading of the Bible, that is a very familiar story indeed.

The last of the minor prophets is Malachi. His final oracle talks about a future time when the prophet Elijah will come again. For Christians this oracle was fulfilled with the preaching of John the Baptist. So Malachi points the way to the New Testament.

Here is a quick profile of each of the twelve minor prophets in order of appearance on the scroll:

Hosea—the heart-to-heart prophet

Joel—prophet of true repentance

Amos—the plumb-line prophet

Obadiah—the how-to-treat-family prophet

Jonah—the reluctant prophet

Micah—a courtroom prophet

Nahum—a prophet of confidence

Habakkuk—prophet of patience

Zephaniah—prophet of the Lord's Day

Haggai—the temple prophet

Zechariah—prophet of vivid images

Malachi—the gateway prophet

HOSEA

Hosea is famous for his marriage to a woman named Gomer. His marriage to this woman was a sign to the people of Israel. Just as Gomer was unfaithful to Hosea, so the people of Israel were unfaithful to God. But just as Hosea spoke to her heart and won her back, so God will speak to the heart of the people and win them back.

The children of Hosea and Gomer are signs for the people. The names given them at birth represent the broken relationship between God and people of Israel. One daughter has the name Lo-ruhama (meaning "not pitied"), representing how God felt toward a sinful people. A boy is given the name Lo-ammi (meaning "not my people").

Because this is a book about God's love, the story does not end on this sad note. In a later oracle, God renames the children. The girl is named Ruhama because God will have pity of the people. The boy is named Ammi because God will call them once again "my people."

Hosea's experience with Gomer sums up the rest of the oracles of this prophet. God wants to have a heart-to-heart talk with the people but they engage God in only superficial conversation because they insist on going their own way.

Dismayed at their lack of spiritual maturity God declares their form of piety to be like "the dew that early passes away." They will not enjoy the life-giving "rain" of God's love until they are willing to truly listen to God.

In the final oracle of the book, the people at last come to their senses. They turn away from their idols and ask God to forgive them. God accepts their apology. The bond between God and people is restored.

The 14 chapters of Hosea:

1 — 3	Hosea's family
4 — 10	What God has to say
11 — 14	God's children

Overcast

Hosea 6:3–4 offers a good example of the way this prophet can use an image. In this case, the image is light. The people think of God coming into their lives like the light of a new day. But from God's viewpoint, the light of the dawn is obscured by the clouds of their imperfect piety.

Hosea on the Clock (BC)

King Jeroboam   786–746

Rise of Assyria   745

Fall of Samaria   721

Hosea's king was Jeroboam II, who ruled over the northern kingdom of Israel from his capital in Samaria. He was enjoying a golden age, chiefly because the great empires of Egypt and Assyria were not strong enough to interfere in his world. But things were about to change dramatically. Within a generation after the death of Jeroboam in 746 BC, his kingdom was gone, victim to a new and more powerful Assyria.

As you read Hosea...

How is Hosea's experience with Gomer a suitable example of God's experience with Israel?

Why do you think the language and imagery in chapters 1 to 3 is so strong?

What do you think the prophet means by saying, "There is no knowledge of God in the land" (4:1)?

How many images for God and for the people can you find in chapters 6 and 7? Which ones do you find most striking?

Note what God really looks for in 6:6. Can you find similar passages in the Bible?

"Reaping the whirlwind" is a well-known expression found in 8:7. What do you think Hosea means here?

How effectively does Hosea use the image of the vine and the fig tree in chapters 9 and 10 and in verses 14:5–9?

In Hosea 11 God speaks of the people as a parent might speak about a rebellious child. What is so moving about this passage for you?

Note the images for the frailty of life in 13:3. Could you come up with similar images?

Compare Hosea 13:14 with Paul's message in 1 Corinthians 15:55.

Three Spiritual Lessons From Hosea

- No matter where we have strayed we can always come home to God
- Nothing is more valuable than a relationship with God
- Faith can transform a desert into a garden

JOEL

"[R]end your hearts and not your clothing" (2:13). Sound familiar? This is the challenge we hear at the beginning of Lent every year. It is a good summary of the important biblical lesson that religion should reach into our hearts.

The oracles of Joel move from devastation to plenty. The prophet paints a bleak picture of a field filled with locusts devouring the crops. You are not likely to see a swarm of hungry locusts, but if you have ever seen your favorite plants disappear because some bug decides to munch on them, you have a good idea of what Joel is talking about. It is a good image of the spiritual blight that can plague a people who do not rely on God but turn only to earthly resources to solve their problems. Joel wants to make an impression; he urges his readers to pass on the message:

> Tell your children of it,
>> and let your children tell their children,
>> and their children another generation. (1:3)

But prayer makes a big difference. Seek a close bond with God and you will be surprised at the gifts you will recognize in your life. Joel holds out to his readers an alternate scene of mountains and hills flowing with cool drinks:

> In that day
> the mountains shall drip sweet wine,
>> the hills shall flow with milk,
> and all the stream beds of Judah
>> shall flow with water. (3:18)

The 4 chapters of Joel:

1 — 2	Famine
3 — 4	Plenty

Spirit-Filled Generations

Peter quoted a passage from Joel in his Pentecost sermon of Acts 2:14–21. The oracle reads,

Then afterward
    I will pour out my spirit on all flesh;
your sons and your daughters shall prophesy,
    your old men shall dream dreams,
    and your young men shall see visions. (2:28)

Peter declared that the time for fulfillment of those words had arrived with the gift of the Holy Spirit.

Joel on the Clock (BC)

Exile to Babylon 587

Return from Exile 537

Second temple c. 515

If we knew when the crops of the Holy Land were ruined by a plague of locusts, we could better place Joel's oracles in time. But such devastation was unfortunately not that uncommon. Joel's reference to the temple with no mention of a monarchy suggests that Joel's temple is the second one constructed after the Exile. A date close to the beginning of the fifth century is often proposed for Joel's oracles.

As you read Joel…

The name *Joel* means "the Lord is God." Do you find this name appropriate to the message of this book?

Identify as many images for destruction as you can in the first chapter. Which ones do you find especially impressive?

Joel 2:12–18 is the first reading for Ash Wednesday. What makes this an appropriate text for the beginning of Lent?

Note the contrast between Joel 3:10 and Isaiah 2:4. What is Joel's message to his people?

How many positive images can you identify in the final verses of Joel?

After reading the oracles of Joel, what do you think the phrase Day of the Lord meant to him?

Three Spiritual Lessons From Joel

- True repentance is a rending of the heart
- All the resources of heaven are on our side for salvation
- We need a world filled with people who enjoy the Spirit of God

AMOS

Any builder knows the value of a plumb line, a line with a weight at one end. In Latin the word for the heavy metal we call lead is *plumbum*. Builders use a plumb line to make sure a vertical wall is straight.

When you think about it, a plumb line is the perfect tool to represent a prophet. The prophet stands among the people to make sure they are "straight" with God. This is precisely what Amos does for the people of his day. God places Amos among the people to teach them they are not yet "straight" with God. Unfortunately, the people did not want to listen to Amos. They preferred to keep to their crooked ways.

Amos begins his book with a series of oracles directed at the nations, rebuking them for their abuses. Israel and Judah are no exception; in fact, Amos is especially harsh with them because they should know better. In subsequent oracles, Amos rebukes them for their extravagances and their mistreatment of the poor. Later oracles include a series of visions announcing God's judgment against them.

But Amos is not discouraged. He concludes his book with an oracle about the days to come when God will rebuild the nation into a people close to God.

The 9 chapters of Amos:

1 — 6	Warning of judgment
7 — 9	Judgment carried out

The Unimaginable

Amos asks some curious questions: "Do horses run on rocks? / Does one plow the sea with oxen?" (6:12). The answer in each case is "of course not." The prophet's point is it should be just as unimaginable for God's people to misuse justice. But the prophet says that is precisely what they did.

Amos on the Clock (BC)

King Jeroboam	786–746
Rise of Assyria	745
Fall of Samaria	721

Like the prophet Hosea, Amos also preached during the prosperous reign of Jeroboam II in the middle of the eighth century before Christ. Both prophets preached in the northern kingdom of

Israel. But Amos was from the southern kingdom of Judah. God sent him north to preach the word. Like Hosea, Amos warned the people about letting the comforts of life smother them spiritually; he had especially strong words for the wealthy people in the capital city of Samaria.

As you read Amos...

If your Bible has a map, locate the places Amos preaches against in the first two chapters. Where do Judah and Israel fit into the pattern?

What does Amos 3:3–8 reveal about the power of the prophet's word?

Note the recurring refrain in chapter 4. What does God look for in the people?

The rabbis taught that Amos 5:4 summed up all 613 laws in the Torah. Do you agree?

Amos 6 is read as the companion text for the parable of the rich man and Lazarus (Luke 16:19–31). What connections do you see between the two readings?

What progression do you see in the series of five visions in Amos 7—9?

How does Amos defend his role as a true prophet in 7:10–17?

How would you apply Amos's oracle against greed in Amos 8:4–14 to the present day?

How do the images in 9:8–14 contribute to the theme of restoration?

Three Spiritual Lessons From Amos

- God's Word is our surest guide in life
- The gifts of this world lead us closer to God
- God's love embraces all the nations of the world

OBADIAH

The oracles of this prophet take up just one chapter in the Bible. Look at a statistical chart of the books of the Old Testament and poor Obadiah will be highlighted as the shortest of them all. But don't let that fool you. Obadiah has a major message against pride. He has a powerful warning against any nation that forgets we all belong to the family of God.

> For the day of the LORD is near against all the nations.
> As you have done, it shall be done to you;
> > your deeds shall return on your own head. (1:15)

When Obadiah looks at nations, he does not think of them as lands or governments. He thinks of them as family. Obadiah remembers that the nations of Edom and Israel can trace their origins back to the twin sons of Isaac and Rebecca. Edom traced its origins back to Esau; Israel of course traced its origins back to Jacob. Obadiah criticizes the nation of Edom for mistreating its neighbor Judah after the fall of Jerusalem in 587 BC. He points an accusing finger at Edom for forgetting this family history: "For the slaughter and violence done to your brother Jacob, / shame shall cover you, / and you shall be cut off forever" (verse 10).

This is strong language. But Obadiah's purpose is not to gloat over the destruction of an enemy. He wants to break the cycle of violence by showing a prideful nation what lies in store for it if it does not change its ways.

The 21 verses of Obadiah:

1 — 14	Mortal deeds
15 — 21	Divine response

Safety

Edom was noted for its rocky cliffs east of the Dead Sea, which seemed to offer them lasting protection. But time changes everything. By the fourth century, the Nabateans overcame the Edomites and carved out of the sandstone cliffs their famous city of Petra (meaning "rock" in Greek).

Obadiah on the Clock (BC)

Jacob and Esau   c. 1700

Kingdom of David   c. 1000

Fall of Jerusalem   587

Obadiah criticizes the nation of Edom for mistreating its neighbor Judah after the fall of Jerusalem in 587 BC. Obadiah himself may have been a witness to this mistreatment. If so, his book reaches back some five centuries before the time of Jesus.

As you read Obadiah...

The name *Obadiah* means "servant of God." Can you find evidence that he lives up to his name?

In verses 3 and 4 Obadiah has this warning: "you that live in the clefts of the rock.... / From there I will bring you down / says the Lord." Cite other passages in the Bible where people seek refuge in earthly resources instead of trusting in God.

Obadiah lists eight things Edom should not have done (verses 12–14). What does this list reveal about the character of Edom?

According to verse 8 Edom was famous for its wisdom. But does Edom seem wise to you?

Why do you think Obadiah concludes with praise of Mount Zion?

Finding satisfaction in the misfortunes of others is a common human emotion. Why does Obadiah speak against it?

Three Spiritual Lessons From Obadiah

- This world is a gift from God to be enjoyed
- Human plans should be in accord with the plans of God
- The misfortunes of others should stir up within us feelings of compassion

OBADIAH

125

JONAH

Jonah does not enjoy being a prophet, at least if being a prophet means he has to offer an opportunity for forgiveness to a people he believes does not deserve the chance. God directs Jonah to go to Nineveh, a city belonging to Israel's worst enemy, the kingdom of Assyria. Jonah instead takes a boat out to sea. Of course, Jonah's plan does not work. The famous great fish swallows him up and takes him back where he belongs.

When Jonah at last arrives in Nineveh and preaches the Word of God, the entire city pleads to God for forgiveness. Any other prophet would have been absolutely thrilled to have been so successful. But Jonah is not happy. In a rage, he blurts his reasoning out to God: "O LORD! Is not this what I said while I was still in my own country? That is why I fled to Tarshish at the beginning; for I knew that you are a gracious God and merciful..." (4:2).

Jonah is so angry he wants to die. But God does not grant his wish. Instead God tries to educate him on the topic of compassion. When Jonah expresses appreciation for a plant that shades him from the hot sun, God suddenly sends a little worm that attacks the plant and kills it. When Jonah complains about this, God takes the opportunity to teach a lesson.

If Jonah can be upset about the loss of a plant, does it not makes sense that God can be upset about the potential loss of an entire city? Maybe we are to think of Jonah as a little worm that would threaten the existence of Nineveh the same way the worm threatened the life of the plant. Jonah certainly does seem to be a very small angry person in the big world God loves so much.

The 4 chapters of Jonah:

1 — 2	Jonah's way
3 — 4	God's way

A Big Book

The author of Jonah likes to describe things as "big." The city of Nineveh is called "big" throughout the book. A "big" storm surrounds Jonah's boat. The sailors are filled with a "big" fear. Of course, everyone knows Jonah was swallowed by a "big" fish. And in the final chapter, Jonah is angry with a "big" anger.

Jonah on the Clock (BC)

Nineveh restored by Sennacherib   c. 700

Nineveh destroyed   612

Nineveh was a flourishing city some seven hundred years before the time of Jesus. Sennacherib chose this beautiful city to be his capital. His building program included a massive royal palace of nearly eighty rooms. The walls of Nineveh enclosed an area of more than 1700 acres. But Jonah was not impressed with the grandeur of the city. His interest was in preaching the Word of God. The actual writing of Jonah's book seems to come from a later time; it was known to Jesus ben Sirach who lived around two hundred years before the birth of Jesus.

As you read Jonah...

What do you think is Jonah's reason for not going to Nineveh as God directed him?

Later in the book (4:2) Jonah reveals the actual reason for his flight. What do you think of him after hearing his real reason?

Compare the attitude of the sailors toward Jonah with Jonah's attitude toward the people of Nineveh.

Jonah calls out to God from the belly of the fish. Does he say what you expected him to say?

The people of Nineveh respond to God's word more devoutly than the people of Israel usually did. What lesson can be drawn from this?

Jonah's book ends with God speaking to Jonah about divine mercy. We are not given Jonah's response. Why do you think the book ends this way?

Three Spiritual Lessons From Jonah

- Every nation belongs to God's family
- God's love is much wider than our love
- A sense of gratitude to God helps us see others differently

JONAH

MICAH

This prophet gives us one of the most quotable lines from the Bible:

> …and what does the LORD require of you
> but to do justice, and to love kindness,
> and to walk humbly with your God? (6:8)

It might be surprising to learn that this line belongs to a complaint God makes against the people for their failure to remain faithful to the covenant. God, on the other hand, has always been faithful to the covenant. Micah's oracles, challenging the people to change their ways, is further evidence of God's ceaseless efforts to win the people over.

We can read Micah as a trial scene unfolding in stages. It begins with God summoning the people to the trial: "…let the Lord GOD be a witness against you…" (1:2).

Following this is a list of charges including idolatry, injustice, misguided leadership and false prophecy. Then comes this sentence leveled against them:

> You shall eat, but not be satisfied,
> and there shall be a gnawing hunger within you;
> you shall put away, but not save,
> and what you save, I will hand over to the sword. (6:14)

But the book ends with an affirmation of God's mercy and forgiveness. It seems that once more God's purpose in sending a prophet is to give the people every advantage in making a change and returning to God.

The 9 chapters of Micah:

1 — 2	Summons to trial
3 — 4	The charges
6 — 9	God's decision

Messiah

This word means "anointed." In biblical times olive oil was used to anoint people. It was a way of preparing them to do special work for God. Aaron was anointed with oil to prepare him for his task as high priest; kings were anointed to prepare them to serve God's holy people. Jesus is *the* Messiah because he served God more perfectly than anyone else did. The title "Christ" comes from the Greek word for "anointed."

The prophet Micah gives us one of the most familiar passages associated with Jesus as God's anointed one:

> But you, O Bethlehem of Ephrathah,
>> who are one of the little clans of Judah,
> from you shall come forth for me
>> one who is to rule in Israel,
> whose origin is from of old,
>> from ancient days. (5:2)

Micah on the Clock (BC)

Jotham   742–735

Ahaz   735–715

Hezekiah   715–687

Micah must have been a powerful preacher. According to Jeremiah 26:17–20, Micah's message moved the court of King Hezekiah to initiate spiritual reforms. This detail as well as the opening verses of Micah's book places him in the eighth century with three other prophets: Hosea, Amos, and Isaiah. It is worth noting that Micah and Isaiah share the famous passage about beating swords into plowshares (Isaiah 2:4; Micah 4:3).

As you read Micah…

How dedicated is Micah to his mission as a prophet? See 1:8–9.

What do you think of the response the people give to Micah's message at 2:6?

Note Micah's vivid portrayal of injustice in 3:1–4.

In 3:5–8 how does Micah compare his own preaching to the preaching of other prophets?

What does Micah's oracle in 5:1–4 reveal about the character of the Messiah?

In the divine charge against the people (6:1–5), God refers to events from the Exodus to the entrance into the Promised Land. What deeds of the Lord took place within this timeframe?

What is Micah searching for in 7:1–7?

MICAH

In Micah 8:6–8 the prophet speaks plainly about what God expects of the people. How many other passages from the Bible have a similar theme?

The name *Micah* means "Who is like God?" How appropriate is this name to the theme of the book, and especially the final verses of the book?

Three Spiritual Lessons From Micah

- We should give God no cause for a complaint against us
- God is faithful to the covenant with the people
- We are called to walk humbly with God

NAHUM

Nahum has good news for God's people. This prophet confidently announces that the people of God will ultimately enjoy a life free from fear and oppression.

> Look! On the mountains the feet of one
> who brings good tidings,
> who proclaims peace!
> Celebrate your festivals, O Judah,
> fulfill your vows,
> for never again shall the wicked invade you;
> they are utterly cut off. (1:15)

Nahum makes it very clear that powers of this world cannot match the power of God. For this prophet the great imperial city of Nineveh represents any earthly nation that would presume to work against God's saving plan in order to claim the world for itself. Such great schemes will fail in the end.

The 3 chapters of Nahum:

1	Divine power
2 — 3	Human weakness

Sleepy Shepherds

Nahum warns the nation of Assyria that its shepherds "are asleep." What he means is that the earthly resources to which they turn for security will prove unreliable. For this prophet there is only one true source of security—the Lord God of Israel.

Nahum on the Clock (BC)

Fall of Thebes   663

Fall of Nineveh   612

We can date Nahum between the fall of two cities. The first was Thebes, taken by Assyria in 663 BC; the second was Nineveh, taken by Babylon in 612 BC. Nahum has this to say about them:

> "Nineveh is devastated; who will bemoan her?"
>> Where shall I seek comforters for you?
> Are you better than Thebes
>> that sat by the Nile,
> with water around her,
>> her rampart a sea,
>> water her wall? (3:7–8)

As you read Nahum…

Nahum announces that the Lord is "a jealous God." Do you think of God this way? What positive meaning could this portrayal of God have for the people of Israel?

What image of God comes to mind as you read 1:1–11?

Note the number of images this prophet uses to represent Nineveh between verses 2:9 and 3:7. Which ones do you find most powerful?

In 3:14 the prophet satirizes the building of a brick wall for defense. What other passages in the Bible satirize the choice to seek defense behind walls instead of in God?

The name *Nahum* is associated with the Hebrew word for "comfort." What do you find comforting about the message of this prophet?

131

Three Spiritual Lessons From Nahum
- A close bond with God is the only real source of security
- There is wisdom in recognizing our limitations
- God offers us peace and comfort

HABAKKUK

Be sure to pronounce his name properly. Put the accent on the second syllable—Ha-BAK-kuk. This prophet has been compared to Job because of his plea to God:

O LORD, how long shall I cry for help,
and you will not listen? (1:2)

Habakkuk is waiting for an answer from God. He is distressed over the hardships of his people and wants to know when God is going to do something about it. Haven't we all felt that way at one time or another?

It is not as if Habakkuk believes his people to be thoroughly innocent. He understands that God may wish to allow a wayward people to learn from their mistakes. But he wonders why God allows an enemy to make life endlessly miserable for those who are more righteous.

Habakkuk is so determined to get an answer from God that he announces that he is going to station himself in a tower and just wait to see what God will say. He does not have to wait long.

Then the LORD answered me and said:
Write the vision;
make it plain on tablets,
so that a runner may read it.
For there is still a vision for the appointed time;
it speaks of the end, and does not lie.
If it seems to tarry, wait for it;
it will surely come, it will not delay. (2:2–3)

God's answer to Habakkuk seems to be that there will come a time of reckoning for the oppressor, but it will take place on God's time not the prophet's. Habakkuk's task is to wait with confidence and understand that God has a plan.

Appropriately, Habakkuk's oracles conclude with a prayer of total trust in God. The prophet believes that even in the face of all evidence to the contrary, God's plan of salvation will prevail.

> Though the fig tree does not blossom,
>> and no fruit is on the vines;
> though the produce of the olive fails
>> and the fields yield no food;
> though the flock is cut off from the fold,
>> and there is no herd in the stalls,
> yet I will rejoice in the LORD;
>> I will exult in the God of my salvation. (3:17–18)

The 3 chapters of Habakkuk:

1 — 2	Concern
3	Confidence

A Special Mission

Habakkuk makes a guest appearance in the book of Daniel. In the last chapter of Daniel, Habakkuk has prepared a meal for people working in the fields of Judea. Then God transports Habakkuk to Babylon where he is directed to give the food to Daniel in the lion's den. His mission accomplished, Habakkuk is transported back to his own place.

Habakkuk on the Clock (BC)

Nebuchadnezzar   605–562

Fall of Jerusalem   587

Nebuchadnezzar, king of Babylon from 605 to 562 BC, was a force to be reckoned with. He expanded his father's kingdom and transformed the city of Babylon into one of the seven wonders of the ancient world. This king's forces are most likely "the Chaldeans" the prophet Habakkuk complains about to God (Habakkuk 1:6). Nebuchadnezzar is a throne name meaning "May Nabu (God of wisdom) protect my kingdom." But Habakkuk knew that true protection came only from the God of Israel.

HABAKKUK

As you read Habakkuk…

Habakkuk complains because he cries to God for help but God does not listen. When have you shared this prophet's feelings?

Read over this prophet's description of an approaching army (Habakkuk 1:7–11). What images are especially moving for you?

What answer would you give to Habakkuk's question to God at 1:13?

In chapter 2, Habakkuk lists examples of people who rely only on the resources of this world for happiness. What examples from our present time could you add to his list?

What wisdom would you want to see written on tablets of stone (Habakkuk 2:2)?

This prophet boldly announces that the just will live because of faith (2:4). What does this statement mean for you?

Paul quotes Habakkuk 2:4. Read Romans 1:17 to discover the lesson Paul finds in the words of this prophet.

At 2:6–20 Habakkuk has words of warning for five groups. What spiritual weakness do the five share?

What do you think of Habakkuk's statement about his faith in 3:17–19?

Three Spiritual Lessons From Habakkuk

- Questions addressed to God can lead to new spiritual insights
- Human plans have limitations
- Faith is the key to life

ZEPHANIAH

When Zephaniah spoke about the Lord's Day he was not thinking of a bright sunny day filled with worshippers on their way to church. For Zephaniah the Day of the Lord was a time of judgment, a day on which God takes action against the proud people who seek their own will instead of the will of God. As Zephaniah saw things, there had to be a thorough house cleaning first. After that, God could rework the nation into the ideal people of faith they were supposed to be.

When Zephaniah spoke about pride, he was thinking mainly of leaders who looked for security in earthly resources instead of in God. Policies of this kind were doomed to fail. A much more promising alliance for security was to be found in a right relationship with God. For this to happen, God would work with a remnant of Israel, a small number of people loyal to God:

> For I will leave in the midst of you
>> a people humble and lowly.
> They shall seek refuge in the name of the LORD—
>> the remnant of Israel;
> they shall do no wrong
>> and utter no lies,
> nor shall a deceitful tongue
>> be found in their mouths.... (3:12–13)

Such humble service to God will lead to a new day. And so Zephaniah's oracles conclude on the happy theme of restoration for the people:

> At that time I will bring you home,
>> at the time when I gather you;
> for I will make you renowned and praised
>> among all the peoples of the earth,
> when I restore your fortunes
>> before your eyes, says the LORD. (3:20)

The 3 chapters of Zephaniah:

1 — 2	Judgment
3	Restoration

Dregs

Zephaniah says some of the people were only concerned about drinking the dregs at the bottom of the barrel (1:12). What he means is they had grown complacent about life. They were neglecting their true purpose in life: to serve God and to reach out to their brothers and sisters in this world.

ZEPHANIAH

Zephaniah on the Clock (BC)

Josiah 640–609

Fall of Jerusalem 587

The first lines of this book place Zephaniah's oracles during the reign of Josiah (640 to 609 BC) just before the preaching of Jeremiah. Josiah was one of the few kings who received favorable remarks from the author of Kings. Perhaps it was Zephaniah's message that helped motivate Josiah to introduce his religious reforms. Unfortunately, these reforms did not last and the kingdom eventually collapsed.

As you read Zephaniah…

This prophet is often pictured with a lantern in his hand. Read 1:12 to discover what he is looking for.

In 2:14–15 Zephaniah describes a deserted city. How effective is his description?

At 3:3–5 how does this prophet use morning and evening to contrast God and people?

On the Fourth Sunday of the Year, Zephaniah 3:12–13 is paired with the Beatitudes from Matthew 5:3–12. What do you discover from reading the two together?

This prophet has two different descriptions for the Day of the Lord. Compare 1:14–16 with 3:14–18.

Three Spiritual Lessons From Zephaniah

- Time is a gift from God to be used wisely
- Walk in the light of God's lamp
- Wait for God

HAGGAI

This prophet's curious name is connected with the Hebrew word for "festival." This seems appropriate since Haggai certainly does have something to celebrate. But that comes only later in the book. As the book begins, Haggai is busy trying to light a fire under the people.

He wants his people to get their priorities straight. If they really want things to go well, they must first concentrate on building the temple of the Lord. Of course, Haggai is not naïve enough to think the physical presence of a building is going to automatically change the fortunes of the people. But he is prophet enough to know that if the people put God first in their lives many good things will follow.

Things are not going so well as Haggai begins his prophecies. We can see this from the harsh conditions he describes at the beginning of his book.

> You have sown much, and harvested little;
> you eat, but you never have enough;
> you drink, but you never have your fill;
> you clothe yourselves, but no one is warm;
> and you that earn wages earn wages to put them
> into a bag with holes. (1:6)

Clearly, something has to change and Haggai sees that change coming with an inner transformation of the people. Haggai got results. Before long, the people were busy rebuilding the temple of the Lord in Jerusalem. It was a good start. The people were finally putting their efforts into rebuilding a right relationship with God. Little wonder Haggai's final oracles include this very happy announcement: "From this day on I will bless you" (2:19).

The 2 chapters of Haggai:

| 1 | Call to faith |
| 2 | Future blessings |

A Dynamic Duo

Zerubbabel and Joshua were two movers and shakers in the community after the Exile. Their leadership provided the energy and motivation to get that temple built. Zerubbabel belonged to the royal family of David and was appointed by Persia to serve as governor of Judah. Joshua apparently belonged to a priestly line. His father Jehozadak was also a high priest.

HAGGAI

Haggai on the Clock (BC)

Darius I of Persia   522–486

Second temple   c. 515

Haggai dates his oracles to a three-month span in the second year of Darius. This is probably Darius I, who ruled over Persia from 522 to 486 BC. On our calendar, Haggai's oracles cover a period from late summer to early winter in the year 520. This was the planting season in Haggai's world. He seems to be saying that if the people want a rich harvest they must turn to God. The people were listening. Three weeks after Haggai's first oracle, work on the temple was already underway (Haggai 1:14–15).

As you read Haggai…

How is lack of religion exhibited in 1:4–11?

What tangible results flow from God's blessing in 2:18–19?

How does Haggai use the image of a signet ring in 2:23?

Three Spiritual Lessons From Haggai

- Put God first in life
- The best gift to God is humble service
- The only lasting honor comes from God

ZECHARIAH

Riders on horses, a lampstand of gold, even a scroll flying through the air—these are just a few of the images we find in the opening oracles of Zechariah. He is clearly a prophet with a vivid imagination. But his purpose is not to entertain. Zechariah uses such brilliant pictures to convince us that our minds should be filled with thoughts about God. Only then we will be able to enjoy a future of lasting peace.

What do the images mean? All of them contribute to Zechariah's message of hope based on turning human hearts toward God. The riders represent God's ministers patrolling the earth to secure peace within it. The golden lampstand represents the light of God illuminating the world. The flying scroll is the Word of God soaring over the earth to remove all falsehood.

Obviously, Zechariah has great expectations for the world. He wants to see it transformed from a place of darkness and oppression to a place of light and freedom. But Zechariah is also a realist. He knows such a thorough transformation can happen only when people change their hearts. That is why the central chapters of his book urge the people to put their faith into action. Until that happens, all Zechariah can do is try to motivate them by continuing to fill their minds with images of the wonderful transformation that will take place when God's way prevails over the earth. Among those images is the one of a king entering Jerusalem to inaugurate a kingdom of peace:

Rejoice greatly, O daughter Zion!
  Shout aloud, O daughter Jerusalem!
Lo, your king comes to you;
  triumphant and victorious is he,
humble and riding on a donkey,
  on a colt, the foal of a donkey. (9:9)

The Gospels declare this prophecy to be fulfilled on the day Jesus entered Jerusalem on Palm Sunday.

The 14 chapters of Zechariah:

1 — 6	Anticipation
7 — 8	Sincere religion
9 — 14	Visions of hope

Divine Steeds

Horses are featured prominently in this book. We see red, sorrel and white horses in the opening chapter. Chariots drawn by red, black, white and gray horses appear in chapter 6. And in the final chapter (14:20–21), we see horses decorated with bells on which are inscribed the words "Holy to the Lord." It seems that in this final scene the steeds of heaven have finished their service in battle.

ZECHARIAH

Zechariah on the Clock (BC)

Darius I of Persia   522–486

Second temple   c. 515

Darius the Great ruled Zechariah's world. The reign of Darius I lasted for over thirty-five years, from 522 to 486 BC. But in the book of Zechariah, the greatness of Darius is just a footnote when compared to the wonderful plans God has in store for a faithful people.

As you read Zechariah…

Zechariah 1:3 is a good summary of the Bible. What other passages from the Bible does it bring to mind?

Which images in the first six chapters of Zechariah impress you most?

What do you learn from the dialogue in 7:3–7?

Read 7:9–10 to discover Zechariah's definition of true religion. Can you find others passages from the Bible that support what the prophet says here?

What brought about the change in God's attitude in chapter 8?

What do you think of the description of the Prince of Peace in 9:9–10?

As you read Zechariah 11—14, how many New Testament images do you find?

Three Spiritual Lessons From Zechariah

- God invites us to return
- True repentance is the first step towards a brighter future
- Faith in God leads to peace

MALACHI

In the traditional order of the Christian Bible, the oracles of this prophet bring the Old Testament to a close. That means the oracles of Malachi lead the way to the New Testament. And Malachi is just the prophet to do this because he looks forward to a time when a messenger of God will come to prepare the way of the Lord. The Gospels see this fulfilled in the person of John the Baptist.

The oracles of Malachi are arranged as a series of dialogues between God and the people. Usually the people are busy making excuses for their lack of enthusiasm for religion. God keeps reminding them that, if they persist in their indifference, they will continue down the road to destruction and they will never enjoy the great things God has in store for them.

Because of their limited viewpoint, the people see no advantage in making the sacrifices that are so much a part of a life lived for God. But God assures them that one day there will definitely be a distinction between the just and the wicked because God's plan of salvation will be carried out. This opens the way to the birth of Jesus Christ.

The 3 chapters of Malachi:

| 1 — 2 | Excuses |
| 3 | Time for action |

Moses and Elijah

Moses and Elijah appear in the final verses of Malachi. This makes them the last figures mentioned in the Old Testament. In the Gospels, they appear again, this time conversing with Jesus in the scene of the Transfiguration. This seems to be another dramatic example of the New Testament bringing fulfillment to the Old.

Malachi on the Clock (BC)

Fall of Jerusalem   587

Second temple   c. 515

By Malachi's time, the second temple had replaced the great temple of Solomon destroyed by Babylon in 587 BC. Although, according to Haggai 2:3, the second temple—dedicated in 515 BC—could not match the grandeur of Solomon's day. We can imagine

MALACHI

how thrilled the people must have been to once again have a place to offer their sacrifices. But their initial enthusiasm seems to have soon faded away. Malachi challenges his people to put new life into their worship of God.

As you read Malachi...

 In Malachi 1:6–14 how have the people despised God's name?

According to Malachi 2:17 how have the people wearied God?

In Malachi 3:3 God refines the people like a worker refines precious metals. Can you find other examples of God "refining" people in the Bible?

God calls the people robbers in Malachi 3:8–10. Why?

How does God answer the question, "Why practice religion?" in Malachi 3:14–18?

Malachi 4 is the last chapter of the Old Testament. What is its message?

Three Spiritual Lessons From Malachi

- God wants to keep the dialogue with us going
- God seeks ways to bless us
- A sound relationship with God leads to life

PART SIX

THE GOSPELS

Our word *gospel* comes from Old English. It means "good news" and serves us as a near perfect match for the Greek word *euaggelion* appearing in the very first line of Mark's Gospel. Our word *evangelist* comes from this same Greek word. The news in the four Gospels certainly is good. We learn that Jesus came to save us from our sins, that he has won the victory over death and that believing in him leads to eternal life.

We can think of the four Gospels as the centerpiece of the entire Bible. They announce the fulfillment of God's word in the Old Testament; they are the foundation for all that follows in the New Testament.

Readers of the first three Gospels in the order tradition has handed them down to us—Matthew, Mark and Luke—will recognize a general similarity among them. All three record the major events in the Lord's early life in much the same way. They begin with the events leading up to the public ministry of Jesus, including the preaching of John the Baptist, the baptism of Jesus and his temptation in the desert. Then comes the Lord's mission in Galilee. After this Jesus proceeds by stages to Jerusalem where he fulfills his mission at Passover through his suffering, death and resurrection. Because of the likeness between them, these three Gospels are called "synoptic," meaning they can be viewed together.

John's Gospel has a character all its own. John carries the mission of Jesus over three separate Passovers instead of highlighting just one like the Synoptic Gospels. John prefers to gather details from the Lord's ministry around certain feasts in the Jewish calendar, especially the Passover. He includes no major parables but concentrates on a select number of miracles that Jesus worked, some of them—notably the changing of water into wine and the raising of Lazarus—not even mentioned in the other Gospels.

Our earliest copies of the Gospels come in small book form, typically containing just one or two Gospels. But we have all four Gospels together in one book already just two centuries after the time of Jesus. There are other Gospels from these early years too. One of the best known is the Gospel of James, popular for its special material on the early life and courtship of Mary and Joseph. But only the traditional four Gospels belong to the sacred Scriptures of the church.

MATTHEW

Who could resist a drama about a king's quest to establish his kingdom? Add to the mix a band of loyal followers plus some enemies determined to bring the king down and you have a real blockbuster. Matthew offers us just such a drama. But what makes Matthew's drama especially compelling is that it is not fiction but reality. And on top of all this, the king is none other than Jesus Christ the Son of God.

We can see trouble in store for this king right from the start. Matthew tells us about the royal lineage of Jesus. He belongs to the royal line of David. But Jesus is not recognized in his own capital city. When visitors arrive to pay homage to the newborn king of the Jews, Herod, the reigning monarch, seeks to kill Jesus and so his family must flee for safety.

This opening account about Jesus prepares us for the struggle that characterizes the years of his public ministry. Jesus teaches about the kingdom of heaven, its advantages and the character of its citizens. But people choose to embrace earthly kingdoms far less valuable, kingdoms that will fade away with time.

Jesus chooses his own twelve apostles who have all the potential to carry forward the wonderful message of salvation preached by Jesus. But even these twelve will falter as they struggle to break free from the lure of this world and put their trust in the world that is to come.

We readers begin to grasp the seriousness of the struggle when we read that John the Baptist, herald of the Lord's coming, is himself executed by Herod—an execution foreshadowing the fate of Jesus. But Jesus will not be distracted from his mission no matter what threats face him. He goes about healing the sick, giving sight to the blind and—most importantly—forgiving sins. All of this invites onlookers to recognize what wonderful things await them if they welcome the message of the kingdom of heaven into their hearts.

In the final chapters of this Gospel, Jesus at last enters his royal city as its true king. He continues to invite the people to shift their allegiance from the passing things of this world to the everlasting promises of the next. But now the clash between the kingdom of heaven and the kingdoms of this world reaches a critical point. At the end of the Gospel, the earthly rulers assume they have won the day as Jesus is put to death, his tomb under heavy guard. But the kingdom of heaven prevails. Jesus rises from the dead and sends his loyal apostles out to spread the good news to the entire world.

The 28 chapters of Matthew:

1 — 4	Jesus is not recognized in his royal city
5 — 7	The nature of Christ's kingdom
8 — 13	The advantages of the kingdom
14 — 20	The power of the kingdom and the character of its members
21 — 28	Jesus enters his royal city and establishes his reign

A Real Treasure

The oldest textual fragment of a Synoptic Gospel is now known as Papyrus 64. It includes twenty-four lines from Matthew 26. The manuscript dates from the late second to the early third centuries of our era. It is preserved at the Magdalen College Library in Oxford, England, and called—appropriately enough—the Magdalen Papyrus.

The Tax Collector

By tradition, the author of this first Gospel was Matthew the tax collector. And it seems this Gospel does reflect the viewpoint of someone familiar with the value of things. Only in this Gospel, for example, does Jesus compare the kingdom of heaven to a buried treasure. Matthew alone uses the precise names for certain coins circulating in his day: the double-drachma and the stater.

Contrasts

Matthew seems to relish contrasts. The royal banquet of Herod contrasts with the Lord's feeding of five thousand (Matthew 14). The request of the two sons of Zebedee contrasts with the request of two blind people (Matthew 20). Even at the end of the Gospel, the guards' report contrasts with the proclamation of the Gospel (Matthew 28).

The Prophecies of Isaiah

Matthew gives special attention to the prophecies of Isaiah and how they were fulfilled by Jesus. This is true of Isaiah's prophecy about the birth of Immanuel (Isaiah 7:14; Matthew 1:23); his prophecy about a light for the nations (Isaiah 9:1–2; Matthew 4:15–16); his prophecy about the suffering servant (Isaiah 42:1–4; Mathew 12:18–21); and his prophecy about resistance to the divine word (Isaiah 6:6–9; Matthew 13:14–15).

Matthew on the Clock (AD)

Christ's public ministry   c. 30–33

Fall of Jerusalem   70

Saint Ignatius of Antioch dies   c. 107

Since Matthew relies on Mark, his Gospel must come after Mark, which is usually dated just before the fall of Jerusalem. Matthew's Gospel also must have been in circulation by AD 100 since Ignatius of Antioch knew of it. Many specialists date it between AD 80 and 90, since they find within it evidence of the strained relationship between Christians and Judaism characteristic of that decade.

As you read Matthew…

How could you describe the first two chapters as a clash between two kingdoms?

As Matthew begins his account of the earthly ministry of Jesus in chapter 4, he quotes from the prophet Isaiah about the dawning of light on the nations. How fitting is this image for the Gospel?

After reading the Sermon on the Mount (Matthew 5–7), what would you say are some of the distinguishing character traits of those who belong to the kingdom of heaven?

Matthew presents Jesus as the New Moses. What evidence for this do you see in the Sermon on the Mount?

What are the advantages of faith as you find them in chapters 8 and 9?

What do we learn about the kingdom of heaven from the parables of chapter 13?

Matthew alone preserves the parable of the unforgiving servant (18:21–35). What does it reveal about the kingdom of heaven?

What is revealed about the kingdom of heaven in Matthew's distinctive parable of the workers (20:1–16)?

What wisdom distinguishes the wise bridesmaids from the others in the parable of 25:1–13?

What do we learn about the kingship of Jesus from the parable of the Last Judgment in 25:31–46?

In the account of the Lord's passion, Matthew alone records details about the death of Judas (27:3–10). How does this passage contribute to Matthew's message about the kingdom of heaven?

In the final chapter of Matthew, guards are bribed to spread a story while the apostles are sent by Jesus to proclaim the Gospel. Why do you think Matthew ends his Gospel with these two very different passages?

Three Spiritual Lessons From Matthew

- The kingdom of heaven is more valuable than any treasure on earth
- Let your light—your witness to Jesus— shine before the world
- Use your gifts to work for the kingdom of heaven

MARK

How do fishermen become fishers of men? Mark has the answer. They do so by believing that Jesus is the Son of God. Mark affirms the divinity of Jesus in the very first line: "The beginning of the good news of Jesus Christ, the Son of God." And at the death of Jesus on the cross, a centurion announces, "Truly this man was God's Son!" (Mark 15:39). So the entire Gospel of Mark is framed by this testimony to the Lord's divinity.

Peter and Andrew are fishermen; they know how to use nets to catch fish. Their first step in becoming fishers of men is to leave those nets behind. As they follow Jesus, they learn to take up a different kind of net altogether—the gospel of Jesus Christ, the Son of God.

All the chapters of Mark are exhausted before Peter, Andrew and the other apostles are prepared to cast the net of the gospel into the sea of humanity to draw them closer to God. And in fact, one of the twelve never learns to rely on Jesus. But this is getting ahead of things. Let's go back to the beginning and consider how Mark presents this wonderful account.

Appropriately, the sea is the special place of instruction for the chosen twelve. They observe Jesus teaching the crowds from a boat on the sea, as if his word were a net tossed from the boat to draw his listeners closer to himself. While on the sea in the boat with Jesus the master fisherman, they—apprentices in training—are examined on their understanding of the true significance of his words and his miracles.

The apostles are slow to catch on to the full meaning of his mission. Peter at least shows signs of understanding when he declares boldly that Jesus is the Christ. He does not yet fully grasp the meaning of this declaration, but he has taken a giant leap forward. Peter and the rest will learn more as they follow Jesus on the road to Jerusalem.

Mark seems to have a particular interest in emphasizing the struggle of learning to walk by faith. Only Mark, for example, includes the parable of the seed and its slow growth, suggesting that faith grows slowly too. Only Mark provides details like the Lord needing to place his fingers into the ears of a man to open them or the detail that Jesus needed to twice apply his fingers to the eyes of a blind man so that he could see. Such details seem to emphasize the gradual process of conversion, something the reader can plainly see in the halting progress of the apostles.

Once they arrive in Jerusalem, the apostles witness the bold pronouncements of Jesus as he exhibits his authority in taking on his opponents. But because they are still attached to the physical realm, the apostles fall away as Jesus is seemingly overpowered by the rulers of this world. But on the third day, they discover that the truth has only begun to be proclaimed. Empowered by the Risen Lord they are at last qualified to go out and proclaim the good news to the entire world. They have at last become fishers of men.

The 16 chapters of Mark:

1 — 4	Jesus chooses apostles to teach them to be fishers of men
5 — 10	Lessons for the apostles on land and sea
11 — 13	Jesus teaches in Jerusalem
14 — 16	Jesus is victorious over death and sends the apostles to preach the gospel

Caution

Throughout this Gospel, Jesus cautions others not to speak of him. Scholars sometimes refer to this as the "messianic secret." The reason for such caution may be that only after the resurrection will the disciples have the understanding to proclaim the good news with effect. Until that time, their limited viewpoint would impede the message.

It's All in the Details

Mark has an eye for detail. He alone tells us that the woman with the hemorrhage exhausted her resources in her search for a cure (5:25–27). He alone gives his readers the finer points of Jewish cleaning practices (7:3–4). Mark alone includes an extended dialogue between Jesus and the father of the boy with epilepsy (9:21–24).

Urgency

The word "immediately" appears over and over again in this brief Gospel. It adds a kind of breathless quality to the account, as if Mark cannot wait to get the message out. There is a real urgency since the world is in such dire need of the healing presence of the Lord.

The Fugitive

Mark alone tells us about the man in the linen cloth who runs off naked to escape on the night of the Lord's arrest. Many wonder who this fugitive is. Some suggest it is Mark himself. But whoever he is, he represents a would-be disciple. With nothing material to interfere with his progress, all this man needs to overcome is the inner fear that stands between him and complete faith in Jesus.

Mark on the Clock (AD)

Christ's public ministry   c. 30–33

Death of Peter   c. 67

Fall of Jerusalem   70

Mark may be our earliest complete Gospel, finished just over three decades after Jesus rose from the dead. One indication of Mark's early date is that it speaks of the destruction of Jerusalem (70 AD) as something that will happen in the future. Another indication of an early date for Mark is that it must precede the Gospels of Matthew and Luke, since both of them borrow from it extensively. A final indication of an early date for this Gospel comes from the tradition that Mark was the disciple and interpreter of the apostle Peter. If Mark wrote down his message shortly after Peter died (late 60's of the first century), then this Gospel would be early indeed.

As you read Mark…

In the first two chapters, Mark recounts many scenes in rapid succession. What impression does this make on you?

Mark 4:1–20 contains the parable of the seed. As you read the rest of the Gospel, look for people who exemplify the different soils in this parable.

Only Mark records the parable of the growing seed (4:26–29). What does it contribute to your understanding of discipleship?

In his account of the healing of the woman who touched the garment of Jesus, Mark alone adds details about the woman's search for a cure (5:26–27). How do these details make you feel about the woman?

Mark 6 records two feasting scenes. At which one would you want to be a guest?

In Mark's account of the healing of the man who could not hear or speak, Jesus puts his fingers in the man's ear and touches the man's tongue. What do these details add to the account for you?

Why do you think Jesus is so critical of his disciples as he questions them in Mark 8:14–21?

In his account of the healing of the boy (9:14–29), Mark alone includes an extended dialogue between Jesus and the boy's father. What does this dialogue add to the account for you?

In Mark 10:35–52, how does the request of James and John compare to the request of Bartimaeus?

How is the figure of the withered tree illustrated by the responses to Jesus in chapters 11 and 12 of Mark?

Mark stresses how important it is to be watchful for the master's coming (13:35–37). How is this lesson on preparedness illustrated in Mark's account of the Lord's passion?

Only Mark's account of the Lord's passion includes the scene about the young man who flees (Mark 14:51–52). What does this scene mean to you?

After reading this Gospel, discuss how Jesus has fulfilled his promise to make his apostles fishers of men.

Three Spiritual Lessons From Mark
- It takes time to learn to live by the values of heaven
- Our lives should inspire people to faith
- We should not hesitate to seek God's healing touch

LUKE

Be careful! As you read this Gospel, you may find yourself being lifted up to a new way of thinking. There is a definite lightness to Luke's Gospel; its message carries us above this world forcing us to view it differently, removed from the things that may weigh us down.

This should come as no surprise since Luke's Gospel—just like his Acts of the Apostles—gives special attention to the power of the Holy Spirit. References to the Spirit are more frequent in Luke than in any of the other Gospels.

What does the Spirit do? It carries forward God's plan of salvation. Luke's special interest is the march of salvation history. Luke explains in his opening paragraph that he writes about all that was fulfilled. He keeps track of things that take place "in the fullness of time."

There is a sense of irresistible energy in this Gospel. Some people, Luke tells us, try to stop the Gospel's advance, but adversity only leads to further progress. People cannot really interfere with the progress of the Good News. So why resist? Take full advantage of God's power in this world.

If you still have doubts about the buoyant character of this Gospel, consider the fact that there are no fewer than three songs in the opening chapters. The first is Mary's Magnificat celebrating her role in God's wonderful work of salvation. Then there is the song of Zechariah as he looks forward to the things his son John will do to prepare the way of the Lord in the hearts of the people. Finally, there is Simeon's song of thanksgiving to God for allowing him to see the child who will be a light to the nations.

God's plan of salvation sets a new standard for the people of the world. Success is measured in terms of attachment to God rather than to the fleeting things of this world. This new standard is exhibited in the lives of men and women who accept Jesus (Luke 7—9). Jesus breaks the boundaries of human limitation. He touches a leper; he touches a corpse; he dines with sinners. He urges authorities to accept this new standard by offering for their reflection parables such as the Prodigal Son (15:11–32) and the Pharisee and the Tax Collector (18:9–14).

Luke fills his Gospel with special people not mentioned in the other Gospels, people who stride ahead of so many others spiritually because they live by the new viewpoint preached by Jesus. The Good Samaritan surpasses others by making himself a neighbor to others (10:30–35). Zacchaeus may be short physically but spiritually he is ten feet tall because he listened to the Lord (19:1–10). There is even a good thief who reaches out to Jesus for salvation even as his own life draws to a close (23:39–43).

Luke includes unique parables in his Gospel too, parables about success. A worldly steward becomes an example of the sort of cleverness people ought to exhibit with regard to the things of God (16:1–9). Angels rejoice over sinners who take advantage of grace and change their lives for the better (15:8–10). There is no one more pitiable for Luke than someone like the rich fool of 12:16–21 who measures success in terms of this world only.

If it were not for the power of the Spirit, things would have been quite different; the limited viewpoint of this world would have prevailed. Children and foreigners would have been given limited access to Jesus. Our brothers and sisters would be forgiven just seven times.

The compassion of Jesus is clearly apparent in Luke's Gospel even during his last hours on earth. When Peter denies any association with him Jesus turns and looks at his apostle, connecting with his own even as they flee from him out of fear. And we have already mentioned the dialogue with the good thief, offering him everlasting life in the kingdom of heaven.

At the end of the Gospel, Luke gives special attention to the way the Risen Lord reaches out to his still-troubled disciples. He walks with the two to Emmaus explaining to them all the Scripture passages concerning him. He does the same with the apostles gathered with others in Jerusalem. As the Gospel concludes, we get the distinct feeling that things have only just begun.

The 24 chapters of Luke:

1 — 4	Celebrating God's plan of salvation
5 — 8	Responses to Jesus in Galilee
9 — 19	The journey to Jerusalem
20 — 24	Victory over death

Part One

Luke's Gospel is the first of a two-part series. The second part is his Acts of the Apostles. As Luke writes his Gospel, he is apparently already thinking of connections with Acts. Both accounts, for example, give prominence to the power of the Holy Spirit. In his Gospel account of the Lord's passion, Luke alone includes a hearing before Herod (23:6–12); in Acts, Luke records that Paul also had a hearing before a figure named Herod (Acts 27). Just as Jesus prayed for his persecutors (Luke 23:32–34), the martyr Stephen prayed for his enemies even as they picked up stones to kill him (Acts 7).

Lazarus and Dives

This pair is one of the most recognizable in the Bible. But the rich man does not even have a name in the Gospel account (Luke 16:19–31). The popular name Dives comes from the Latin word for "rich man." The lesson from this most popular parable is that despite all appearances to the contrary, the greatest advantages belong to those who are close to God.

Emmaus

The journey to Emmaus is one of the best-known resurrection accounts. It is found only in Luke. It illustrates the role of Jesus as the Good Shepherd who goes after the strays within the flock. It also serves as an example of the kind of instruction Jesus gave his followers after his resurrection.

Simeon and Anna

These two seniors represent the old Israel longing for the age of the Messiah. Both of them live out their lives waiting to see the fulfillment of God's promises. Their dedication to God serves as an example for every reader of this Gospel.

Jerusalem

Luke gives special emphasis to the Lord's journey to Jerusalem. In this portion of his Gospel (9:51—21:38) Luke includes many lessons on discipleship. The journey to Jerusalem is an ideal opportunity to learn what it takes to follow the Lord.

Samaritans

These people were scorned by some Jews on the grounds that their bloodline was not pure. Even the apostles seem to display a dislike for them. But in Luke's Gospel, Samaritans become models of faith. Of ten lepers healed by Jesus, only a Samaritan returns to give him thanks. In the Lord's parable about neighbors, the ideal neighbor is the Good Samaritan.

Luke on the Clock (AD)

Christ's public ministry   c. 30–33

Fall of Jerusalem   70

Matthew   c. 85

This Gospel must come from a time after Mark since, like Matthew, it relies on that first Gospel extensively. Luke also seems to have been familiar with the details of the fall of Jerusalem in AD 70. On the other hand, Luke's Gospel does not exhibit, like Matthew's, evidence of the strained relationship between Christians and Judaism so prominent in the last two decades of the first century. So Luke is usually assigned a date around AD 80.

As you read Luke...

In what ways do Zachary and Elizabeth remind you of Abraham and Sarah?

Do you get the feeling that a new age is dawning as you read Luke's first chapters?

How is Mary's response to the angel Gabriel superior to the one Zachary gave?

What is the theme of the three canticles of Mary, Zachary and Simeon?

Mary announces that she magnifies the Lord. Could you do this too?

After reading the parable of the Good Samaritan (10:30–35), describe in your own words what it means to seek the kingdom of God.

LUKE

Much material unique to Luke is included in the journey narrative that begins at 9:51. Why do you think he chooses this journey narrative for his special material?

Luke includes a number of lessons from the Lord about people who act unwisely (12:16–21 and 14:28–32). Read them and discuss what makes these people so unwise.

Luke alone records the parable of the Prodigal Son (15:11–32). What lessons do we learn from the father and from the elder brother?

What spiritual lessons do you discover in the parable about the rich man and Lazarus (16:19–31)?

What do we learn about prayer from the Lord's parable (found only in Luke 18:9–14) about the Pharisee and the tax collector?

What spiritual lessons can be drawn from the story of Zacchaeus, found only in Luke 19:1–10?

Only Luke includes the scene of the trial before Herod. What lesson do you see in it?

Luke alone includes the crucified Lord's dialogue with the good thief. What do you learn from this passage?

How does the Risen Lord prepare his disciples to receive the Holy Spirit?

How does Luke's conclusion prepare us for his second work—the Acts of the Apostles?

Three Spiritual Lessons From Luke

- Mary's "yes" to God is the kind of response for which we should strive
- Discipleship calls us to a new set of standards, like imitating the Good Samaritan
- Prayer will open our hearts to the power of the Spirit

JOHN

The traditional symbol for John the evangelist is the eagle. Like an eagle, John certainly does take us up to the heavens with his message. The very first line speaks of Jesus, the Word of God, in heaven with the Father. As we read the rest of John's Gospel, we feel an upward sweep, lifting us above the earth and toward heaven. The eagle is definitely a suitable symbol for John.

John's Gospel has two major parts: the Book of Signs (2—12) and the Book of Glory (13—20). The first book includes the miracles of Jesus that serve as signs of his glory. We find here the very first of the Lord's signs: the turning of water into wine at Cana (John 2:1–11). We also find the healing of the lame man at the pool (John 5:1–18); the miracle of the loaves (John 6:1–15); the healing of the man born blind (John 9:1–41); and the dramatic raising of Lazarus from the dead (John 11:1–44).

In the book of glory we witness the details of "the hour" when Jesus fulfills his Father's saving plan. John provides us with an extensive account of the Lord's last supper with his disciples concluding with a prayer asking his heavenly Father to see them through the difficult days ahead (John 13—17). The concluding chapters record the passion, death and resurrection of the Lord. We also witness here the inspiring encounter between the Risen Lord and his closest followers: Mary Magdalene, the Beloved Disciple, Thomas and Peter.

All this testimony is given to draw us closer to God. John even steps out of the picture from time to time to address us readers, making sure we grasp the true significance of what we read. Consider for example this verse near the end of the Gospel: "But these are written so that you may come to believe that Jesus is the Messiah, the Son of God, and that through believing you may have life in his name" (John 20:31).

One of the great joys of reading John comes from the dialogue in the Gospel. Often people misunderstand what Jesus is telling them so that Jesus has to spell it out more clearly. We find a very familiar example of this in the Lord's dialogue with the scholarly Nicodemus. When Jesus tells him of the need to be born "from above," Nicodemus struggles with the anatomical implications of being born a second time. He even asks Jesus this question: "How can anyone be born after having grown old? Can one enter a second time into the mother's womb and be born?" (3:4).

The spiritual awkwardness of Nicodemus makes us readers feel all the more confident about our ability to grasp the true meaning of what Jesus is saying. To do this means that we have successfully shifted from an earthly to a spiritual understanding of things. In this case, for example, we recognize that Jesus is speaking about becoming children of God by committing ourselves to total reliance on God. By doing so, we are born "from above" because we now value God's viewpoint on life in this world instead of limiting our worldview to satisfying our wants and desires.

As John's Gospel progresses, we readers become more and more adept at making these shifts to the heavenly plane. The more readily we do this the more assured we can be that we are learning to see the world as John wants us to see it—through the eyes of faith.

John's Gospel does not include a Christmas narrative, although he does make a clear statement about the Lord's coming into this world: "And the Word became flesh and lived among us, and we have seen his glory, the glory as of a father's only son, full of grace and truth" (1:14).

But John does offer a beautiful prologue that carries us to the timeless realm of God before the world was even created. John announces that the Word was in the beginning and that the Word was with God and was God. By speaking of Jesus as the Word, John places the accent on God's will to communicate with us. The Word seeks to engage with us and evoke a response of faith from us.

We can see this emphasis on communication surfacing all throughout John's Gospel. Jesus, for example, identifies himself to the woman at the well (4:26) and the man born blind (9:37) as "the one who is speaking" to them. When officers are sent to arrest Jesus, they return to their superiors empty-handed; they offer as their excuse this wonderful testimony: "Never has anyone spoken like this!" (7:46).

Jesus describes his mission as one very much connected with proclaiming the Word of God:

> ...for I have not spoken on my own, but the Father who sent me has himself given me a commandment about what to say and what to speak. And I know that his commandment is eternal life. What I speak, therefore, I speak just as the Father has told me. (John 12:49–50)

By the time we readers reach the end of his Gospel, John has given us every advantage for responding faithfully to the Word of God so well presented in his eyewitness account of the earthly ministry of Jesus.

The 21 chapters of John:

I	The Word
2 — 12	Book of Signs
13 — 20	Book of Glory
21	Faithful responses

Nicodemus

This religious leader comes to listen to Jesus only at night. But he does speak up on the Lord's behalf at a meeting with his peers (John 7:51). And in the end Nicodemus comes into the light to anoint the body of Jesus and help place him in a tomb.

John the Baptist

In this Gospel, John is the ideal witness to Jesus. He draws no attention to himself, but directs everyone he meets toward the Lord.

The Woman at the Well

We never learn her name, but she becomes a model of faith. She comes to draw water from a well and meets Jesus, the fountain of living water. Leaving her water jar behind, she returns to Samaria to lead others to Jesus.

Peter

His faith journey is a prominent feature of this Gospel. In the final chapter, his threefold affirmation of love for Jesus erases his earlier denials. And Jesus declares that Peter will glorify God by dying as a witness to the Gospel.

Sign of Glory

Jesus chooses a wedding feast as the occasion for his first miracle. By doing so, Jesus shows quite clearly that marriage is a very suitable symbol for the bond between God and us. But it is also true that a relationship with God brings so much more into a person's life. It begins already with the rich wine Jesus provides after the limited resources at the wedding run out. This first miracle foreshadows others. We can expect to see many more instances in which Jesus surpasses the former things with a great bounty from above. And the bride and groom from Cana could tell their children and grandchildren that it all started at their wedding!

Bread From Heaven

This is a wonderful example of Jesus surpassing the former things. The people of Israel had the manna to nourish them for the journey to the Promised Land. Jesus offers himself as the bread of life. If people believe in his word and eat this bread, they will live forever. Those who hear Jesus make this startling announcement are skeptical because they try to understand it in earthly terms. But Jesus is challenging them to move beyond the limited thinking of this world and to have faith that what he tells them is absolutely true. Jesus asks the twelve if they, too, will abandon him. That's when Peter steps forward and says, "Lord, to whom can we go? You have the words of eternal life" (6:67).

Life

The raising of Lazarus is the most dramatic of the Lord's miracles in the Gospel. John records it just before his testimony about "the hour" of the Lord's passion, death and resurrection (John 13–20). This makes the raising of Lazarus the final entry in the Book of Signs. After it, begins the Book of Glory. Jesus had purposely delayed his arrival at the home of Martha and Mary until Lazarus died. He wanted this great miracle to be the one that would at last break through the barrier of resistance he encountered in so many. He wanted Martha and the rest to understand that he had the power to give life. We readers immediately recall the testimony of John 3:16. We have certainly reached a peak moment in John's Gospel.

Did You Know?

One of the oldest fragments of a New Testament text is a portion of John's Gospel (18:31–33, 37–38 to be exact) on papyrus dating to about AD 125 and discovered in Egypt. It is now known as Papyrus 52 and is in safekeeping at the John Rylands Library in Manchester, England.

The Grapevine

According to the Jewish historian Josephus, Herod's temple displayed a carved vine over the entranceway. It was covered in gold and was as big as a man. The apostles may have thought of this golden vine when Jesus said he was the vine and they were the branches.

John on the Clock (AD)

Christ's public ministry   c. 30–33

Fall of Jerusalem   70

Papyrus 52   c. 125

John's Gospel is generally regarded as the last of the four Gospels. Passages about expulsion from the synagogue (John 9:22; 16:2) may reflect a time near the end of the first century when the rift between Christians and Jews was becoming more pronounced. Fragments of a manuscript of John's Gospel (Papyrus 52) testify to its circulation already in the first quarter of the second century. A date near the end of the first century of our era seems likely for this Gospel.

As you read John…

What are the advantages gained by those who receive the light according to John 1:1–18?

What do you think Peter is thinking when he hears Jesus give him a new name?

What does the first sign at Cana reveal about Jesus?

How does Jesus help Nicodemus understand the meaning of being born from above?

John 3:16 is often quoted. How is it illustrated in other passages from this Gospel?

How does the woman at the well change as a result of her discussion with Jesus?

Look for parallels with the Exodus in John 6.

What do you think Jesus was writing in the sand while others stood around watching (7:53—8:11)?

How does John 9 reveal the spiritual blindness of some people?

What are the special characteristics of the Good Shepherd in John 10?

How are Martha and Mary similar? How are they different?

How does Jesus encourage and strengthen his apostles during his last supper with them?

What do you learn from the dialogue between Jesus and Pontius Pilate?

If you were standing with the disciples at the Sea of Tiberias in John 21, what would you want to tell Peter?

How effectively does Jesus bring Peter to full faith after his triple denial?

Three Spiritual Lessons From John's Gospel

- Let the Word of God sweep you up to heaven
- God invites us all to become children of heaven
- Jesus is the way, the truth and the life

PART SEVEN

ACTS OF THE APOSTLES

The title says it all. In this book, the apostles are fully active and engaged in the work of Jesus Christ. In the Gospels, they worried and fretted about the things Jesus was saying and the direction his life was taking. But here in Acts these same apostles are completely without fear as they go about preaching the Good News and facing all sorts of obstacles in the process.

How do we account for this startling change in these apostles? The Holy Spirit is the key. The power of the Spirit is so prominent in this book that it really could be entitled The Acts of the Spirit. In fact, if things had been left to human initiative alone, little would have changed. But the Holy Spirit carries the plan of salvation forward.

Without the sort of zeal that derives from the power of the Spirit, a number of things would have been different. Peter may not have preached to the Gentiles. Paul undoubtedly would have continued persecuting the church. Without a push from the Spirit, Paul would not have expanded his mission to Europe. Without a push from the Spirit, the church would have continued to impose the Mosaic law on Gentile converts to Christianity.

Resistance, threats and even chains cannot impede the progress of God's Word in this book. As we work our way though its chapters, we see the Good News expanding in ever-widening circles, like ripples on the surface of a pond: first in Jerusalem, then beyond that city and finally to the world as Paul preaches in Europe and at last in Rome, the central city of the empire.

Details in this book strongly suggest that Luke wanted us readers to make parallels between the work of Jesus and the work of his disciples. Like Jesus, Stephen prays for those who wish him dead. Like Jesus, Peter heals the sick and raises the dead. Like Jesus, Paul is dragged before the court of someone named Herod. By the time we finish this book, we understand that the Lord's work will go on.

The book begins with the apostles receiving the wonderful gift of the Holy Spirit on the first Pentecost. Subsequent chapters (Acts 4 and 5)

ACTS OF THE APOSTLES

trace the advance of the gospel among the Jews in Jerusalem especially through the preaching of Peter.

In chapter 6, we learn how the gospel began to reach beyond Jerusalem. Through the Holy Spirit, the church selects seven men to see to the temporal needs of the church. But soon Stephen and Philip are preaching the word. By chapter 10, Peter is led by the Holy Spirit to preach the gospel to the household of a Roman centurion.

Thus begins the mission to the Gentiles. Luke now turns his attention to the missionary work of Paul. Chapters thirteen and fourteen record Paul's initial missionary journey to Asia Minor. His successes raised the critical question about whether the Mosaic law was to be imposed on Gentile converts. The church in Jerusalem affirmed that salvation came not though the law but "through the grace of the Lord Jesus" (Acts 15:11).

Paul's next missionary journey took him again to Asia Minor but then the Holy Spirit directed him to cross over into Greece. In this portion of Acts (16—18), we see Paul preaching in cities familiar to us from his letters: Philippi, Thessalonica and especially Corinth. After a brief return to the Holy Land, Paul is once again in Asia Minor, spending considerable time in the city of Ephesus (19—20).

The concluding chapters of Acts record the circumstances that eventually brought Paul to Rome. He was arrested in Jerusalem but was transferred to Caesarea on the coast out of concern for his safety. Two years later Paul appealed to Caesar before the newly appointed governor of Judea. After a perilous sea voyage, Paul arrives in Rome where we last see him preaching the kingdom of God to everyone who visited him.

The 28 chapters of Acts:

1 — 7	The Word of God in Jerusalem
8 — 15	The Word of God reaching beyond Jerusalem
16 — 28	The Word of God embracing the world

Pentecost

Luke's account of Pentecost can be read as a reversal of the Babel account in Genesis 11. At Babel, God makes it impossible for one person to communicate with another because they are not promoting faith in God. But at Pentecost God removes all barriers to communication. The gospel is something everyone needs to hear.

Cornelius

This Roman officer was hungry for the Word of God. As Peter proclaims the gospel to him, Cornelius and his entire household receive the gift of the Holy Spirit. This scene marks a significant step in the advance of the gospel. For the first time it reaches a Gentile audience.

Transformation

Paul's dramatic conversion to Christianity is recounted no less than three times in Acts. Luke first recounts it as Paul makes his way to Damascus (9:1–19). Next Paul himself gives an account of it as he addresses his fellow Jews while standing on the steps of the temple (22:6–16). Paul does so again in Caesarea before Festus the governor and King Agrippa (26:12–18). Despite popular tradition, in no account is there mention of Paul falling from his horse.

Gallio

Gallio was the chief Roman official in Corinth at the time of Paul's stay there in the year AD 52. When a group of troublemakers brought charges against the apostle Paul, Gallio refused to hear the case on the grounds that it was a religious rather than a civil matter (Acts 18:12–18). Gallio's brother was the famous Roman philosopher Seneca.

A Popular Speaker

If you had been in Ephesus in the mid-fifties of the first century, you could have heard Paul speak in a place called "the lecture hall of Tyrannus." According to Acts 19:10 Paul preached there on a daily basis for two years.

A Loyal Nephew

We never learn the name of Paul's sister or of her son. But this nephew of Paul played an important role in the events that led to the apostle's voyage to Rome. Learning of a plot by some forty zealots to assassinate his uncle, this nephew took action. He warned Paul and then the Roman commander Claudius Lysias. The commander made immediate arrangements to have Paul transferred from Jerusalem to Caesarea, a port on the coastline of Palestine and residence of the Roman governor Felix. It's all there in Acts 23:16–35.

The Herod Family

This dynasty wielded power in the Jewish homeland for many years. Unfortunately, this family never tapped the power of faith. Herod the

Great, founder of the dynasty, gave orders to find and kill the baby Jesus. A son named Antipas ordered John the Baptist to be beheaded. Agrippa I, a grandson, executed James, the son of Zebedee; he also imprisoned the apostle Peter (Acts 12:1–6). Agrippa II, a great-grandson, heard Paul's witness to Jesus (Acts 26:28) but found it merely amusing.

Acts on the Clock (AD)

Christ's earthly ministry   c. 30–33

Paul in Rome   c. 63

Saint Irenaeus   c. 180

The events recorded in this book span the time from the resurrection of Jesus all the way down to Paul's residency in Rome. In terms of years, this span would begin around AD 33 and end sometime around AD 68. Luke wrote this book as a sequel to his Gospel. Since the Gospel is commonly dated between AD 80 and 85, Acts must come some time after that and certainly before the end of the second century when other ancient witnesses like Saint Irenaeus, a priest in Lyons, make reference to it.

As you read Acts…

What change do you notice in the apostle Peter as he addresses the others in Acts 1:15–20?

How would you interpret the events of the first Pentecost as a reversal of the Babel account in Genesis 11?

In what ways does the work of Peter and John (Acts 4–5) remind you of the work of Jesus?

What parallels do you see between the account of Stephen's death (Acts 7) and the passion of Jesus?

How does Luke's Gospel prepare us for Philip's mission to the Samaritans in Acts 8?

How is the power of the Holy Spirit revealed in the account of Paul's conversion in Acts 9:1–31?

Try to imagine how it would feel to be part of the household of Cornelius and hear Peter's proclamation in Acts 10:34–43.

Luke tells us in Acts 11:26 that it was in Antioch that the disciples were first called Christians. What do you suppose was the character of the faith community in Antioch?

As you read about Paul's first missionary journey in Acts 13–14 what do you find most inspiring about it?

What crisis threatens the unity of the church in Acts 15 and how does the church resolve it?

Look at a map of Greece and trace the stages in Paul's missionary work there (Acts 15:36—18:17).

What challenges must Paul face in Philippi and Corinth?

What do you find inspiring as you read about the final years of Paul's missionary work in the East (Acts 18:18—20:38)?

What parallels do you see between Paul's experiences in Jerusalem and what happened to Jesus there (Acts 21—23)?

In what ways do the Roman governors Felix and Festus remind you of Pontius Pilate (Acts 24—26)?

How does God protect Paul during the journey to Rome (Acts 27—28)?

How does Paul's preaching in Rome remind you of the way he preached during his other missionary journeys?

Three Spiritual Lessons From Acts

- Be confident that the Holy Spirit can help
- Prayer can lead to insights that take us beyond our limited viewpoints
- Hardships can lead to spiritual gains

PART EIGHT
THE LETTERS

The letters of the New Testament apply the gospel to daily life in much the same way the wisdom books apply the message of the Old Testament to daily life.

The first letters in this section are those written by Paul. The apostle wrote them to take care of problems in the early churches and to encourage them to remain faithful to the gospel of Jesus Christ. It appears that Paul began writing letters during his second missionary journey. As far as we can tell, he continued to write letters the rest of his life. Some of his letters are addressed to specific communities like Rome, Corinth or Philippi. Others are addressed to individuals like Timothy, Titus and Philemon. Galatians seems be directed at a cluster of communities in Asia Minor (present-day Turkey).

After the letters of Paul, we find the letter to the Hebrews. It is sometimes associated with Paul and, in fact, a third-century manuscript of Paul's letters places Hebrews after Romans. But today Hebrews is usually separated from the letters of Paul. The main theme of this letter is that Jesus is the one who brings to fulfillment all that preceded him in the history of salvation.

The next letters in the New Testament are known as the Catholic Letters. The term "catholic" in this context means "general" or "universal" since these letters have a wider range than Paul's letters addressed to specific churches. James and 1 John may be familiar to us already; the other letters in this group are 1 and 2 Peter, 2 and 3 John, and Jude.

THE LETTERS OF PAUL

Tradition has given us thirteen letters from Paul. Specialists in the field regard just seven of these thirteen as authentically the work of Paul on the basis of style, content and theological outlook. It is good to know such things since it is helpful for getting a clear idea of what people regard as the essential Paul. But for our purpose, which is merely to gain an overview of the literature of the Bible, we will follow the traditional count of Paul's letters.

First, we should keep in mind that Paul's letters make up a considerable part of the New Testament. Nearly half, if you consider the number of books—thirteen out of twenty-seven. In terms of actual verses, Paul's letters account for just about 25 percent of the New Testament. Understandably, Paul has a considerable influence on the way we understand the message of the New Testament.

Among Paul's contributions to theological thinking are his image of the church as the body of Christ; the cardinal virtues of faith, hope and charity; and the portrait of Jesus as the New Adam. Without Paul, we would not possess such memorable texts as the passage on Christ's humility in Philippians 2:6–11 or the passage on love in 1 Corinthians 13.

In the Bible, Paul's letters are not arranged in chronological order. If they were, 1 Thessalonians would definitely begin this list. It was written just twenty years after the resurrection of Jesus Christ, making it the oldest book in the New Testament. But the list of Paul's works in the Bible begins with his Letter to the Romans, written late in Paul's career when he was wrapping up his preaching in the east and planning a preaching tour to the western provinces of the Roman Empire.

The church seems to a have assigned Romans its primary place in the list very early on. The earliest example of New Testament literature of any size is a papyrus manuscript of over two hundred pages, dating to the early part of the third century of our era. It contains eight of Paul's letters. The manuscript arranges the letters of Paul in this order: Romans, 1 and 2 Corinthians, Galatians, Ephesians, Philippians, Colossians and 1 Thessalonians. If you look at your own personal copy of the Bible, you will see that the first eight letters of Paul are listed in this same order. Now you know how old that order is!

If you count the number of verses in each of Paul's letters, you will immediately recognize that they are listed in our Bibles according to length. Romans and 1 Corinthians come first with over 430 verses each. Then comes 2 Corinthians with over 250 verses. Last in the list is Philemon with just 25 verses.

Connecting Paul's letters with his several journeys can be quite a challenge. It may be consoling to know that this task is even challenging for the specialists. To help you out, the following paragraphs offer an overview of Paul's journeys and where the letters might be placed in relation to them.

Just fifteen years after the resurrection of Jesus Christ, Paul and Barnabas began preaching the gospel in Cyprus and Asia Minor. They set out from Antioch in Syria, home to a very vibrant Christian community, which sponsored their work.

After a brief stay on the island of Cyprus, Paul and Barnabas sailed to Asia Minor where they followed the main east-west road, the Via Augusta, preaching to the communities they encountered on the way: Antioch, Iconium, Lystra and Derbe.

From the city of Derbe, Paul and Barnabas could have continued on to Paul's native city of Tarsus and then by land to their starting point of Antioch in Syria. But they felt it was much more important to retrace their steps, returning to the communities already established and encouraging them to remain faithful to the Gospel. Then Paul and Barnabas returned to Antioch.

About the year AD 50, Paul set out on another journey, this time with Silas as his companion. They went by land this time, following the Roman road north from Antioch, and then turning west into Asia Minor. They arrived first at Derbe then moved on to Lystra where Timothy joined their company.

Paul probably intended to continue west to visit the other communities he had established on his first missionary journey. But instead, the Spirit of God led him northwest to the coastal city of Troas. There Paul had a vision of a man urging him to preach the gospel in Macedonia. And so Paul crossed the Hellespont into Europe.

In Macedonia and Greece Paul established faith communities in cities familiar to us from his letters: Philippi, Thessalonica and Corinth. Paul stayed eighteen months in Corinth as a guest of Aquila and his wife Prisca. Like Paul, they were skilled at tent making.

The dating for Paul's stay in Corinth can be fairly well established because we know it overlapped in its concluding months with the governorship of Gallio in AD 52. While in Corinth, Paul wrote 1 Thessalonians and, just a little later, 2 Thessalonians (if this letter was, in fact, written by Paul). Both letters gave clarity to that community's understanding of the Lord's Second Coming. Later that same year Paul returned to Antioch.

By AD 54, Paul was once again in Asia Minor, spending most of the next three years in Ephesus, capital of the Roman Province of Asia. From Ephesus, Paul wrote a number of letters to churches established on previous journeys: Galatians, 1 and 2 Corinthians and perhaps Philippians, though others believe this last letter came later during Paul's time in Rome. The apostle found it increasingly necessary to counter claims from others that his form of the gospel was incorrect because it did not include compliance to such Jewish practices as circumcision. Paul may also have written his friend Philemon at this time (perhaps while imprisoned in Ephesus) seeking reconciliation for a former slave now converted to Christianity. Eventually Paul visited Corinth again, and probably from there he wrote his Letter to the Romans.

Paul's plan was to use Rome as a base for missionary journeys to the western provinces of the Roman Empire. But first, he returned to Jerusalem to present the money collected from the Gentile churches. Disputes with Jews led to Paul's arrest. He was held prisoner in the port city of Caesarea for two years until he appealed, as a Roman citizen, to the court of the emperor. This appeal was made before Porcius Festus, the new procurator of Judea, who probably assumed his post in AD 60. The next year Paul arrived in Rome, where he remained for two years under house arrest.

According to tradition, Paul wrote Colossians and Ephesians (and possibly Philippians) during his time in Rome. Tradition also holds that Paul later returned to Asia Minor where he wrote his associates Timothy (twice) and Titus to offer them pastoral guidelines. However, many believe these letters (as well as 2 Thessalonians) were not written by Paul himself, although they do reflect his thinking. Paul's death is not recorded in the New Testament. Tradition holds that he was beheaded in Rome during the time of the Emperor Nero (ruling from AD 54 to 68) and probably late in Nero's reign.

ROMANS

Mention Rome today and people think of St. Peter's or the Colosseum. For Paul, Rome seems to bring to mind a stepping-stone. After many years of preaching in the eastern portions of the Roman Empire, Paul was ready to proceed westward. The city of Rome was the logical place to begin this new undertaking.

In his other letters, Paul had to address issues presented to him by the many faith communities he established during his missionary journeys: concerns about the Second Coming of Christ; about discrimination during the celebration of the Eucharist; about how to respond to pressure from dissident groups; or even about whether or not it was proper to eat meat sacrificed to idols.

But in Romans, Paul does not have to concern himself with topics proposed to him by others. In Romans, Paul has the freedom to write about the one thing that gave meaning to everything he said and did: salvation through the death and resurrection Christ. For so many years, he had preached about the Lord Jesus Christ. Now at last he had the time to put his message down in writing.

Paul's main message is that Jesus died for the people of Israel and all the nations. If we want a concise summary of what Paul has to say, we need look no further than the first chapter of this letter: "For I am not ashamed of the gospel; it is the power of God for salvation to everyone who has faith, to the Jew first and also to the Greek" (Romans 1:16).

Paul starts by explaining how much the people of the world need the salvation won for them by Jesus Christ. Left on our own we have a deplorable record of remaining loyal to God. Despite the fact that there are plenty of clues in creation pointing us in the right direction, steering us toward God, challenging us to recognize our utter dependence on God, we have a definite inclination to go our own way.

So the initiative for salvation belongs to God. Paul appeals to the story of Abraham to prove his point. As great a figure as he was, this patriarch could never have claimed that he earned all the wonderful gifts God gave him, especially the gift of a child. In fact, God was making promises to Abraham even before the patriarch accepted circumcision as the sign of his covenant with God. That is how gracious God is. Abraham simply needed to express the slightest degree of belief, and God was more than ready to regard this as proof of full-fledged faith.

To later generations God gave the Law of Moses. But good as it was, this law could not transform the people of Israel into perfect covenant partners with God because the people continually failed to live up to all the ideals expressed in the Law.

Fortunately, Jesus came into the world to show us the way. His perfect devotion to God, even to the point of death, won salvation for us all. And so deliverance comes to us not through the Law of Moses but through the Lord Jesus Christ. If we are bonded to Christ, we live by the power of the Holy Spirit.

Of course, Paul is only too familiar with human nature. He knows that people will presume from this that if they express faith in Jesus they are free to do whatever they please. So Paul concludes with some practical guidelines, a catalog of things people can do to display to God and to others that they are servants of God.

Gifted preacher that he is, Paul offers his readers this wonderful image likening Jesus to a protective garment of light:

> Let us then lay aside the works of darkness and put on the armor of light; let us live honorably as in the day, not in reveling and drunkenness, not in debauchery and licentiousness, not in quarreling and jealousy. Instead, put on the Lord Jesus Christ, and make no provision for the flesh, to gratify its desires. (13:12–14)

The 16 chapters of Romans:

1 — 3	Our need for Jesus
4 — 8	What Jesus means for us
9 — 11	What Jesus means for Israel
12 — 16	Putting our faith into practice

The Power of Words

Paul knows how to use words. Look how he expresses our bond with Jesus:

> For I am convinced that neither death, nor life, nor angels, nor rulers, nor things present, nor things to come, nor powers, nor height, nor depth, nor anything else in all creation, will be able to separate us from the love of God in Christ Jesus our Lord. (Romans 8:38–39)

Building Blocks

Paul enjoys linking clauses together like building blocks. Consider these examples:

> ...but we also boast in our sufferings, knowing that suffering produces endurance, and endurance produces character, and character produces hope, and hope does not disappoint us.... (5:3–5)

> And those whom he predestined he also called; and those whom he called he also justified; and those whom he justified he also glorified. (8:30)

> But how are they to call on one in whom they have not believed? And how are they to believe in one of whom they have never heard? And how are they to hear without someone to proclaim him? And how are they to proclaim him unless they are sent? (10:14–15)

The New Adam

A celebrated passage from Romans is the one in which Paul connects Adam and Jesus. The sin of Adam enveloped everyone in sin and death; the saving work of Jesus brings all people life. Paul, of course, expresses it so much better: "For just as by the one man's disobedience the many were made sinners, so by the one man's obedience the many will be made righteous" (Romans 5:19).

A Snapshot

In Romans 16:5, Paul mentions the church that meets in the house of Prisca and Aquila. Praying to God in private homes was the standard for the church until the early fourth century, when the church was favored by the state and even supported by it. That is when churches as we know them were constructed.

Some Terms

Paul speaks a great deal about justification and righteousness. It may be helpful to think of these terms as different facets of the gem of salvation. Justification is a way of describing all that Jesus did for us to make us just in God's eyes. Righteousness is a way of saying we are in right relationship with God again because of the death and resurrection of Jesus Christ.

ROMANS

Good Works

Paul teaches that salvation comes from faith in the Lord Jesus Christ and not from works in accord with the Law of Moses. But Paul also recognizes that faith in Christ must lead to action: "For he will repay according to each one's deeds: to those who by patiently doing good seek for glory and honor and immortality, he will give eternal life..." (Romans 2:6–7).

Romans on the Clock (AD)

Paul writes Romans   c. 58

Paul in Rome   c. 61

By the year AD 58, Paul had been preaching for nearly ten years and traveling extensively. It has been estimated that on his second missionary journey alone Paul traveled over three thousand miles. But Paul was planning another missionary journey to the provinces in Spain. Paul was thinking of using Rome as his base of operation. So, probably while staying with a believer named Gaius in Corinth (Romans 16:23), Paul wrote to the community in Rome. He arrived there about three years later.

As you read Romans...

As you read over the portrait of people without the Spirit in Romans 1:29–31, how does it make you feel?

In Romans 2 and 3 Paul presents his reasons why the Law of Moses is ultimately ineffectual for salvation. What impresses you about his argument?

Note how many references to the Old Testament Paul makes in Romans 3:10–18. Look at the footnotes in your Bible to discover from what books they come.

How does the biblical account of Abraham contribute to Paul's lesson that we are justified by faith (Romans 8)?

In Romans 8 Paul talks about the struggle between the flesh and the spirit. How do you see this struggle in your own life?

How does Paul see God's mercy working with the people of Israel in Romans 9—11?

In Romans 14 and 15 Paul presents his plan for making a community stronger. How could his plan be applied to your own community?

Three Spiritual Lessons From Romans
- Nothing can separate us from God
- The beauty of creation can lead us to God
- God's plans are bigger than our own

1 CORINTHIANS

The church in Corinth demanded a great deal of Paul's attention. Why? A little background may be of help. Corinth was one of the busiest seaports in the Mediterranean. In fact, Corinth had two ports, one on the Adriatic Sea, the other on the Aegean Sea. Just four miles separated the two ports by land. The flow of commerce between the two ports generated a great deal of income for the city. It had public baths, theaters, temples and even hosted the second-best games, after the Olympics. Little wonder Paul devoted so much energy to this community.

Paul also knew this community very well. He stayed there for eighteen months, probably between the years AD 49 and 51. It is likely that during this time he lived along the busy corridor between the two ports. Archaeology reveals a number of shops along the route. The commerce along this busy thoroughfare would have provided Paul with an ideal setting to bring in an income through his work as a leather worker and maker of tents. Paul makes a point of telling his readers that he supported himself through his skill as an artisan. He was determined not to be a financial burden to the communities he served.

Paul begins this letter on a positive note. He compliments the faithful in Corinth for their many spiritual gifts. This sets the tone for the rest of the letter. Paul wants his Corinthians to concentrate on nourishing their spiritual gifts and avoid weakening their commitment to Christ by entertaining things that are unspiritual.

What were some of the unspiritual things Paul was concerned about? He begins with their attachment to people rather than to God. They seemed to attach more importance to the names of Paul or Apollos or Cephas than they did to the name of Jesus Christ. The community was even splitting apart into camps based on the different people who baptized them.

Another unspiritual trait was exhibited in their practice of going outside the community to settle disputes. Paul encourages them to remember that they have been set apart from the world through baptism. They ought to work out differences between themselves rather than bring civil judges into the matter.

Paul also urges them to keep a proper perspective on what they do. As believers baptized into Christ they should not view the world as if its joys and sorrows were the only measure of what is meaningful in life. They should look for meaning in their relationship with Jesus who will come in glory at the end of time. They should be concentrating on the lasting values of heaven. Paul would rather see them promoting a spirit of sacrifice for the sake of others. This is the very thing he sought to do while he was among them.

In the latter portion of this letter, Paul returns to the theme of spiritual gifts with which he began the letter. He reminds them again how blessed they are to have so many gifted members among their number. But he also reminds them to use their gifts not to promote themselves but to build up the community. The greatest gift is the kind of love that Jesus has for them, a love that guides people closer to God.

At the end of the letter, Paul assures them of the truth about the resurrection of Jesus Christ. It should transform the way they live their lives.

The 16 chapters of I Corinthians:

1 — 6	Unity in Christ
7 — 14	Nourishing God's gifts
15 — 16	The power of the Resurrection

Love Never Fails

Paul's own devotion to the spiritual well-being of the faith community in Corinth is a fine example of the kind of love he describes in 1 Corinthians 13. Altogether he wrote at least four or five letters to the church in Corinth. He also visited them personally on several occasions after his eighteen-month stay with them during his second missionary journey.

Corinthian Column

You may remember that a Corinthian column has the most elaborate decoration on its capital. The community of believers in Corinth seems to have been equally elaborate with all the different twists and turns among its members.

Fund-Raising

One of Paul's favorite projects was raising money for the needy in the home church in Jerusalem. In 1 Corinthians 16:2 Paul suggests a plan for generating funds. He advises each church member to put aside a little something on the first day of each week.

The Lord's Supper

In 1 Corinthians 11:23–25, we have the oldest account of the Lord's Supper in the New Testament:

> …the Lord Jesus on the night when he was betrayed took a loaf of bread, and when he had given thanks, he broke it and said, "This is my body that is for you. Do this in remembrance of me." In the same way, he took the cup also, after supper, saying, "This cup is the new covenant in my blood. Do this, as often as you drink it, in remembrance of me."

House Churches

The early church worshiped in the homes of certain members of the community. In 1 Corinthians 1:11 Paul refers to one group as "Chloe's people." This may refer to the community that met in the home of this Christian woman. As we noted in the previous chapter, the church met in private homes until Christianity became a legally recognized religion in the time of Constantine (fourth century AD).

Apollos

Paul credits this learned man for "watering" the garden he himself had planted in Corinth (1 Corinthians 3:6). Apollos was noted for his knowledge of the Bible. He was from Alexandria, Egypt, the place traditionally associated with the translation of the Torah from Hebrew into Greek.

Single

This letter reveals that Paul was indeed single. He tells the Corinthians: "To the unmarried and the widows I say that it is well for them to remain unmarried as I am" (1 Corinthians 7:8).

I Corinthians on the Clock (AD)

Paul's first stay in Corinth   c. 50–52

I Corinthians   c. 57

Four or five years after his first stay in Corinth (probably between 50 and 52 AD), Paul begins writing letters to the church in Corinth. The letter we now call 1 Corinthians was preceded by a least one other. Paul refers to this earlier letter in 1 Corinthians 5:9. It urged its readers to take care to preserve their character as people devoted to the Lord. We know the present 1 Corinthians was written from Ephesus sometime before the Feast of Pentecost (16:8). It may have been composed in the year AD 57.

As you read 1 Corinthians...

In 1 Corinthians 1—6 Paul addresses issues weakening the Christian community in Corinth. How are communities today similar to the one in Corinth?

In chapter 7, Paul offers his advice on human relationships. What is his guiding principle?

Regarding the journey to heaven, Paul advises us to run so as to win the race. How does his own life serve as an example?

In Paul's time and long after, the church worshiped in the private homes of believers. What light does this shed on the things Paul remarks on with regard to the Eucharist in Corinth?

In your opinion what is attractive about Paul's image of the church as the body of Christ?

Chapter 13 is often chosen as a reading at weddings. What makes this reading so fitting for the occasion?

In chapter 15 Paul speaks about the resurrection of the body. What do you find powerful for you in his message?

Three Spiritual Lessons From 1Corinthians

- Nourish the spiritual gifts God has given you
- Work to bring people together in the name of Jesus
- Live life with a view toward the Second Coming of Jesus

2 CORINTHIANS

If we want to do any bragging, we should brag about the good things people are doing in the Lord's name. This advice is a big part of Paul's message to the church in Corinth in this second letter to them. But how did this concern with boasting even become an issue?

A lot happened between Paul's first letter and this second one. To begin with, certain self-proclaimed experts showed up in the community. We do not know the details about their teachings but we do know Paul did not at all agree with them. It was their bragging about credentials that set the tone for this letter.

Paul was so concerned about the impact of this group of experts—he refers to them as "super-apostles" later in the letter (11:5)—was having on the community that he visited Corinth himself in an attempt to set things straight. This visit did not go well since Paul remembers it as a "painful" visit in 2 Corinthians 2:1.

As a result of this unfortunate visit, Paul sent Titus to the community with a letter. Paul felt uneasy about this letter but still felt it was necessary. Some believe 2 Corinthians 10—13 is the text of that letter, or at least a portion of it.

At last, perhaps as much as a year after 1 Corinthians, Paul wrote them the letter we now know as 2 Corinthians. Things appear to have settled down enough that Paul felt comfortable writing again, letting them know how much he cared for them and how proud he was of their spiritual progress in spite of the setbacks. Paul even boasted about their progress. In so doing, he may have intended to give the community an example of the kind of boasting they should be impressed with: not the self-promoting bombast of the experts, but sincere pride in the spiritual accomplishments of their bothers and sisters in the Lord.

In some translations, the word *boast* appears more than twenty times in this letter. Paul boasts about the sincerity of his relationship with the church in Corinth (1:12); he boasts about the fine character of the Corinthian church (7:14); he boasts about their eager support for his campaign to raise funds for the Jerusalem church (9:3).

In the final four chapters of the letter, Paul boasts even more, this time about his own ministry for the Lord. Of course, this is in no way a reflection of Paul's true character. He boasts in these chapters to show how foolish is it for mortals to take on such pretensions. He wants to bring down a few notches those "super-apostles," who promote themselves in the guise of preaching a true version of the gospel.

In this letter, Paul also concerns himself with things included in his first letter to this church. He urges the community to remain loyal to the great gift of faith they received. He explains the significance of the Resurrection for their lives. He urges them to be generous in their contributions for the Jerusalem church.

But this letter differs from the first in its emotional energy. Paul allows his readers to hear about his sometimes unbearable suffering for the faith, his frustration at the attempts of others to influence the community in the wrong way, his anger at having to defend his work from the attacks of others, but, above all, his deep love for them.

Overall, this letter allows us to experience Paul's character as a true shepherd of his people. He is deeply concerned about their spiritual welfare. And nothing seems to irritate him more than the news that others are leading the people in the wrong direction while presenting themselves as true preachers of the gospel.

The 13 chapters of 2 Corinthians:

1 — 7	Promote Jesus rather than self
8 — 9	Reach out to others
10 — 13	Humbly serve the Lord

Marketing

Paul was bothered by marketers, too: not the kind that sell commercial products, but the kind who preach the Word of God only to make a profit. In 2 Corinthians 2:17 he calls them "peddlers of God's word."

A Special Burden

Paul mentions a thorn in his flesh at 2 Corinthians 12:7. Many regard this as a reference to some speech impediment because in the same letter Paul refers to his failings as a speaker. But Paul may also have in mind some particular member of the community in Corinth who is generating much of the trouble there.

Gentle Persuasion

Paul was very dedicated to his project of collecting money to aid the needy in the home church of Jerusalem. When it came to asking for funds he could be as smooth as velvet: "Each of you must give as you have made up your mind, not reluctantly or under compulsion, for God loves a cheerful giver" (2 Corinthians 9:7).

The Sorrowful Letter

In 2 Corinthians 2:4 Paul speaks of a letter he sent to Corinth that was very painful for him to write but at the same time was very necessary for him to write. The purpose of the letter was to address a problem associated with one particular person in the community.

2 Corinthians on the Clock (AD)

Paul's first stay in Corinth   c. 50–52

1 Corinthians   c. 57

2 Corinthians   c. 58

There was quite a bit of give-and-take between Paul and the church in Corinth in the months that followed 1 Corinthians (possibly sent in AD 57). Church members in Corinth took offense at the first letter. This motivated Paul to actually go there himself, but things did not go well since Paul describes the visit as "painful" (2 Corinthians 2:1). After returning to Ephesus, Paul sent another letter, which he admits (in 2 Corinthians 2:4) was very difficult for him to write. But then Paul's associate Titus seems to have been instrumental in working things out between the apostle and the church. Encouraged by this news, Paul wrote to them again. This is 2 Corinthians. According to 8:10 of this letter, a full year had passed since the writing of 1 Corinthians. Sometime later Paul visited Corinth again.

As you read 2 Corinthians…

Throughout this letter Paul boasts about the good things being done to promote the gospel. What would you boast about within your church community?

In 2 Corinthians 2:14–17 Paul speaks about the "fragrance" of the gospel. What makes this image appropriate?

In 2 Corinthians 3:1–6 Paul says the Corinthians themselves are his "letter of recommendation." What does he mean? Could you say the same about people in your life?

What are present-day examples of people walking by faith and not by sight?

2 CORINTHIANS

183

In 2 Corinthians 6:3–10 Paul talks about what it is like to be a servant of God. How would you describe being a servant of God?

Paul was very excited about the collection he was taking up for the poor within the church. What work is your community excited about?

This letter reveals how much effort Paul exerted to bring about healing between himself and the community in Corinth. Do you put effort into healing relationships?

Three Spiritual Lessons From 2 Corinthians

- Our greatest honor is to serve the Lord
- Efforts toward healing relationships may sometimes be painful
- Generosity of spirit goes a long way when it comes to building community

GALATIANS

How do you spell "freedom"? Paul spells it with the letters of the name of Jesus. He wants the churches in Galatia also to spell it that way. But he fears that some of them are in danger of losing their freedom because some church members were taking on the burdens of the Law, convinced that obedience to the Mosaic Law went along with commitment to the Lord Jesus Christ.

Paul, of course, had worked very hard to assure believers that once baptized they were free from the Law. The reason for this, to put it simply, was that in baptism believers died and rose to new life in Christ. So life was now gained through Jesus and not the works of the Law.

But there were influential people circulating among the churches in Galatia who taught that circumcision was still necessary for salvation. Paul insisted that accepting this sign of the covenant was not necessary. Of course, Paul's position on this was entirely in line with the teaching of the apostles in Jerusalem.

Paul begins this letter with a vigorous defense of his credentials as an apostle. He had to do this because some in the community questioned his authority, arguing that Paul was not among the witnesses of the earthly ministry of Jesus. Paul responds that he received his mission directly from the Risen Lord and that is enough.

In the rest of the letter, Paul moves from one example to another in an effort to convince the believers in Galatia that salvation comes through faith in Jesus.

His favorite example is Abraham, whom God recognized as a man right with God simply because of his faith in what God promised him. And most importantly for Paul's argument, this happened before Abraham was circumcised. The lesson Paul wants his readers to take away from this example is this: Faith is the key to salvation. For Paul salvation no longer comes through circumcision and commitment to the Law of Moses. It should come as no surprise that Paul chooses this letter to include the details of a dispute he once had with Peter over this very matter. While visiting Antioch, Peter had no difficulty sharing a meal with Gentiles. But once certain representatives from the Jerusalem church showed up, Peter drew away from the Gentiles. Paul told Peter and everyone else in no uncertain terms that this sort of thing was not at all in line with the message of the gospel.

In another example of salvation through faith in Jesus, Paul explains to his readers that through Christ we have become adopted children of God. This means we are no longer slaves but children of God and therefore heirs of the kingdom of heaven. This example leads to one of Paul's most famous lines: "There is no longer Jew or Greek, there is no longer slave or free, there is no longer male and female; for all of you are one in Christ Jesus" (3:28).

Paul returns to the book of Genesis to find yet another example of freedom. Abraham had two sons. The first was Ishmael who did not inherit the promise; the second was Isaac who did inherit the promise because he was a child born to an Abraham filled with faith. Those who believe in Jesus are like Isaac; they too are born into freedom.

By the end of his letter to the Galatians, Paul is feeling better, confident that his words will have the desired effect of protecting the Galatians from the influence of misguided teachers.

The 6 chapters of Galatians:

1 — 2	Listen to the truth
3 — 6	Seek freedom in Jesus

Emotion

You can feel Paul's emotion in the words of this letter. He expresses his astonishment at how quickly they abandoned the true gospel.

GALATIANS

He even calls them foolish for allowing themselves to be taken in by another gospel.

Branded for Jesus

Paul talks about the marks of Jesus he bears on his body. He is probably referring to the hardships he has endured for the sake of the gospel.

True Freedom

For Paul freedom in Jesus is no license to do whatever we please. True freedom is found in serving the Lord.

Large Letters

Near the end of Galatians, Paul draws attention to the large letters in his writing. This may be due to his lack of training as a scribe; it could also be due to the strong emotions surging in Paul as he writes these words.

Galatians on the Clock (AD)

Paul's first journey   c. 49– 50

Paul at Ephesus in Asia Minor   c. 54–58

By AD 54 Paul was once again in Asia Minor—modern-day Turkey. He made Ephesus his home base this time, staying there for three years according to Acts 20:31. At this time in his missionary work, Paul had to defend his position on salvation in Christ against those who insisted that following the Mosaic Law was also necessary. This was the occasion for writing Galatians. This issue also surfaces in other letters from this period in his life, notably Philippians and Romans. However, some scholars believe Paul wrote this letter at the end of his first missionary journey. That would make Galatians the earliest of Paul's letters.

As you read Galatians…

In 1:10 Paul states that he seeks to please God rather than people. Can you identify others in the Bible who could say the same?

Paul found the grace of God very much at work in his life (1:11—2:21). How is God's grace at work in your life?

At 3:27 Paul declares that in baptism we have put on Christ. How is this exhibited in the church's baptism ceremony?

How does Paul draw a lesson about spiritual freedom from the biblical account of Sarah and Hagar (4:21–31)?

Discuss the fruits of the Holy Spirit as described by Paul in 5:22–23.

What practical advice does Paul leave us with in 6:1–10?

Three Spiritual Lessons From Galatians:

- We are heirs to the kingdom of heaven
- Let your Christian values shine through
- Let the Holy Spirit be your guide in life

EPHESIANS

Get out your spiritual telescopes! This letter has us looking at "the heavenly places" where Jesus sits in glory at the right side of his Father. Paul wants us to understand quite clearly that Jesus has already won the victory over sin and death. But Paul also wants us to understand that this is not something Jesus accomplished for his own sake. He did it for us that we might have a share in his victory. Of course, we could never claim to have deserved such a wonderful gift. It was all done through God's great love for us.

This letter offers a sweeping overview of God's plan of salvation. It moves from the vast expanse of heaven all the way down to our family connections on earth, from the countless ages before the creation of the world to the moments ticking away as we read this letter.

The wonderful message emerging from this all-embracing portrait of creation is God's love for us. Paul wants his readers to know how fortunate they are to be living at a time when God's plan of salvation, reaching way back even beyond the beginning of time, has been fulfilled in Jesus Christ. All of this is a wonderful gift from God. And our part is to show our gratitude by living lives that reflect the great honor given us by God's grace.

The letter explores some of the striking aspects of this gift from God. For one thing, we were completely undeserving of this gift, living in sin and subject to death, when God graciously raised us to new life in Christ. It is also striking that the Gentiles, once distinct from God's chosen people and ignorant of the covenant relationship between God and Israel, now share in the fulfillment of that covenant. All have become one through the saving power of God.

For his part, Paul is so grateful to serve God as a minister of the gospel that he regards his current hardships, including confinement to a prison, as nothing compared to the joy he has known in serving God. He prays that the recipients of his letter will be guided by God's grace to appreciate what God's love has done for them.

How do we show our gratitude for this gift of divine love? Paul urges us to use our God-given gifts to promote the gospel and the church. It will demand setting aside the pursuit of personal interests and concentrating instead on all that benefits our brothers and sisters in the Lord. Since we belong to the family of God, we should reflect in our lives the love of God. In this way the love between husband and wife, children end parents, servants and masters will serve as a model of faith for others.

Finally, Paul advises his readers to be ready to stand against anything that would work against the ideals of the gospel. The good news, if we recall the opening paragraphs of this letter, is that we have all the advantages in this struggle because the God of all creation is on our side.

The 6 chapters of Ephesians:

1 — 3   God's loving plan
4 — 6   Our loving response

Ready for Battle

Paul imagines the various spiritual components of our lives as pieces of armor to protect us. We have truth for protective clothing; righteousness for a breastplate; the gospel of peace for boots; faith for a shield; salvation as a helmet; and the Word of God for a sword.

Ephesus

The letter itself does not mention the church at Ephesus as the recipient of this letter. For this reason, some believe this letter was intended to circulate among a number of churches in the western portion of what we now call Turkey. The specific connection with Ephesus came only later, perhaps because of the prominence of that city. As a center of commerce in the ancient world, Ephesus certainly qualified as an ideal place to send a letter intended for a wider audience.

The Family

Modern readers might feel uncomfortable with Paul's call for wives to be submissive to their husbands. It might help to keep in mind that Paul also calls for husbands to love their wives. Paul is not working on a handbook for domestic relations here, he is stressing that the Christian family should exhibit the kind of self-giving love that Christ has for the church.

Our Advantage

Paul refers to Satan as "the ruler of the power of the air" (2:2). This curious expression comes from the belief, popular in Paul's day, that the realm between heaven and earth was controlled by evil powers. But Paul preaches the Good News that the Risen Lord has broken the influence of Satan. Jesus sits at his Father's right hand "in the heavenly places, far above all rule and authority and power and dominion" (1:20–21). People "in Christ" now have all the advantages in the struggle over evil.

Trinity

Although he does not use the word, Paul definitely thought of God as a trinity. The Father is the originator of the plan of salvation. Jesus fulfills that plan and in turn bestows upon his followers the gift of the Spirit (Ephesians 2:18–20).

A Life Worth Living

Paul provides his readers with a description of the kind of life he regards as worthy of their Christian calling. It is a life lived "with all humility and gentleness, with patience, bearing with one another in love, making every effort to maintain the unity of the Spirit in the bond of peace" (Ephesians 4:2–3).

Early Church

From Ephesians 4:11 we get some idea of the kind of ministries exhibited in the communities Paul founded. They include apostles, prophets, evangelists, pastors and teachers.

Ephesians on the Clock (AD)

Paul stays in Ephesus   c. 54–57

Paul in Rome   c. 61–63

Paul dies   c. 67

It is not easy to assign a date to this letter. The traditional view is that Paul wrote this letter while under house arrest in Rome. He wrote to encourage his dear companions in Ephesus to never lose sight of the great gift of salvation offered them through the Lord Jesus Christ. It was sometime between AD 61 and 63. But according to another view, this letter comes from the hand of a disciple sometime after Paul's death.

As you read Ephesians…

What do you find striking in Paul's description of God's plan of salvation (1:3–14)?

Describe how the passage from death to life (2:1–22) is exhibited in your life.

How could you make your own the prayer Paul makes in Ephesians 3:14–19?

Note Paul's powerful assertion of Christian unity in 4:1–6.

Is there anything about your "old nature" (4:22) that needs to be set aside?

How closely does Paul's portrait of the Christian home (5:21—6:4) reflect your home or church community?

What do you find meaningful in Paul's lesson about the armor of God (6:10–20)?

Three Spiritual Lessons From Ephesians

- We are surrounded by God's protective love and care
- Life is filled with gifts from God
- Words have the power to bring people closer to God

PHILIPPIANS

This is a bittersweet letter. The sweet part is the mutual love that so obviously exists between Paul and the faithful in Philippi. They have taken such good care of him, sending him much needed assistance from time to time. And Paul is so very grateful for the way they have lived by gospel values from the very first time they heard about them.

The bitter part comes with the realization that Paul wrote this letter from prison. His situation seems so critical that he is not sure how things will turn out. If he is to die, he is ready to be with Christ. But he would rather remain alive, not for his sake but for the sake of communities like the one at Philippi.

While he awaits the outcome of all this, Paul resists being trapped in self-pity. Instead, he pours out his attention on his fellow Christians, like those in Philippi. He understands that devotion to Jesus demands sacrifices. This conviction leads Paul to one of the most recognizable passages from his letters. He describes the way Jesus makes a complete gift of himself for the sake of others. You will recognize it immediately:

> Let the same mind be in you that was in Christ Jesus,
>> who, though he was in the form of God,
>>> did not regard equality with God
>>> as something to be exploited,
>> but emptied himself,
>>> taking the form of a slave,
>>> being born in human likeness. (2:5–7)

In the realm of possibilities, Jesus could have chosen not to enter this world of time as one of us. But God's love for us is so great that Jesus did become one of us. And this great gift of love challenges all of us, in our own limited way, to do something similar with our own lives.

The bittersweet character of this letter surfaces again when Paul suddenly shifts his focus and warns the church in Philippi: "Beware of the dogs…" (3:2). He is thinking of certain Christians who insist that circumcision is still required for salvation. Paul resists this teaching with all his might. He makes an issue of the fact that he is the most likely person of all to make a case for circumcision given his deep-seated Jewish background. But he is not going to make a case for this ritual because he has gained everything in Christ. Jesus is the way.

The letter concludes with a call for joy. There is reason for celebration in their faith in Jesus. There is reason for celebration in the love and support Paul and this church in Philippi have for one another.

Paul's own joy gives rise to another burst of eloquence as he offers his dear Philippians this list of things to concentrate on: "…whatever is true, whatever is honorable, whatever is just, whatever is pure, whatever is pleasing, whatever is commendable…" (Philippians 4:8).

PHILIPPIANS

The 4 chapters of Philippians:

1 — 2	Live as Jesus lived
3 — 4	Stay focused on the Lord

A Prayer

In this letter Paul makes a statement that is now included in the ordination right for deacons in the church. "I am confident of this, that the one who began a good work among you will bring it to completion by the day of Jesus Christ" (Philippians 1:6).

Euodia and Syntyche

These are certainly not household names. But they were well known in the church at Philippi. Paul pleads with them not to allow their differences over some issue spoil all the good work they have done in the Lord's name.

Epaphroditus

Paul holds this member of the Philippi church in high regard. He calls him "my brother and coworker and fellow soldier." He was the one the Philippians entrusted to carry their gift to the imprisoned apostle.

Gaudete Sunday

Philippians 4:4–7 was traditionally read on the third Sunday of Advent. Paul's call for them to "rejoice" (*gaudete* in Latin) gave rise to the popular title: Gaudete Sunday.

Philippians on the Clock (AD)

Paul's first visit to Philippi   c. 50

Paul in Ephesus   c. 54–58

Paul in Rome   c. 61–63

This letter may have been written sometime during Paul's three-year stay at Ephesus between AD 54 and 58. His concern with those insisting on strict adherence to the Mosaic Law seems to fit this time in his life. But others find in Paul's reference to the Praetorian Guard (1:13–14) evidence for dating this letter during Paul's house arrest in Rome.

As you read Philippians...

What would you gain by thinking of your own hardships as somehow advancing the gospel (1:12)?

Paul declares that for him "living is Christ and dying is gain" (1:21). Is this a viewpoint you could embrace?

What good work do you want God to bring to completion in you?

Paul famously describes the saving work of Jesus in Philippians 2:1–11. Comment on its power for you.

Paul speaks highly of Epaphroditus as a "fellow worker and soldier" (2:25–30). Is there anyone in your life you would describe in similar terms?

What do you count as loss for the sake of Jesus Christ (3:7)?

The church reads verse 4:4 on the Third Sunday of Advent. What makes this passage appropriate for that Sunday?

What do you think Paul means when he describes the peace of God as something that "surpasses all understanding" (4:7)?

Paul urges the community in Philippi to focus on everything that is spiritually positive (4:8–9). How would you achieve this in your community?

Three Spiritual Lessons From Philippians

- Live life in gratitude to God
- Imitate the self-giving of Jesus
- We are citizens of heaven

COLOSSIANS

Paul wants us to be well dressed. But for Paul being well dressed has nothing to do with fashion and everything to do with Christ. So what would the well-dressed Christian look like? Paul has drawn up this description for us: "…clothe yourselves with compassion, kindness, humility, meekness, and patience…. Above all, clothe yourselves with love, which binds everything together in perfect harmony" (Colossians 3:12, 14).

Paul probably had his inspiration for this passage from the rite of baptism in which the faithful died with Christ and rose with him to new life. But the image of new clothing would have been especially appropriate for the community in Colossae since that locality had once been a famous garment center in antiquity noted especially for the purple wool garments produced there.

Paul also drew up a list of things believers should take off and leave off: anger, malice, insults, foul language and lying. This list addresses relationships within any community, but the list may represent actual shortcomings in the community at Colossae. Paul wants the Colossians to realize that through baptism they have all become one in the Lord. Any distinctions that existed before—based on origin, appearances or social rank—should no longer carry any weight with them.

In this letter Paul also takes on the role of a spiritual pilot steering the community clear of dangerous waters. For the Colossians the danger seems to have come from the world of idolatry that surrounded them. Paul steers them toward the safe waters of the true Gospel. He urges them to be faithful to the teaching they received that Jesus Christ is Lord. This tradition is far superior to any "philosophy" generated by mortals. The apostle cautions his readers not to be taken in by mere human fabrications, no matter how clever or seductive they may be.

Some of the trouble may have revolved around attachment to certain cosmic influences that some imagined encircling the earth at different levels. People ascribed to them some degree of mediation between God and humanity. Paul wants his readers to know that Jesus is the only authentic Mediator between God and humanity.

The apostle recommends music as a special form of giving thanks to God. What kind of lyrics did he have in mind for his songs? A passage from the first chapter of this letter may in fact be the text of a hymn celebrating the role of Christ in creation. It reads in part:

> He is the image of the invisible God, the firstborn of all creation; for in him all things in heaven and on earth were created, things visible and invisible, whether thrones or dominions or rulers or powers—all things have been created through him and for him. (1:15–16)

As Paul concludes this letter, he returns to one of his favorite themes— the harmony that should exist in the Christian household. Paul believes the relationship between husband and wife, children and parents, slave and master should reflect the love of Christ.

In the final paragraphs Paul provides us with an example of the kind of love and respect that should exist among believers as he sends greetings from his associates in the faith complimenting them for their devotion to the gospel.

The 4 chapters of Colossians:

I — 2   Avoid falsehood

3 — 4   Put on Christ

A Triumph

Paul's description of the Lord's victory over certain "principalities and powers" (2:15) seems to be inspired by the military triumphs celebrated by victorious generals in Roman times.

Pass It On

There must have been constant communication between the various churches established by Paul. He wants the churches in Colossae and Laodicea to be sure and circulate the letters he sent each of them. In the Middle Ages people read a popular work that some regarded as the lost letter of Paul to the Laodiceans. It is just some twenty lines long. But scholars today regard it as inauthentic.

A Close Community

In the final chapter of this letter, Paul mentions by name no fewer than eleven people: Tychicus, Onesimus, Aristarchus, Mark, Barnabas, Justus, Epaphras, Luke, Demas, Nympha and Archippus. Such listings suggest how closely knit faith communities were in Paul's time.

Beloved Physician

In Colossians 4:14 Paul identifies Luke as "the beloved physician." Some think Luke's vocabulary does in fact suggest that he was associated with medicine. Others find his vocabulary no more distinctive than that of other authors. Of course, there is always the possibly that Paul meant Luke was gifted at healing people spiritually.

Christ the Head

In this letter and in Ephesians, Paul's image of the church as the body of Christ receives further nuance. Jesus is described as the head of the body. Some believe this new feature indicates that these two letters were not authored by Paul himself.

A Good Bonding Solution

Paul recommends love as the best bond for connecting all our spiritual strengths: "Above all, clothe yourselves with love, which binds everything together in perfect harmony" (3:14).

COLOSSIANS

Colossians on the Clock (AD)

Paul's house arrest in Rome   c. 61–63

Paul dies   c. 67

Tradition has Paul writing this letter during his confinement in Rome between AD 61 and 63. Others argue—on
the basis of vocabulary, style and theological viewpoint—that this letter
was written after the apostle's death by someone very familiar with
Paul's writings.

As you read Colossians...

Paul begins this letter with a lengthy thanks to God.
What gifts from God are you thankful for?

Paul gives thanks to God the Father who "has rescued us
from the power of darkness and transferred us into the
kingdom of his beloved Son..." (1:13). How has this
been exhibited in your life?

What impresses you in Paul's hymn about Jesus in Colossians 1:15–20?

What would you gain by thinking of your own hardships as somehow
"completing what is lacking in Christ's afflictions for the sake of his
body, that is, the church" (1:24)?

Paul cautions his readers against the empty notions of his day (2:8).
What do you identify as empty notions in the world today?

In 2:12 Paul tells the Colossians, "...when you were buried with him in
baptism, you were also raised with him through faith in the power of
God, who raised him from the dead." Have you ever thought of baptism this way? What does it contribute to your understanding of this
sacrament?

Paul associates his own suffering with the suffering of Jesus (1:24).
How have you responded to suffering?

What do you think Paul means when he says we should "seek the
things that are above" (3:1)?

What would you need to change within yourself to be dressed for
Christ as Paul urges in 3:12–17?

How would you reflect in your life what Paul says about conduct,
speech and the use of time (4:5–6)?

Three Spiritual Lessons From Colossians
- Seek to be spiritually well-dressed
- Lead a life worthy of the Lord
- Our lives should become a hymn of praise to God

1 THESSALONIANS

This letter is filled with energy, the kind of energy that comes from anticipating that something good is about to take place. For Paul and the recipients of this letter, that something good is the Second Coming of Christ.

Paul anticipates the Lord's coming any day, but he does not pretend to know when that day will come and he discourages anyone from speculating about it. In place of idle speculation, Paul recommends active engagement in everything that promotes the gospel. Such devotion to gospel values will make us ready for the Lord whenever he comes.

What is the character of someone who lives by the gospel? This letter gives us the following traits: a readiness to accept hardships for the sake of the gospel; love and respect for one another; commitment to all that is holy; a good work ethic to avoid becoming a burden to others; a readiness to forgive personal injury; a spirit of gratitude; and constant prayer.

If this is Paul's earliest letter—and therefore the earliest surviving book of the New Testament—it was written less than twenty years after the resurrection of Jesus Christ. It allows us to see what a powerful impact the gospel had on the lives of people so soon after the earthly ministry of Jesus.

In spite of the early date for this letter, it appears that distortions of the gospel message were already surfacing in the community. Paul reminds the Thessalonians that he did not preach the gospel to enrich himself or to gain the approval of others. Apparently, there were some in the community who did. So Paul advises his readers to be discerning as they listen to others preach the Word of God.

Near the end of this letter, Paul addresses a particular question from the community. Apparently, some expected the Lord's coming to be so soon that they were concerned for dead family and friends, thinking that they might be at some disadvantage when the Lord comes. Paul gives them assurance: "…we who are alive, who are left, will be caught up in the clouds together with them to meet the Lord in the air…" (1 Thessalonians 4:17).

Paul concludes the letter with a blessing for all and a request for prayers for himself. He also asks that this letter be circulated among them.

The 5 chapters of 1 Thessalonians:

1 — 3   The character of faith
4 — 5   The coming of the Lord

Caring Images

Paul's strong language in some of his letters reveals that he could be quite forceful in his proclamation of the gospel. But this letter reveals a softer side of Paul. He describes himself as caring for their welfare the way a nurse or a father would care for them.

Battle Readiness

Paul encourages the community at Thessalonica to prepare for the spiritual struggles that lie ahead by putting on suitable armor. Faith and love will serve as a breastplate; the hope of salvation will serve as a helmet.

24/7

Paul was very careful not to burden the communities with the task of caring for him. He reminds the Thessalonians that he worked night and day to support himself while at the same time preaching the gospel to them.

A Brave Man

From the Acts of the Apostles, we know that while he was in Thessalonica Paul stayed in the home of a man named Jason. Jason was prepared to endure a lot for the gospel. Angry citizens hauled Jason before the magistrates of the city and accused him of disloyalty to the Roman emperor because he accepted Jesus as king. Jason had to post bond before being released.

The Rapture

Some derive the notion of the Rapture from a literal reading of 1 Thessalonians 4:17, "Then we who are alive, who are left, will be caught up in the clouds…". Connecting this passage with Revelation 20:4, they understand the Rapture to begin an actual thousand-year reign of Christ. The traditional interpretation holds that Paul is teaching

the Thessalonians about the glorious Second Coming of Christ at the
end of time.

I Thessalonians on the Clock (AD)

Paul's first visit to Thessalonica   c. 50

Paul in Corinth   c. 50–52

Paul wrote this letter during his stay in Corinth; that visit
lasted for eighteen months and is usually dated between AD
50 and 52. These dates are fairly secure because of the connection with
the Roman official Gallio who was in Corinth at that time as proconsul
of the Roman province of Achaia. In the letter Paul speaks of his visit
with the Thessalonians as a very recent one (2:17). This suggests that
Paul wrote this letter soon after his arrival in Corinth making this his
earliest letter, though some would say that distinction belongs to his
letter to the Galatians.

As you read 1 Thessalonians…

Note Paul's reference to the three cardinal virtues
in 1:2–4.

Paul speaks of his courage to declare the gospel in
the face of great adversity (2:2). Where is this true
for the faithful today?

What does it mean to you to lead, as Paul says, "a life worthy of
God" (2:12)?

How is Paul's devotion to the community at Thessalonica exhibited
in 2:17—3:10?

What difference would it make in your life to anticipate the
Second Coming of the Lord as vividly as Paul does at 3:11–13?

Paul urges his readers to put on "the breastplate of faith and love,
and for a helmet the hope of salvation" (5:8). What do these strong
images suggest to you?

In 4:13–18 Paul comforts his readers with his message about the
day of Lord. What comfort do you find in his message?

Three Spiritual Lessons From 1 Thessalonians
- Be devoted to things that promote the gospel
- Make the values of the gospel your protection
- Our destiny is to be with God

2 THESSALONIANS

Something has changed. This second letter is filled with energy just like the first letter to Thessalonica. But this time the energy belongs more to Paul than to his readers. It seems the enthusiasm of some believers has begun to weaken. But Paul seems to draw strength from their weakness. It serves only to motivate him to preach the word all the more.

The lack of energy in the community is due to a misunderstanding. Some in the community seem to have interpreted Paul's teaching in the first letter to mean that the Lord's Second Coming will be very soon. This gives some members the excuse to do nothing to build up the community. They simply await the end while relying on the generosity of the community in the meantime.

In spite of Paul's caution about trying to predict the Second Coming, some in the community were doing just that. In this letter the apostle encourages his community not to be "so easily agitated or terrified" by the arguments of others or by letters claiming to carry his authority.

Paul provides his readers with a list of things that must happen before the coming of the Lord. Specifically he speaks about "the apostasy" and "the lawless one." The apostle's precise references here are difficult to determine but the general sense is that the community must be prepared to stand up to the hardships and adversity they will surely encounter because of their devotion to the truth.

Paul urges his readers to adhere to "the traditions" they received from him when he was personally present among them or which they learned from the letters he has sent to them.

Finally, Paul offers a prayer that God will give them the strength they need to live out their commitment to Christ in both word and deed. The apostle is certainly thinking of the struggles they face as Christians. But the context of this letter also suggests that Paul is hoping God's grace frees them from the fears they had concerning the Day of the Lord.

Paul urges his readers to follow the example he gave them while he was with them. The apostle worked "to the point of exhaustion" so as not to be a burden on them. He may be referring to his craft as a leather worker. But the whole context of this letter seems to suggest that Paul is speaking about his commitment to preaching the gospel. In other words, he actively contributed to the faith life of the community.

The apostle gives them some advice about how to handle the disorderly among them. They should not treat them as enemies but instead try to persuade them as family in the Lord. This letter itself could serve them well as a model.

In his closing remarks, Paul prays that the Lord of peace will grant peace to them. His wish is not that they would be free of adversity and hardship. He knows all too well that commitment to the gospel includes many struggles. The peace Paul speaks of is the inner calm stemming from the conviction that they have devoted themselves to the truth of the gospel.

The 3 chapters of 2 Thessalonians:

1	Live for the gospel
2	Cherish the tradition
3	Pray

Good Example

Paul begins all his letters with a blessing for grace and peace. It displays Paul's deepest wishes for his churches, even those with which he has disagreements. What a good example for all of us to follow.

End-Time Thinking

Paul seems to employ the standard language of end-time literature when he writes that the last judgment must be preceded by a time especially remarkable for its evil character. He explains, "…that day will not come unless the rebellion comes first…" (2:3).

The Lawless One

Paul's accent on the coming of "the lawless one" at the end of the ages has sparked a great deal of speculation about who this may be. It seems best to see this as a symbolic person representing all that stands opposed to God (2:4)

2 THESSALONIANS

Personal Note

At the conclusion of this letter, Paul directs attention to a personal greeting written in his own distinctive style. A similar note at the end of Galatians (6:11) refers to Paul's large letters. The major part of such letters would have been written down by a trained scribe.

2 Thessalonians on the Clock (AD)

Paul's first visit to Thessalonica   c. 50

Paul in Corinth   c. 51–52

Paul dies   c. 67

Paul's first letter to this community must have stirred up a lot of discussion. It seems he had to write this second one shortly after (probably around AD 51) to warn them about becoming too preoccupied with predicting precisely when the Lord would come again. On the other hand, some regard this letter as the work of someone other than Paul, written after his death, when the apostle's letters were a recognized collection. Note the words "every letter of mine" in the final paragraph.

As you read 2 Thessalonians…

What comfort does Paul find in the Lord's Second Coming as he describes it in 1:5–12?

In 2:1–12 how does Paul explain the delay of the Second Coming of Christ?

Paul urges his readers to hold onto the traditions he taught them (2:15). How do the traditions of the church influence your life?

Why do you think Paul uses such strong language against those living in idleness (3:6–13)?

In 12:1–3 Paul advises his readers not to be distracted from living the faith by trying to predict the Lord's coming. How does Paul's advice apply to our own age?

Three Spiritual Lessons From 2 Thessalonians

- We should work for God without drawing attention to ourselves
- Faith can lead us through hardships and adversity
- Prayer makes a difference

1 TIMOTHY

This is a letter from one pastor to another. Timothy was closely associated with much of Paul's missionary effort. He was Paul's trusted representative to the Christian communities in Corinth and Thessalonica. By the time Paul wrote this letter, Timothy was shepherding the community in Ephesus, a prominent port on the western coast of Asia Minor. Paul writes to his younger associate advising him on the task of being a spiritual shepherd.

Paul's first concern is the influence of distortions to the truth of the gospel. It seems some members of the community were more interested in impressing others with their knowledge than in promoting the love of the gospel.

Paul understands their position quite well because he himself was once like them. He was once a proud and arrogant man, "a blasphemer, a persecutor, and a man of violence" (1:13). But by God's mercy a marvelous transformation took place in his life. Now he is grateful that through God's grace he has become a servant of God.

Such a wonderful transformation can happen for others, too. So Paul recommends to Timothy the power of prayer. He also advises that leaders in the community be people of prayer. If they are given to displays that call attention to themselves rather than to God, they should not be entrusted with positions of influence in the community.

Paul goes on to offer Timothy practical advice in dealing with the wide range of people in his church. He even has opinions on the way people dress. It may be of help to remember that the typical community in these early years of the church met in private homes. In such intimate settings seemingly insignificant things—like dress or hairstyle—could draw attention to self rather than contribute to the worship of God.

In the final paragraphs of the letter, Paul compares the advantages of this world to the advantages of faith. In a wonderful and memorable phrase, Paul reminds Timothy that there is "great gain in godliness" (6:6). Of course, he is not thinking of material gains but of spiritual ones like those he lists a few verses later: righteousness, godliness, faith, love, endurance and gentleness (6:11).

If Timothy put Paul's sound advice into practice, he certainly transformed his community into the kind of church that could serve as a model for others.

The 6 chapters of I Timothy:

1 — 2   The power of prayer
3 — 6   The character of the church

Security in God

The church's profession of faith in one God raised suspicions among some leaders in the Roman Empire. This certainly made life difficult for Christians. But Paul looks for security in God; he recommends prayer and intercessions for kings and civic leaders so that the church may carry on its work without interruption.

Early Creed

This letter includes what appears to be an early creed outlining the ministry of Jesus from incarnation to resurrection:

He was revealed in flesh,
  vindicated in spirit,
    seen by angels,
proclaimed among Gentiles,
  believed in throughout the world,
    taken up in glory. (3:16)

Money

This letter includes in verse 6:10 the famous line about the root of all evil. It should be noted that money itself is not the source of the problem, but the love of money.

Mercy

Only in his letters to Timothy does Paul add the term "mercy" to his standard introduction. This is surely due to the profound gratitude he expresses in this letter over the marvelous transformation in his own life through the grace of God.

Witness

Paul speaks of the "noble profession" Jesus made before Pontius Pilate. Paul likewise professed the faith before representatives of the Roman Empire. He stood before Gallio in Corinth, Felix and Festus in Caesarea, and finally the imperial court in Rome. In each case, Paul certainly must have drawn inspiration from the Lord's "noble" witness to the truth.

The Only One

Paul makes it very clear that "the man Jesus Christ" is the only mediator between God and humanity. The reason for Paul's emphatic declaration of this may come from the fact that some citizens of Ephesus worshipped a host of mediators between heaven and earth. Archaeology has revealed a number of amulets and the like to secure the favor of these mediators.

I Timothy on the Clock (AD)

Paul meets Timothy   c. 50

Paul in Rome   c. 61–63

Paul dies   c. 67

Tradition holds that Paul wrote to Timothy after AD 63 when his confinement in Rome was a thing of the past. Paul is apparently in Macedonia when he sends this letter offering Timothy advice on how best to shepherd the community in Ephesus (1 Timothy 1:3). But there is also the possibility that this letter was written by a disciple of the great apostle sometime after his death.

As you read 1 Timothy…

Paul marvels at the wonderful transformation in his life through the mercy of God (1:12–17). Have you discovered this in your life too?

Notice Paul's emphasis on the necessity of prayer in chapter 2.

Paul lists the qualifications for serving God (1 Timothy 3:1–13). Would you qualify as a servant of God? What changes might you need to make?

Paul's opinion about money in 6:10 is often misquoted. What is Paul really saying?

Three Spiritual Lessons From 1 Timothy

- The greatest honor is service to God
- Real advantages come from faith
- Work to build community

I TIMOTHY

2 TIMOTHY

As we know only too well, stress can wear us down. This is apparently what happened to Timothy. Paul writes this second letter to encourage him. As a seasoned apostle, Paul is well acquainted with the hardships that must be faced by loyal servants of God like his good friend Timothy.

Apparently, one problem for Timothy is his habit of getting embroiled in heated discussions with certain members of the community. Two members in particular—Hymenaeus and Philetus—seem to have had a unique interpretation of the Resurrection that Timothy could not accept. Paul advises his young associate to avoid getting into arguments with these two.

Later in this letter, Paul runs through this litany of adjectives describing the kind of people who give Timothy trouble:

> ...lovers of themselves, lovers of money, boasters, arrogant, abusive, disobedient to their parents, ungrateful, unholy, inhuman, implacable, slanderers, profligates, brutes, haters of good, treacherous, reckless, swollen with conceit, lovers of pleasure rather than lovers of God, holding to the outward form of godliness but denying its power. (3:1–4)

With people like this in his community, it is perfectly understandable that Timothy felt overwhelmed at times. In an effort to console Timothy, Paul reminds his good friend of his own struggles. It has become a kind of epitaph for Paul:

> I have fought the good fight, I have finished the race, I have kept the faith. (4:7)

So Paul offers his own victory over adversity as encouragement to Timothy. If his younger associate can persevere, he, too, will be able to enjoy the spiritual crown of glory that awaits him in the next world.

In the meantime, Paul encourages Timothy to come to see him as soon as possible. While they are both still on this side of time, they can give encouragement to each other.

The 4 chapters of 2 Timothy:

Concentration

Paul holds up to Timothy a series of images to encourage him to stay focused on Jesus (2:4–6). First, there is the soldier's attention to his superior officer. Next, there is the athlete's careful compliance with the rules of competition. Finally, there is the farmer's hard work to ensure a rich harvest.

Personal Library

Paul reminds Timothy to bring the books and the parchments he left in Troas (4:13). The apostle could not bear to be separated from his personal library for long.

Onesiphorus

This fellow Christian appears to have offered his house as a gathering place for believers. Paul also commends him for taking care of him during his stay in a Roman prison. Onesiphorus was apparently quite willing to put his faith into action.

Jannes and Jambres

Who were these two figures mentioned by Paul in 2 Timothy 3:8? They are the names rabbinic tradition assigned to a pair of Pharaoh's magicians who tried to match what Moses was doing in the name of the God of Israel. It seems there were quite a few legends about these two floating about even in Paul's time. According to one such legend, they foretold to Pharaoh the birth of Moses.

Successor of Peter

Linus, mentioned at the end this letter (4:21), is by tradition the first successor of Saint Peter as bishop of Rome. Tradition also holds that Tuscany was his place of origin and that he served as chief shepherd for twelve years.

Timothy on the Clock (AD)

Paul meets Timothy c. 50

Paul released from Rome c. 63

Paul dies c. 67

This letter appears to be Paul's last. Paul is again in Rome, this time awaiting the outcome of another trial in the imperial courts. Paul seems to be preparing for the worst. But for Paul it will be the best, since the apostle speaks of the crown of glory that awaits him after fighting the good fight and finishing the race. These circumstances place this letter about the year 67 AD, the traditional date for Paul's execution during the reign of the emperor Nero. But there is also the possibility that this letter was written by a disciple of Paul's in the years following his death.

As you read 2 Timothy…

Paul mentions Timothy's mother, Eunice, and grandmother Lois as models of faith for him (1:5). Are you a model of faith for members of your family?

In 2:1–7 Paul uses a number of images to represent being strong in Christ. Which of them do you find especially meaningful?

Paul's skill with words is evident in 2:11–13. Read it aloud and then reflect on its meaning for you.

What do you think of Paul's images in 2:20 for the different sorts of people in the church?

Paul's declaration on the inspiration of Scripture (3:16) is often quoted. With regard to what passages from the Bible do you find it easy to agree with Paul? Are there any passages about which you find it challenging to agree with him?

At 4:7 Paul declares that he has fought the good fight. Could you say the same?

Three Spiritual Lessons From 2 Timothy

- Stay focused on the Lord
- Make your life a source of inspiration for others
- Work for a spiritual reward

TITUS

Paul writes to Titus about truth. By truth, Paul means the reliable Word of God that leads to eternal life. Paul spent his career as an apostle defending that truth from distortion. Now he encourages Titus, shepherd of the community on Crete, to give special attention to the teaching of sound doctrine.

Titus was one of Paul's most trusted associates. We can see this in the fact that Titus was the one Paul chose to carry to Corinth one of the most difficult letters he had to write and one that could make or break his relationship with a community he knew so well.

Paul writes to Titus that one way to secure the truth among believers is to lead an exemplary life. Such traits as moderation and self-control are especially appropriate for a Christian because one of the most fundamental convictions of the faith is that we live our lives awaiting the glory of the world to come.

Paul encourages every generation within the community to regard itself as a model of faith for others. Before embracing the faith, they were preoccupied with earthly interests, the slaves of passion and pleasures. Now, enlightened by the faith, their vision reaches beyond the horizons of this world to the promise of eternal life. And that promise is a sound one because—as Paul states at the beginning of this letter—God never lies (Titus 1:2).

The 3 chapters of Titus:

I —2	Hold on to the truth
3	Be models of faith

Genealogies

Paul warns both Timothy and Titus about genealogies. We might wonder what is wrong with tracing down a family tree. It may be that Paul is concerned about those who use their family histories to claim superiority over others.

Grace

This letter offers us a very helpful summary of God's gracious love:

> But when the goodness and loving kindness of God our Savior appeared, he saved us, not because of any works of righteousness that we had done, but according to his mercy, through the water of rebirth and renewal by the Holy Spirit. This Spirit he poured out on us richly through Jesus Christ our Savior, so that, having been justified by his grace, we might become heirs according to the hope of eternal life. (3:4–7)

Résumé

Paul offers a résumé of requirements for leadership in the church. It includes respect for the bond of marriage; a disciplined family; and

TITUS

detachment from material things. The candidate must also be "hospitable, a lover of goodness, prudent, upright, devout, and self-controlled" (1:8).

Coming Into Focus

Church offices familiar to us today are beginning to take shape in this letter (also in 1 Timothy). Paul talks about elders (the Greek term is *presbyter*) and bishops. Over time, the order of priest and bishop would become more distinct, but in this letter, they appear to be almost interchangeable.

Titus on the Clock (AD)

Paul works with Titus   c. 50–58

Paul released from Rome   c. 63

Paul dies   c. 67

If this letter is from Paul, he must have written it after his house arrest in Rome because he is free to meet with Titus in a city called Nicopolis in Asia Minor (3:12). Tradition thus dates this letter shortly after AD 63. But current thinking is that this letter was written after Paul's lifetime by one of his followers. In that case, the letter to Titus dates from around the turn of the century, since writers in the middle of the second century are familiar with it.

As you read Titus...

As the letter begins, Paul identifies himself as a servant of God. Could you say the same about yourself?

In referring to the divine promises in the Bible, Paul says that God "never lies." What divine promises do you think Paul was thinking of?

Paul stresses knowledge of sound doctrine. Can you identify the basics of the doctrine of the church?

Interpreters debate about the character of the false teachers mentioned in this letter. What insights would you add to the debate?

Paul offers an ideal profile of the people who make up the Christian community. What is it about their character that most impresses you? What important role does Paul find for women in the Christian community?

The oldest list of New Testament books that we have—it is known as the Muratorian Fragment—praises this letter to Titus for the lessons on discipline it offers the church. What lessons do you find within it for yourself?

Three Spiritual Lessons From Titus

- The Word of God is truth
- Lead a life that serves as a model of faith for others
- Remain attached to the things of heaven

PHILEMON

This letter reads very much like the sort of letter any of us might write. First, it is just about as long as one of our letters. Second, Paul has a favor to ask, just as we might write a letter to ask a favor of a friend. Finally, Paul seems to have written this letter entirely in his own hand, just as we do. Paul's other letters were probably dictated to a scribe.

Paul writes this letter to a friend named Philemon (pronounced Phi-LEE-mon). His address is Colossae, a city in what in Paul's day was known as Asia Minor. We know this part of the world today as Turkey.

What is the favor Paul seeks? He wants his friend Philemon to welcome a former slave as an equal in the Lord and then allow him to return. The slave's name is Onesimus. He was a young man who left his master and ended up with Paul. The precise circumstances for his leaving are unknown to us. Was he unhappy? Was he feeling unappreciated? We simply do not know. What we do know is that while he was with Paul, Onesimus became a Christian.

Paul seems to be playing the role of reconciler. He tells Philemon that he is sending Onesimus back to him. He understands that Philemon may be reluctant to take his former slave back. But Paul wants him to consider the fact that Onesimus was away for just a brief time. And he should weigh that brief time against the fact that he can now think of Onesimus forever as a fellow believer.

Paul seems confident that his request will be granted because of the mutual respect Philemon and he have for each other. Paul even takes the liberty to make a lighthearted play on words in his letter. The name

Onesimus means "useful," but Paul hopes it is Philemon who will prove "useful" to him by allowing Onesimus to return. We cannot know whether Philemon appreciated Paul's sense of humor or not. We do not even know if he allowed Onesimus to return. But the cordial tone of the letter suggests that Paul anticipated his request would be granted.

In any case, this letter displays the kind of ideals Christianity inspired in the hearts of people. Paul was asking Philemon to appreciate the fact that he and his former slave were now members of the body of Christ; they were spiritual equals.

For all we know the early church cherished this letter and retained it in its library of sacred literature precisely because the ideal of human equality is expressed within it. But what makes the appeal in this letter unique from other appeals for equality is the fact that the argument is based on our common bond in the Lord Jesus Christ.

The 25 verses of Philemon:

1 — 7	Paul's gratitude
8 — 25	Paul's request

Epaphras

This curious name means "charming" or "favored." From what we know of this figure from Paul's letter, the name seems to fit. Epaphras was one of Paul's close associates. The apostle describes him in this letter as "my fellow prisoner in Christ Jesus." Epaphras was apparently a prominent figure in the church at Colossae. In fact, from Paul's remarks in Colossians 1:7, it was the preaching of Epaphras that got the church started in that city.

Philemon

This is another figure in the early church who seems to have lived up to his name; *Philemon* means "loving." He apparently offered his home as a gathering place for the church in Colossae. From Paul's letters we know of other house-churches: the home of Priscilla and Aquila in Ephesus (1 Corinthians 16:19) and in Rome (Romans 16:3–5); and the home of Nympha in Laodicea (Colossians 4:15).

Philemon on the Clock (AD)

Paul in Ephesus   c. 54–58

Paul in Caesarea   c. 61

Rome in Rome   c. 61–63

Paul writes this letter while confined to a prison. But where? We know that Paul was under house arrest in Rome, but the apostle's plan to visit Philemon—perhaps at Colossae in Asia Minor—seems to imply that he is closer than Rome. We know Paul was also imprisoned in Caesarea by the sea, but it is just too far away for a visit. Ephesus fits the situation best—just over a hundred miles from Colossae—making Philemon one more letter from the productive three years he spent there (AD 54–58). One problem with Ephesus as the place of origin for this letter is that there is no explicit mention in Acts of Paul being in prison in that city. On the other hand, other letters from Ephesus—those to Corinth and Philippi—seem to suggest that Paul did endure hardships there.

As you read Philemon…

In length this letter is just like letters you have written. But have you given thanks to God in your letters as Paul does?

How would you describe the relationship between Paul and Philemon?

What kind of person do you think Onesimus was?

Do you think Paul condones slavery in this letter?

Three Spiritual Lessons From Philemon

- Value others as children of God
- Live a life that inspires others to believe in God
- Work for reconciliation

PHILEMON

213

THE LETTER TO THE HEBREWS

If you are looking for a boost in your spiritual life, you will find it in this book! The author of Hebrews wants to light a fire in our hearts. He knows our struggles; he knows some of us may even be on the verge of giving up altogether. His advice to us all: Stay focused on the Lord because the Lord is the perfect mediator between God and humanity.

The book begins with an assortment of passages from the Bible showing how Jesus is above the angels. Then the author of Hebrews turns to the Exodus account and explains to us how Jesus surpasses Moses as servant of God. In the first exodus, the Israelites followed Moses out of a land of oppression into the Promised Land. In the new exodus, the people of God follow Jesus out of this world of suffering and death into eternal life. The central portion of the letter defends Jesus as the perfect priest whose sacrifice surpasses the sacrifices of the temple in Jerusalem. The letter puts it this way: "For by a single offering he has perfected for all time those who are sanctified" (Hebrews 10:14).

As the author draws near to his finale, he puts together for us a list of people from Israel's past who were faithful to God in the face of every adversity. The author imagines them to be in the stands of the great stadium of life. They make up "a cloud of witnesses" (12:1) surrounding us and cheering us on as we run the race that lies before us. If we are burdened by sin, this author urges us to put those burdens aside. Let's not give up! Our coach tells us: "…lift your drooping hands and strengthen your weak knees, and make straight paths for your feet, so that what is lame may not be put out of joint, but rather be healed" (12:12–13).

So if you are beginning to feel weary on the journey of faith, pick up your Bible, turn to Hebrews and let its author inspire you to continue toward the finish line.

The 13 chapters of Hebrews:

1 — 4	Jesus is the mediator
5 — 10	Jesus is the priest
11 — 13	Follow Jesus

The Glory of God

Hebrews announces that Jesus is the reflection of God's glory. In the Bible God's glory always has some connection with the plan of salvation. When God's glory shines there is something happening for our spiritual benefit.

Victory

The author wants us to be successful in our faith journey. The people of Israel did not do so well when they got to the borders of the Promised Land; many of them failed to enter into that place of rest and fulfillment. Fortunately, we have Jesus to follow. If we are loyal to him, we will succeed.

Sacrifice

The priests of Israel offered prayers and sacrifices for the benefit of their people. But Jesus offers the perfect sacrifice of himself. This gives us great confidence in our own journey of faith. We can make it.

The Author

From earliest times, this letter was associated with Paul. A second-century manuscript, now known as Papyrus 46, includes Hebrews among Paul's letters, placing it right after Romans. Paul's trusted companion Timothy appears in the final chapter of Hebrews (13:23). However, the letter itself makes no claim to have been written by Paul. The prevailing opinion today is that Paul was not the author.

His Bible Was in Greek

The author of Hebrews uses the wording of the Greek Old Testament to make his arguments. For example, at 9:16 he says the word for "covenant" can also mean "testament." This is true for the Greek word for covenant, not the Hebrew word. At 11:29–40 there are probable references to Judith and to the book of Maccabees, both of them belonging to the Greek Bible.

Melchizedek

This Old Testament figure has special meaning for the author of Hebrews because so much about him foreshadows the perfect priesthood of Jesus. The name *Melchizedek* includes the word for "righteousness," and Jesus was the most righteous of all. Melchizedek was also the king of Salem, which means "peace," and Jesus brought a lasting peace to the world. And Melchizedek appears suddenly without any details about his origins, and Jesus, of course, as the Son of God has no beginning and no end.

Hebrews on the Clock (AD)

Nero   54–68

Fall of Jerusalem   70

Domitian   81–96

This letter reflects a time of great difficulty for believers. The outlook is so grim that some Christians seem to be on the brink of abandoning their faith. Such circumstances could reflect the oppressive reigns of either Nero or Domitian, but a date closer to Nero seems very likely since Hebrews makes no reference to the destruction of the temple. And that would be surprising in a book focusing so much on high priests and sacrifice.

As you read Hebrews...

Can you think of some of the "many and various ways" God spoke through the prophets in the Old Testament?

Count the number of arguments the author uses in 1:5–14 to prove that Jesus is superior to angels. What significance do you find in the total number?

According to 2:5–18 what makes Jesus the perfect one to help us in our struggle to remain loyal to God?

How does 4:1–14 show that there is "a Sabbath rest" awaiting us?

What do you find especially impressive in the author's argument that Jesus is the perfect high priest (4:14—10:17)?

At 8:8–12 you will find the longest quote from the Old Testament in any book of the New Testament. It comes from Jeremiah 31:31–34. What do you think makes this passage so quotable?

From the list of faith-filled people in Hebrews 11, which ones do you find most impressive?

By the time you reach the end of the letter, has the author succeeded in inspiring you to run the race and win the crown of glory?

Three Spiritual Lessons From Hebrews

- Ask God for the strength to finish the race
- Look for models of faith in the saints
- Remain faithful to Jesus

THE LETTER TO THE HEBREWS

THE CATHOLIC LETTERS

THE LETTER OF JAMES

What are we to do when faced with challenges to our faith? James understands our struggles and he wants to help. Like every other contributor to the Bible, James is committed to giving us every advantage in our journey of faith. He wants us to be successful. He wants us to share eternal life with the Lord.

So what edge does James give us in this struggle? He urges us to turn to God because there is wisdom available to us from above. All we have to do is ask God to give it to us. But James also cautions us to be sincere in our request. He puts it this way:

> But ask in faith, never doubting, for the one who doubts is like a wave of the sea, driven and tossed by the wind; for the doubter, being double-minded and unstable in every way, must not expect to receive anything from the Lord. (1:6–7, 8)

What kind of wisdom-gifts can we expect from God that give us an advantage in the journey of faith? James seems to hold four in special regard. The first gift empowers us to put faith into action. James wants to see our close relationship with God exhibited in the things we do in life. He mentions specifically treating everyone with respect no matter what their social rank in the eyes of the world.

For examples of faith-in-action, James holds up Abraham and Rahab. Abraham put his faith into action by showing his readiness to offer his only son to God to prove he no longer attached any conditions to his faith. Rahab protected the messengers whom Joshua commissioned to spy on Jericho. She even gave them advice about how they could safely return to their people.

As second example of wisdom from heaven is to make good use of the power of speech. James was all too familiar with the damage words can do.

…also the tongue is a small member, yet it boasts of great exploits.

How great a forest is set ablaze by a small fire! And the tongue
is a fire. (3:5–6)

A third example of wisdom from above is detachment from the things
of this world. The desire to possess the things of this world leads to animosity and even warfare. James wants us to pray for the gift to keep this
world in perspective, to resist the temptation to own this world and
instead accept it humbly as a gift from God.

Finally, James urges us to ask for the gift of patience with our brothers and sisters in this world. If we seek examples, James points us in the
direction of the prophets who were patient in their proclamation of the
Word of God. We can also take an example from the patience of Job.

In the final paragraphs of this letter, James returns to the theme of
prayer, this time urging us to pray for each other, especially for those suffering from physical or spiritual ills. As a model for prayer, James directs
our attention to Elijah, the prophet whose prayers brought rain to a
parched earth.

The 5 chapters of James:

1	Pray for wisdom
2	Put faith in action
3	Speak words of blessing
4	Accept the world as a gift
5	Be patient with each other

Twelve Tribes

James addresses his letter to "the twelve tribes in the Dispersion." He
may be thinking of the church as the new Israel. Like the tribes of Israel,
the church too is dispersed among the nations. But, as Acts so well
displays, this dispersion is for the best. It serves to spread the gospel to
the world.

A Deadly Thing

In 1:14–16 James speaks of sin as a kind of parasite within us that when
full grown "gives birth to death." The best defense against it is to seek
wisdom. It protects against harmful desires and makes us worthy to
receive "the crown of life."

JAMES

A Misquotation?

At 4:5 James cites the following as a quote from the Bible: "God yearns jealously for the spirit that he has made to dwell in us." The trouble is, no such text can be found in the Bible as we have it today. But it is certainly a good summary of texts like Exodus 20:5, which speaks of idolatry as something that provokes God's jealous love.

God Willing

James cautions his readers against presuming too much. We typically plan our days from morning to night. But James wants us to remember that in all we do we take for granted the wonderful gift of life. We do well to remember that we are "a mist that appears for a little while and then vanishes" (4:14).

Anointing of the Sick

> Are any among you sick? They should call for the elders of the church and have them pray over them, anointing them with oil in the name of the Lord (5:14).

This is the traditional scriptural basis for the sacrament of healing.

Another James

According to tradition the author of this letter is known a "James the Less." This title distinguishes him from James the son of Zebedee. Acts 12:1–2 records the execution of this other James at the command of King Agrippa I (c. AD 37–44), a grandson of Herod the Great. Perhaps because he was martyred for the faith at this early stage, this son of Zebedee is called James the Greater.

James on the Clock (AD)

The Council of Jerusalem   c. 50

Death of James, brother of the Lord   c. 62

Tradition attributes this book to James, the brother of the Lord and leader of the Jerusalem church. James played an important role in the early church debate over what to do with Gentile converts to the faith (see Acts 15). If this letter was inspired by that occasion, it could be dated to the middle of the first century. The dispute over Gentiles in the church could also explain the book's appeal for mutual respect and the power of words for promoting good. On the other hand, the letter may be the work of a disciple writing decades later in the name of James or perhaps even revising a letter by James.

As you read James...

James enjoys using vivid images. Note all the images in the first chapter. Which ones do you find especially powerful?

Can you accept James's advice (1:5) to ask for wisdom and to be confident that God will grant it to you?

James points to Abraham and Rahab as examples of people who put their faith into action (2:18–26). Can you identify other examples from the Bible and from the present day?

How does James's lesson about putting faith into action apply to you?

Think about the images James uses to represent the power of words (3:6–12). Could you add other images to his list?

How detached are you from the things of the world?

What similarities can you find between the struggles faced by people in this letter and the struggles in your own faith community?

Three Spiritual Lessons From James

- Put faith into action
- Use words to build up the kingdom
- Suffering can lead us closer to God

1 PETER

Anyone who has ever searched for a home knows how difficult it is to find just the right place, a place that feels comfortable, and a place to grow old in. At the time Peter wrote this letter, many Christians felt homeless. Their commitment to Jesus meant that they were in the world but not of the world. They met with animosity from outsiders who did not understand the Christian detachment from the world and looked upon their Sunday celebrations with suspicion. In some pockets of the empire, Christians were persecuted for their refusal to worship the emperor and the host of gods in the Roman pantheon.

I PETER

Imagine then how grateful these Christians would be to hear Peter tell them they have a home. He understood how difficult it was for them to live in a world that did not share their convictions about the fundamental truths of life. But Peter tells them not to let go of their convictions. They belong to Christ who, in the words of Psalm 118, is the stone rejected by the builders but who has become the foundation stone for a new world. Peter puts it this way: "Come to him, a living stone, though rejected by mortals yet chosen and precious in God's sight, and like living stones, let yourselves be built into a spiritual house…" (2:4–5).

Of course, belonging to a spiritual house has a definite impact on the way they are to lead their lives. Peter urges them to keep moving forward in their faith and not to drift back into the patterns they left behind when they became Christians. At one time, they were slaves to the illusions of this passing world. Now they are free. They live for the enduring values of the kingdom of heaven.

As members of the spiritual household of God, Christians should exhibit to the rest of the world a standard of life that models mutual love and respect. The apostle has practical advice for every member of the household—husband, wife, slave, master and elder. He puts it this way: "Like good stewards of the manifold grace of God, serve one another with whatever gift each of you has received" (4:10).

Christians may have to endure hardship for their commitment to the Lord but Jesus endured hardships too. And the advantages are immeasurable: "And after you have suffered for a little while, the God of all grace, who has called you to his eternal glory in Christ, will himself restore, support, strengthen, and establish you" (5:10).

The 5 chapters of I Peter:

I	True holiness
2 — 3	God's household
4 — 5	Suffering for the Lord

Sound Advice

Peter warns his readers to resist the temptation to drift back into a life limited to the things of this world. His advice is quoted in the church's Night Prayer each Tuesday. "Discipline yourselves, keep alert. Like a roaring lion your adversary the devil prowls around, looking for someone to devour. Resist him, steadfast in your faith…" (5:8–9).

God's People

You may recognize a phrase from this letter in one of the Sunday Prefaces. It goes this way: "But you are a chosen race, a royal priesthood, a holy nation, God's own people..." (2:9).

Babylon

The mention of Babylon in 1 Peter 5:13 is believed to be a reference to Rome. This is the only evidence from the New Testament connecting the apostle Peter with the capital of the Roman Empire and the place of his martyrdom.

Preaching to the Spirits

Who are the spirits to whom the Risen Lord preaches in 3:19? One tradition held that they were the souls of repentant sinners, like those of Noah's time. In this tradition, Jesus descended into the realm of the dead to declare them free. Another tradition is that these are hostile spirits believed by some in ancient times to surround the world and influence it toward sin. As he ascends into heaven, Jesus declares the world free of their influence.

I Peter on the Clock (AD)

The reign of Nero   54–68

Death of Peter   c. 65

Tradition holds that this letter was written by the apostle Peter shortly before he died during the Emperor Nero's persecution of the church (around AD 65). The letter does seem to reflect the hardship of the church in those early years when believers were looked upon with suspicion by Rome. But many today doubt the apostle Peter was the actual author of this letter.

As you read 1 Peter...

Peter begins by reminding his readers of the great gift of eternal life that awaits them in heaven. Do you live your life with this in mind? When have you reminded others of it?

Peter warns his readers not to slip back into the way of life they knew before baptism. Each Easter Sunday we renew our own baptismal promises. What does this ritual mean for you?

I PETER

Peter refers to us as a chosen race, a royal priesthood, a holy nation. What does each one of these mean for you?

What practical advice would you have to help people live as the household of God?

What special hardships do Christians endure in today's world? How would you encourage them?

Three Spiritual Lessons From 1 Peter

- Our true home is in heaven
- Lead holy lives as God's holy people
- Think of faith as a precious jewel

2 PETER

Jesus entrusted Peter with the task of shepherding the flock. This letter shows what a faithful shepherd Peter is. He guides the church to spiritual pastures where they will be nourished for eternal life. He is also careful to shepherd them away from pastures that might prove harmful to their spiritual welfare.

Behind the words in this letter is Peter's firm conviction that the day of the Lord is approaching. We cannot calculate the moment of its arrival since, as the apostle reminds us, "with the Lord one day is like a thousand years, and a thousand years are like one day" (3:8). But come it will. And Peter wants the Lord to find us "without spot or blemish" (3:14).

In the course of this letter, we also discover that Peter believes his time on earth is coming to an end (1:14). He leaves this letter with his flock as a kind of last testament expressing his wish that all of them will remain faithful to the Lord and gain eternal life.

Some interpreters wonder if this letter actually came from the hand of the apostle Peter. But even if it was not actually written by him, it certainly reflects Peter's convictions about what really matters in life.

Peter steers his flock away from the dangerous ground of false teaching. Though the precise subject matter of such teaching is not given, it is clear that what makes it dangerous is its power to influence people away from the path of life. At the core of this false teaching is an exclusive attachment to the things of this world and a denial of the truth that there is a world to come. It is the cleverness of this limited viewpoint on the meaning of life that makes this false teaching so harmful.

The apostle has very strong words to describe the false teachers who threaten to lead his flock astray with their denial of a final judgment. His strong words in chapter 2 and the beginning of chapter 3 are borrowed in part from the Letter of Jude, but Peter recasts Jude's language to make it more pertinent to his theme about God's final judgment.

To those who deny a final judgment Peter recommends they take another look at the Bible. He reminds them of several passages in Genesis where God rescues pious people and punishes the wicked. Think for example about Noah and his family versus the rest of the people, or Lot versus the cities of Sodom and Gomorrah.

But Peter is also a gentle shepherd. He takes care to soften the impact of his words with the promise of deliverance for the righteous. He accents God's patience and forbearance "not wanting any to perish, but all to come to repentance" (3:9). As we read these words, we are reminded of the Lord's patience in dealing with Peter's own triple denial.

Where are the safe pastures that nourish people with the truth? Peter points to his own testimony, including his experience of the glory of the Lord on the mountain of the Transfiguration (1:17). He also points to the Word of God expressed in the Scriptures, assuring his readers of its power with these memorable words: "...no prophecy of scripture is a matter of one's own interpretation, because no prophecy ever came by human will, but men and women moved by the Holy Spirit spoke from God" (1:20–21).

By the time we finish reading this letter we can feel assured that Peter has faithfully fulfilled his mission to be a good shepherd. He nourishes his flock with the word of life. He is fully prepared to lay down his life for the sheep.

The 3 chapters of 2 Peter:

1   Peter the good shepherd
2   Dangerous places
3   Safe pastures

2 PETER

New Testament

This letter contains the first reference to a portion of the New Testament as a collection of books on par with the other Scriptures. It is near the end of the letter:

> So also our beloved brother Paul wrote to you according to the wisdom given him, speaking of this as he does in all his letters. There are some things in them hard to understand, which the ignorant and unstable twist to their own destruction, as they do the other scriptures. (2 Peter 3:15–16)

Perfect Specimen

This letter, along with 1 Peter and Jude, is found in the best-preserved ancient manuscript containing part of the New Testament. It is called Papyrus 72 and dates from about the year AD 300. It contains the complete text of all three letters along with some other material not part of the New Testament. Papyrus 72 is so special because ancient books are usually missing some portions of the text due to deterioration over the centuries.

Tartaros

In Greek tradition this was the place deep down in the earth—even below Hades—where the Titans were imprisoned for their misconduct. This letter of Peter is the only biblical book to refer to Tartaros (see 2:4). Perhaps the author wanted to make a connection with his Gentile audience.

Parousia

This interesting word (pronounce it pa-rou-SI-a) is simply Greek for "presence" or "coming." It served as a technical term for the visit of an important person or even a deity. In the church, it became a technical term for the Second Coming of Christ as judge at the end of the world. We find it used this way in 2 Peter, "For we did not follow cleverly devised myths when we made known to you the power and coming [*parousia*] of our Lord Jesus Christ…" (1:16).

2 Peter on the Clock (AD)

Death of Peter the apostle   c. 65

Paul's letters collected   c. 100

Tradition attributes this letter to the apostle Peter. This would date it near the time of his death around AD 65. On the other hand, a later date fits the reference to Paul's letters in 3:15–16 because it would presumably have taken some time for Paul's letters to be circulating as a collection. Although influenced by the letter of Jude, the author of 2 Peter does not make direct references to 1 Enoch or the Assumption of Moses, as does the author of Jude. This suggests the church, by the time this letter was composed, was getting a sense of what books were acceptable for church use. Based on such evidence many today believe 2 Peter to be the latest of the New Testament books. A date after AD 100 seems likely.

As you read 2 Peter...

This letter serves as Peter's last testament to his people. What words would you want to leave as a last testament to the community of faith?

Peter turns to Genesis to find examples of God saving the just and rendering judgment on the impious. Can you identify similar examples from other parts of the Bible?

What present-day dangerous pastures would you want to steer the church away from?

How does your own life exhibit a firm conviction that there is a world to come?

Peter says that Paul's letters contain some things hard to understand. Do you agree?

Three Spiritual Lessons From 2 Peter

- Reflect the kingdom of God in the things you do
- Be zealous for the kingdom
- Take inspiration from the words of the Bible

2 PETER

1, 2 AND 3 JOHN

There are three letters attributed to John in the New Testament. If we read them in sequence, we can detect a progression from a focus on Jesus to his faithful followers. Just as the love of Jesus was embodied in his coming into the world to save us all, so the love of Jesus is embodied in his faithful followers who obey his command to love one another as he has loved them.

This series of letters begins with a near portrait of Jesus and ends with a near portrait of a follower of Jesus named Gaius. Both are portrayals of love. The lesson that emerges from reading these letters in sequence is this: "Beloved, since God loved us so much, we also ought to love one another" (1 John 4:11).

The First Letter

If we received a card inviting us to enjoy eternal life with God, we would certainly accept the invitation. John's first letter is just such an invitation. So how long are we going to wait to reply?

John wants his readers to know that he actually saw and heard Jesus the Lord. His assertion of this in the opening lines of the letter is so vivid and powerful that if the printed page were a pane of glass we could almost expect to see the Lord on the other side. It seems that is precisely the experience John wants us to have. He wants us to see that just as Jesus really came into our world so we, his followers, should do all we can to make him real in our lives.

There is nothing more valuable than a right relationship with God. John has a special word for this. He calls it "fellowship" with the Lord. He writes this letter to strengthen that fellowship. What sorts of things do that? John has a list all prepared and ready: choosing to walk in the light by keeping the commandments; recognizing we need Jesus to save us from our sins; loving God and each other; and being detached from this world.

Within his own lifetime John was concerned that people, even members of the Christian community, were denying that God actually became one of us, that Jesus is the Christ. It seems they could not accept that God loved us so much that God would actually enter our world to show us the way to eternal life.

John has a name for such people. He calls them "antichrists." This is a very appropriate title since in fact they take a stance against the conviction that Jesus is the Christ. The great tragedy in their position is that it deprives them of the joy of recognizing they are children of God. John is very concerned to protect readers like us from the influence of these false teachers. John wants us to live life to the fullest, confident that we are God's children.

First-time readers of this letter are likely to be puzzled by all the repetition within it. John introduces an idea and then returns to it again and again in the course of the letter. A typical example is John's emphasis on loving one another. He introduces this theme in 2:10. In the next chapter he returns to it as a distinguishing characteristic of the children of God (3:10, 11, 14). Then he returns to it again in chapter 4, stressing that such love is indeed a commandment of the Lord (4:20, 21).

By repeating such themes, John works his message deeper and deeper into the mind of the reader. If he were to state such themes just once with a heavy hand we might resist the message. But by repeating a theme as he does, John works it into our minds the way a baker might work yeast into a lump of dough. As we read this letter, we find ourselves being drawn by degrees into the joyful world of which John wants us to be a part.

So as we read this letter we should allow its message to gradually win us over to the point of view John so desperately wants us to accept for our own good. By the time we reach the final line of the letter, we might even find ourselves nodding with approval as John asserts that Jesus is truly God and warns us to keep away from the "idols," the things of this passing world that might draw us away from God.

The 5 chapters of 1 John:

1 — 2	Walk in the light of faith
3	Love one another
4 — 5	Love God

The Second Letter

John wrote his first letter in pursuit of the kind of joy that comes only with faith in Jesus. In this second letter John can confidently announce that he has found the joy he was looking for. In fact, John is "overjoyed" at the faith response he has witnessed in his readers.

He addresses his readers as "the elect lady and her children." We cannot know if this is just one community or several. But what really matters is that they are committed to the truth about Jesus Christ—that he came in the flesh to draw humanity to God.

1, 2 AND 3 JOHN

John applauds the fact that they put their faith into practice by having the kind of love for each other that Jesus had for his disciples. This kind of love seeks all that is spiritually beneficial for people; it draws people closer to God.

The elder—good shepherd that he is—cannot resist a word of caution. He knows there are deceivers circulating among the community trying to draw them away from the path they have chosen. He warns his flock not to receive such people.

But John the elder is only momentarily distracted by such concerns. As he concludes this brief letter, he returns to his theme of joy, expressing his hope that he will be able to greet his readers face to face.

The 13 verses of 2 John:

1 — 6	Love truth
7 — 13	Avoid deceit

The Third Letter

In this work—just fifteen verses long—John is overjoyed once again. This time it is over the example of one person, a man named Gaius. John celebrates the news that Gaius has graciously welcomed missionaries into his house. For John this is a clear example of the kind of love for one another he has always advocated for the churches in his care.

But John has received other news that we might think would lessen his joy. Another church member named Diotrephes cannot find it in his heart to be as gracious as Gaius. John states the issue bluntly: Diotrephes "likes to put himself first."

But John is not disheartened. He seems confident that he will be able to clear things up when he meets with Diotrephes personally. In the meantime, he cautions his friend Gaius not to be influenced by the small thinking of men like Diotrephes. And John looks forward to meeting Gaius face to face too.

The 15 verses of 3 John:

1 — 6	Be generous
7 — 15	Imitate good

The Author

Tradition attributes these letters to John, the Beloved Disciple of the Lord. The emphasis on being an eyewitness of the earthly ministry of

Jesus would make the Beloved Disciple a good candidate. And the title "elder" found in the second and third letters fits nicely with the expectation that the Beloved Disciple would live a long life (see John 21:22–23). But the letters never name their author and so any theory on authorship must proceed with caution.

Three Witnesses

There are three witnesses to God's saving grace in the world, according to 1 John 5:8. They are the Spirit, the water and the blood. All three are associated with the Lord Jesus Christ. Jesus spoke of himself as a source of water offering eternal life (John 5:14). He also said that anyone who drinks his blood has eternal life (John 6:54). The third witness is the Holy Spirit, the gift the Risen Lord gives his faithful followers.

Antichrist

This term appears only in these letters of John. Its basic meaning is someone who is opposed to Christ. John applies this term to persons who deny "that Jesus Christ has come in the flesh" (2 John 7).

1, 2 and 3 John on the Clock (AD)

Death of John the Apostle   c. 95–100

Gospel of John completed   c. 100

Tradition holds that John the apostle wrote these letters in Ephesus sometime after the end of his exile on Patmos and therefore near the end of the first century. But scholars today believe the author of these letters was not the apostle John but some other who held the position of elder in the early church. It is generally agreed these letters date from a time not long after the composition of John's Gospel.

As you read the letters of John…

What are you doing to exhibit fellowship with the Lord in your life as John advocates in the first chapter of his first letter?

What does being a child of God—so prominent a theme in these letters—mean for you?

Where do you find the darkness in today's world? Where do you find the light?

What examples of faith do you celebrate in your community?

When do you find yourself thinking too small? Would reading this letter help?

The second letter urges us to follow the Lord's commandment of love. Is there anything that distracts you from doing this?

How could you display the kind of hospitality exhibited by Gaius in the third letter?

Three Spiritual Lessons From the Letters of John

- Live in the light of the gospel
- We should love one another as God has loved us
- The things of the world lead us toward God

JUDE

This little letter is worth a lot of attention. In just twenty-five verses it pulls together a great deal from the Bible and elsewhere to encourage readers to remain focused on the Lord.

Jude is very worried the faithful will be drawn away from Christ by certain others he refers to as "intruders." Jude says these others deny the Lord. Since they are present at the Eucharist, they must have presented themselves as believers. But the spiritual significance of the Eucharist seems to have escaped them altogether. Instead of giving praise to God, they promote themselves. Jude is especially put off by their habit of flattering people for personal advantage. Jude has some choice images to describe these people: "They are waterless clouds carried along by the winds; autumn trees without fruit, twice dead, uprooted; wild waves of the sea, casting up the foam of their own shame; wandering stars, for whom the deepest darkness has been reserved forever" (12–13).

But Jude is perfectly happy to leave the fate of such "worldly people" up to God. He quotes a passage attributed to Enoch, the one who walked with God during his time on earth (see Genesis 5:21–24). Enoch expresses his conviction that God will bring judgment on the ungodly of this world; Jude agrees.

To keep his readers from being influenced by sinners, Jude reminds them of passages from the Bible that tell the story of three groups who turned away from God and suffered the consequences. These three are the first generation of Israelites who wandered in the desert for forty years until they all died; the fallen angels; and the people of Sodom and Gomorrah.

Jude then continues with three more examples from the Bible, this time targeting the intruders' fondness for using flattery and fancy words to win people over to their side. Jude's three examples are Cain, Balaam and Korah. Each of them used language to steer others into danger. Cain lured his brother out into the field where he killed him. Balaam tried to use language to curse the Israelites. And Korah used language to influence people to join his rebellion against Moses.

Jude also brings into his argument other written works popular in his time but not included in the church's sacred Scriptures. This is similar to people today drawing examples from inspirational works beyond the literature of the Bible.

The first example comes from something called the Testament (or Assumption) of Moses in which the great leader gives advice to his successor Joshua. In the passage cited by Jude, Michael the archangel argues with Satan about the worthiness of Moses to be taken up into heaven. As adamant as Michael was against his opponent, he did not take it upon himself to slander him; he left his opponent's fate up to God. But it is quite different with the "intruders" Jude writes about. They have no qualms about slandering other members of the community.

In the final verses Jude has a triple antidote to all the bad influences in the community. He urges his readers to pray to the Holy Spirit, remain in the love of God, and stay focused on Jesus who leads us to eternal life.

The 25 verses of Jude:

I — 16	Avoid falsehood
17 — 25	Focus on God

Jude

The Jude of this letter is probably not the apostle by that name, since the author speaks of the apostles without including himself among their number. Many think the Jude of this letter is one of the relatives of Jesus mentioned in the Gospels along with James, Joses (or Joseph) and Simon (see Mark 6:3; Matthew 13:55). Jude introduces himself as the "brother of James" perhaps because this James was well known as leader of the community in Jerusalem (Acts 12:17).

JUDE

Tradition

Jude is wary of any innovations on the truth "once for all entrusted to the saints" (Jude 3). The Greek term rendered "entrusted" in this verse can also be translated as "handed down," which is the basic meaning of the word *tradition.*

First Enoch

Jude was familiar with a work we call First Enoch (to distinguish this book from two other books by that name). Enoch was popular among writers of imaginative literature. He was taken up to heaven (Genesis 5:24; Sirach 44:16) and so authors ascribed to him privileged information about the future, especially the last days. First Enoch is 107 chapters long and filled with tours of wondrous places and visions about the end times. Jude 1:14–15 refers to the opening chapter about God's coming to judge the world at the end of time.

Testament of Moses

The parting words of famous figures of the past were a favorite theme among books contemporary with the Bible. The surviving literature includes testaments of the Twelve Patriarchs (Jacob's sons), of Job, of Solomon and even of Adam. There is some debate about the source Jude uses. Is it the Testament of Moses? Or the Assumption of Moses? The problem arises because the segment from which Jude quotes has not survived. It seems Moses was taken up to heaven only after a lively exchange between Michael and Satan about his worthiness. At issue was the fact that Moses had killed an Egyptian early in his career.

Jude on the Clock (AD)

Death of John the Apostle   c. 95–100
Second Letter of Peter   c. 100–125

This letter talks about the apostles as figures from the past. For this reason, it seems best not to date the letter too early in the first century. The Second Letter of Peter—generally regarded as the latest book of the New Testament—borrows material from Jude. So a likely time frame for Jude is the last decade of the first century.

As you read Jude…

Do you find yourself at times not fully appreciating the spiritual significance of the Eucharist?

Read over Jude's images in verses 12 and 13. Which ones do you find most powerful? Could you come up with any images of your own?

Jude was certainly familiar with the literature of his time and could use it effectively to teach a spiritual lesson. What current literature would you use to teach a spiritual lesson?

Jude laments over those who use words to slander other members of the community. What words would you use to build up members of your community?

Three Spiritual Lessons From Jude

- Be a positive influence on the faith of others
- Be nourished by the words of the Bible
- Allow the truth of the gospel to be your guide in life

JUDE

PART NINE

THE FINAL BOOK
OF THE BIBLE

One book remains to be read. It is the book of Revelation, and it is the ideal book to bring the New Testament to a close. All the books we have read up to this point in the New Testament seem to lead up to this breathtaking summary of all that Jesus means for the world.

As the title suggests, this book reveals. It reveals the overpowering majesty of God, from the victory of Jesus over sin and death, across the wide expanse of time, all the way down to the end of the ages. Its purpose is to encourage us to remain faithful to the Lord. If we do so, we will share in God's final victory and enjoy eternal life in the kingdom of heaven.

Positive images, sounds and colors—the Lamb, the rider on the white horse, a woman clothed with the sun, bowls filled with prayers of the saints, hymns of victory, and the glory of the new Jerusalem—all combine to fill us with the strength to face any obstacle. We can be confident that all the advantages belong to those faithful to Christ.

The book of Revelation is also the ideal book to bring the entire Bible to a close because in its final chapter the tree of life is featured once again "with its twelve kinds of fruit, producing its fruit each month" (Revelation 22:2).

We last saw this tree in the opening chapters of Genesis; it was guarded by the cherub with the swirling sword of fire. But now the way to the tree is not guarded. Through Jesus Christ people once again have access to the tree's life-giving fruit. Like a beautiful frame surrounding a picture, the tree of life surrounds the Bible drawing our attention to the wonderful message of life that lies within.

REVELATION

As the title suggests, this book is a real eye-opener. Revelation offers us a clear view straight through to the very end of time. But John's purpose in doing this for us is not to give us predictions of precise events in the future. His purpose is to encourage us to remain faithful to Jesus who is truly Lord of all. He wants us to know that whatever our hardships we should think of ourselves not as victims but as beneficiaries in God's victory over sin and death.

John wrote his book during a time of great difficulty for the church. This seems to give Revelation a timeless character since every age presents some challenge for the church. As Jesus told his followers, there would be hardships in store for them because of their witness to the truth. In the face of such hardships, Revelation promises that the victory belongs to Christ and those who remain loyal to him.

The message unfolds in successive groups of seven. First, there are letters addressed to seven churches urging them to keep the faith. Then comes the vision of a scroll with seven seals. As each seal is broken, more is revealed about God's victory. The scroll vision leads to the sounding of seven trumpets announcing the battle between God and an unbelieving world. The sounding of the seventh trumpet heralds the conclusion as bowls of judgment are emptied out over the earth. In the final chapters we see the New Jerusalem coming down from heaven and God's faithful people enjoying everlasting life.

Throughout the reading of Revelation, we shift back and forth between scenes in heaven and scenes on earth. In heaven the saints and the angels are singing hymns of victory while on earth we see the victory unfold in time. All the vivid colors, breathless scenes and riveting action in this book are guaranteed to keep our attention, making Revelation a powerful testimony to God's saving plan. At the end of it all you want to stand up and declare your allegiance to the kingdom of God. And that is surely just what John had in mind when he wrote the book.

The 22 chapters of Revelation:

1 — 3	Letters to seven churches
4 — 7	The scroll with seven seals
8 — 11	Seven trumpets
12 — 14	Signs of judgment and victory

The Lamb

As John peers through the door to heaven, he sees a figure worthy to open the scroll with the seven seals. It is the Risen Lord, described as the Lamb of God, the perfect Passover sacrifice that supersedes all others. Because Jesus won the victory over death, he is just the one to unseal the text disclosing God's final victory. Later on, John sees the Lamb standing on Mount Zion in Jerusalem surrounded by the faithful who sing a new song celebrating God's final victory (see Revelation 5; 12).

The Woman Clothed With the Sun

John sees her in heaven surrounded by the great lights in the sky. She gives birth to a child who is immediately threatened by God's enemies. But God protects both the woman and her son. This woman represents God's holy people, the church. They give witness to the Lord Jesus Christ in the face of great opposition from the unbelieving world. But God protects them. This woman also represents Mary the Mother of Jesus and Mother of the church.

The Dragon

John tells us plainly that the dragon represents Satan, who deceives the people of the earth with his empty promises. John's description of the dragon mirrors the description of Leviathan, the great monster of chaos portrayed in Psalm 74 with seven heads. The dragon's color is red because so many die a martyr's death as a result of the fierce resistance leveled against the church by powers caught up in Satan's web of lies. In John's time readers probably recognized the Roman Empire in this description of the dragon.

Michael

Michael is the great defender of God's holy people. He leads his angels in battle against the forces of the Dragon and succeeds in throwing them all down to earth. In the book of Daniel (10:13–21), Michael is the great heavenly defender of the Jewish people, protecting them from their enemies. In the Letter of Jude (verse 9) we are told that Michael is an archangel.

REVELATION

239

John

This is the name of the one who receives the visions described in Revelation. In the thinking of scholars today, this visionary is otherwise unknown. But by tradition he is identified with the Beloved Disciple, one of the twelve apostles. John tells us he received this vision on the island of Patmos in the Aegean Sea. He seems to have been banished to that deserted place because of his preaching of the gospel. The visions came to him on Sunday, the very day the church celebrates the Lord's victory over death, a prominent theme in this book of Revelation.

A Challenge

Revelation is not a difficult book to read. John's vocabulary is manageable and his organization of the book is clear. What does make Revelation a challenge is putting together all its vivid images, like working on a puzzle with a thousand pieces. But even a first-time reader will grasp the book's principal message that God will win the victory over all that stands in the way of God's saving plan.

A Thousand Years

Saint Augustine's interpretation of the thousand-year reign of Christ is very helpful. He understood the thousand years to represent the span of time between the Lord's birth and the Lord's Second Coming.

Jesus at the Door

The well-known image of Jesus knocking on the door comes from the letter to Laodicea in which Jesus says, "Listen! I am standing at the door, knocking; if you hear my voice and open the door, I will come in to you and eat with you, and you with me" (Revelation 3:20).

Revelation on the Clock (AD)

Nero   54–68

Domitian   81–96

Some find in the number 666 (Revelation 13:18) a reference to the Roman Emperor Nero and so argue for an early date for this book. But a more probable time frame for the writing of this book is the reign of Domitian (AD 81–96). This emperor insisted on being worshiped as a god even while he was alive. His demands certainly created special problems for Christians.

As you read Revelation…

John begins this book with letters to the churches of his day challenging them to remain faithful to the Lord. What challenges would you include in a letter to a present-day church?

At verse 4:1 John sees the heavens opened above him. If you saw the heavens opened, what would you expect to see?

The prayers of the saints are symbolized by incense offered up to God (5:8). What makes incense so suitable an image for prayer?

Do you share John's distress at the prospect that no one will be found worthy to open the scroll (5:14)?

Silence follows the breaking of the seventh seal (8:1). What does silence mean for you?

On the feast of All Saints the church reads 7:2–14 as a companion text to Matthew's passage about the Beatitudes (Matthew 5:1–12). What connections do you see between the two readings?

John does not identify the two witnesses in 11:1–14. Who do you think they might be? Who are witnesses to the truth of Jesus Christ today?

The sounding of the seventh trumpet is followed by a hymn of praise (11:15–18). What significance do the lyrics of the hymn have for you?

On the feast of the Assumption of Mary, the church reads 12:1–10 as a companion text to Mary's visit with Elizabeth (Luke 1:39–56). What connections do you see between the two readings?

What would the red dragon of 12:3–4 represent in today's world?

John's readers would probably have associated the beasts of chapter 13 and the city in chapters 17 and 18 with the Roman Empire. With what might we associate them today?

In chapter 16 angels empty seven bowls of judgment to bring a sinful world to repentance. How did the people respond? How do you think they would respond today?

What judgment is in store for Satan in chapter 20?

In chapter 21 John describes the New Jerusalem as a bride. What makes this image so appropriate in this book?

In what ways does the New Jerusalem remind you of the Garden of Eden?

Revelation is filled with many colors and images. Which ones did you find most memorable? What do you learn from them for your faith journey?

Three Spiritual Lessons From Revelation

- We should always be ready to open the door to Jesus
- God wants us to enjoy eternal life in the heavenly Jerusalem
- With God's help we can overcome any obstacle

RESOURCES

Here are some resources to get you further introduced to the books of the Bible. Some of them will connect you with other books to take you further on your journey through the Bible.

Print

Arranged by title:

The Bible Speaks Today, a series published by InterVarsity Press (Downers Grove, Ill.: InterVarsity, n.d.)

This series aims at providing readers with a very readable reference for each book of the Bible. As an added feature, the series relates the biblical material to everyday life. The text of each book is broken down into manageable units with eye-catching titles. The only limitation is that it does not include all the books Catholics have in their Old Testament, such as Judith or Tobit.

The Catholic Answer Bible (Huntington, Ind.: Our Sunday Visitor, 2002)

This edition offers you the translation of the *New American Bible.* It includes over twenty helpful inserts on a colorful background. These inserts answer a variety of questions Catholics may have about the Bible and church tradition, such as "Where did the Bible come from?" and "What do the Bible and the church teach about heaven?"

The Collegeville Bible Commentary (Collegeville, Minn.: Liturgical, 1992)

This appears in two volumes, one for the Old Testament and one for the New. They bring together booklets published separately in previous years. The format is easy to follow and the articles are easy to read.

The Collegeville Bible Handbook (Collegeville, Minn.: Liturgical, 1997)

If you are looking for a very friendly, easy-to-use guide to the Bible, this is it. Some of the finest biblical scholars have produced a brief commentary on each book of the Bible. The book also features a host of pictures, maps and drawings that help make the text come alive. There is even a color-coded bar running across the top of each page to help the reader navigate through the many books of the Bible.

A Dictionary of the Bible, by W.R.F. Browning (Oxford: Oxford University Press, 1998)

As you might imagine, there are a lot of Bible dictionaries out there. Most of them are pretty hefty. But a very handy one is this paperback edition published by the Oxford University Press. It is definitely up to the high standards we are accustomed to seeing from Oxford. The entries are refreshingly brief and informative. This is a good start for anyone interested in getting quick background information on things connected with the Bible.

Dogmatic Constitution on Divine Revelation

Catholics will find a good introduction to the Bible in this brief document that came out of Vatican II on November 18, 1965. The entire text is just twenty-six chapters long but it is filled with riches for the Catholic reader. It includes valuable insights about how God speaks to us, about the balance between tradition and Scripture, about the books of the Bible and about the role of tradition and Scripture in the life of the church.

Interfaces, a series published by Liturgical Press

This is a multi-volume series on characters in the Bible. The series editor is Barbara Green, O.P. A very readable volume by Sister Green entitled *From Earth's Creation to John's Revelation* serves as an introduction and companion to the other books in the series. Check their Web site www.litpress.org for further details or to order selections from this series.

The NAB *Catholic Serendipity Bible* (Grand Rapids, Mich.: Zondervan Corporation, 1999)

By "serendipity" they mean what happens when people dialogue about their faith and are open to the Holy Spirit doing something wonderful in their lives. This Bible will certainly help people experience serendipity. It offers many formats for group and for personal study. There are even questionnaires to help readers focus on details.

An especially attractive feature is a segment including two hundred Bible stories for readers to study and learn from. The *Serendipity Bible* is a valuable guide for the interested reader and for Bible study groups.

Arranged by author:

Brown, Raymond E. *Responses to 101 Questions on the Bible* (New York: Paulist, 1990)

If you have a question about the Bible, this is the place to start looking for an answer. Father Brown offers brief and to-the-point responses to over one hundred questions. In case you're curious about that 101st question, it's about the church in the New Testament. What makes this book especially helpful is that the questions are clustered together by subject matter. So, for example, all your questions about how to read the Bible can be found in one place.

Murphy, Roland E. *Responses to 101 Questions on the Biblical Torah* (New York: Paulist, 1996)

This book offers you a very easy-to-read overview of the Pentateuch. The question-and-answer format makes it right for finding just what you are looking for. There are about twenty questions on each of the five books. The last ten questions focus on connections between the Pentateuch and the New Testament.

Scott, Macrina. *Picking the "Right" Bible Study Program* (Chicago: ACTA, 1994)

This book is a real treasure chest. It offers readers a detailed review of 150 programs recommended for Bible study. Sister Macrina's book is the perfect place to begin planning a reading or study program in your parish.

Witherup, Ronald D. *The Bible Companion: A Handbook for Beginners* (New York: Crossroad, 1998)

This book serves as a gentle companion to anyone getting started as a reader of the Bible. The author walks his readers through each book, discussing structure, content and interpretation. There are plenty of easy-to-read tables providing vital statistics on each book. Each section ends with an exercise to help the reader apply the book to life.

Video

Discovering the Bible (n.p.: Gateway Films, 1996)

This informative kit includes four thirty-minute video programs on two video cassettes. The programs are well produced with exciting and vivid images. The dialogue is by the very capable Russell Boulter. Program 1 offers an overview of the Bible. Programs 2 and 3 are about the Old and New Testaments respectively. Program 4 discusses the preservation of the Bible over the centuries. The kit includes handouts and worksheets for listeners as well as a leader's guide. The kit even includes a sample of genuine papyrus from Egypt! The one disadvantage is that kit does not cover the entire Catholic Bible, omitting from its scope books like Tobit, Judith and Sirach.

Scripture from Scratch: *A Basic Bible Study Program* (Cincinnati: St. Anthony Messenger Press)

Virginia Smith and Elizabeth McNamer offer sixteen easy-to-listen-to one-hour presentations giving viewers an overview of the Bible. There are eight videocassettes, each one including two presentations. The videos can be purchased separately or as a unit.

Internet

www.AmericanCatholic.org

This is the Web site for St. Anthony Messenger Press. It will put you in touch with a rich variety of resources to help you get the most out of reading the Word of God.

www.Biblegateway.com

This valuable site makes it possible for you to find any passage, word or phrase in the Bible in whatever translation you choose. It is especially suited for gathering together passages from all over the Bible arranged according to the word or theme you are interested in.

www.nccbuscc.org/nab

This Web site comes to us courtesy of our Catholic bishops. It offers a lot of information. All you need to do is click on the topic you find interesting. One very helpful feature is a calendar from which you can find the liturgical readings for any day of the month. You can also access any chapter of the Bible in the *New American Bible* translation.